The Best
of Me

The Best
of Me

David Sedaris

Little, Brown

LITTLE, BROWN

First published in the United States in 2020 by Little, Brown and Company
First published in Great Britain in 2020 by Little, Brown

3 5 7 9 10 8 6 4 2

Barrel Fever and *Discontents*: "Glen's Homophobia Newsletter Vol. 3, No. 2"; *Holidays on Ice*: "Front Row Center with Thaddeus Bristol," "Christmas Means Giving"; *Naked*: "The Incomplete Quad"; *Me Talk Pretty One Day* and *Esquire*: "You Can't Kill the Rooster," "Me Talk Pretty One Day," "Jesus Shaves"; *Dress Your Family in Corduroy and Denim* and *The New Yorker*: "Us and Them," "Let It Snow," "The Ship Shape," "The Girl Next Door," "Possession," "Nuit of the Living Dead"; *Dress Your Family ...* and *Esquire*: "Repeat after Me," "Six to Eight Black Men"; *When You Are Engulfed in Flames* and *The New Yorker*: "The Understudy," "In the Waiting Room," "Solution to Saturday's Puzzle"; "Solution to Saturday's Puzzle" also appeared in *The Best American Travel Writing 2006*; *When You Are Engulfed ...* and *GQ*: "Town and Country"; *Squirrel Seeks Chipmunk*: "The Motherless Bear," "The Faithful Setter"; acknowledgment is made to Public Radio International's *This American Life*, on which "The Cat and the Baboon" was originally broadcast in a slightly different form; *Let's Explore Diabetes with Owls*: "Think Differenter"; *Let's Explore ...* and *The New Yorker*: "Dentists Without Borders," "Memory Laps," "Loggerheads," "Easy Tiger," "Laugh, Kookaburra," "A Guy Walks into a Bar Car," "Standing By," "Understanding Understanding Owls"; "A Guy Walks into a Bar Car" also appeared in *The Best American Essays 2010 and The Best American Travel Writing 2010*; *Let's Explore Diabetes ...* and *GQ*: "Just a Quick E-mail"; *Let's Explore ...* and *Prospect*: "If I Ruled the World"; *Let's Explore ...* and *Esquire*: "Dog Days"; *Calypso*: "A House Divided"; *Calypso* and *The New Yorker*: "Now We Are Five," "The Perfect Fit," "Leviathan," "A Modest Proposal," "Why Aren't You Laughing?"; *Calypso* and *The Paris Review*: "The Spirit World"; *The New Yorker*: "Girl Crazy," "Card Wired," "How to Spend the Budget Surplus," "Undecided," "Unbuttoned."

A CIP catalogue record for this book is available from the British Library.

Hardback ISBN 978-1-4087-1389-1
Trade paperback ISBN 978-1-4087-1388-4

Typeset in Sabon by M Rules
Printed and bound in Great Britain by Clays Ltd, Elcograf S.p.A.

Papers used by Little, Brown are from well-managed forests
and other responsible sources.

Little, Brown
An imprint of
Little, Brown Book Group
Carmelite House
50 Victoria Embankment
London EC4Y 0DZ

An Hachette UK Company
www.hachette.co.uk

www.littlebrown.co.uk

For my brother, Paul

Contents

Contents

The Best
of Me

Introduction

I'm not the sort of person who goes around feeling good about himself. I have my days, don't get me wrong, but any confidence I possess, especially in regard to my writing, was planted and nurtured by someone else—first a teacher, then later an agent or editor. "Hey," he or she would say, "this is pretty good."

"Really?" This was my cheap way of getting them to say it again. "You're not just telling me that because you feel sorry for me?"

"Yes . . . I mean, no. I really like it!"

Still I never quite believed them.

What lifted me up was writing for *The New Yorker*. While this had always been a fantasy of mine, I did nothing to nudge it along. I'd been told that if the magazine wanted you, they'd find you, and that's exactly what happened. I started my relationship with them in 1995, when an editor phoned and asked if I might write a Shouts & Murmurs piece on then-President Bill Clinton's welfare reform proposal. I was given one day to complete it, and when I was told that it would run in the next week's issue, something inside me changed. It wasn't seismic, like an earthquake, but more like a medium-sized boulder that had shifted a little. Still I felt it. When the magazine came out, I opened it to my piece, arranged it just so on the kitchen table, and strolled past it, wanting my younger, twenty-year-old self to see his name at the top of the page.

"Wait a minute ... is that ... me? In *The New Yorker?*" Thirty nine years it had taken the magazine to notice me. Good thing I wasn't in any rush.

If you read an essay in *Esquire* and don't like it, there could be something wrong with the essay. If it's in *The New Yorker,* on the other hand, and you don't like it, there's something wrong with *you.* That said, you're never going to please everyone. It's hard to think of a single entry in this book that didn't generate a complaint of one sort or another. And it could be anything—"How dare you suggest French dentists are better than American ones!" "What sort of monster won't swap seats on a plane?" Many were angry that I'd inadvertently killed a couple of sea turtles. Granted, that was bad, but I was child at the time, and don't you have to eventually forgive someone for what he did when he was twelve?

There is literally nothing you can print anymore that isn't going to generate a negative response. This, I believe, was brought on by the internet. It used to be that you'd write a letter of complaint, then read it over wondering, *Is this really worth a twenty-five cent stamp?* With the advent of e-mail, complaining became free. Thus people who were maybe a tiny bit offended could, at no cost whatsoever, let you know that they were NEVER GOING TO BUY ANY OF YOUR BOOKS EVER AGAIN!!!!

They always take the scorched earth policy for some reason. Of all the entries in this book, the one that generated the most anger was "The Motherless Bear." Oh, the mail I got. "How dare you torture animals like this!"

"It's a fictional story," I wrote back to everyone who complained. "The giveaway is that the title character speaks English and feels sorry for herself. Bears don't do that in real life."

That wasn't enough for a woman in England. "I urge you not to mock these intelligent and sentient creatures," she wrote, demanding that I atone by involving myself with the two bear rescue organizations she listed at the bottom of her letter.

Just as we can never really tell what our own breath smells like, I will never know if I would have liked my writing. If I wasn't myself, and someone sent me one of my essay collections, would I recommend it to friends? Would I stop reading it after a dozen or so pages? There's so much that goes into a decision like that. How many times have I dismissed something just because a person I didn't approve of found it enjoyable? Or maybe I decided it was too popular. That's the sort of snobbery that kept my younger self slogging through books I honestly had no interest in, the sorts I'd announce had taken me "six months to finish," but were only two hundred pages long. If something is written in your native language, and it's taking you *half a year* to get through it, unless you're being paid by the hour to read it, I'd say there's a problem.

One thing that I would like about my writing is that so much of it has to do with family. It's something that's always interested me, and is one of the reasons I so love Greeks. You could meet an American and wait for months before he begins a sentence with the words, "So then my mother ... " It's the same in France and England. Oh, they might get around to it eventually, but it never feels imperative. With Greeks, though, it's usually only a matter of seconds before you hear about someone's brother, or what a pain his sister is.

There's a lot of talk lately about "the family you choose." It's a phrase often used by people who were rejected by their parents or siblings, and so formed a group of supportive, kindred spirits. I think it's great they're part of a tight-knit circle, but I wouldn't call it a family. Essential to that word is that the people you're surrounded by were *not* chosen. They were assigned by fate, and now you must deal with them in one way or another until you die. For me, that hasn't been much of a problem. Even when I was a teenager, I wouldn't have traded my parents for anyone else's, and the same goes for my brother and sisters.

It bothers me, then, when someone refers to my family as "dysfunctional." That word is overused, at least in the United States, and, more to the point, it's wrongly used. My father hoarding food inside my sister's vagina would be dysfunctional. His hoarding it beneath the bathroom sink, as he is wont to do, is, at best, quirky and at worst unsanitary.

There's an Allan Gurganus quote I think of quite often: "Without much accuracy, with strangely little love at all, your family will decide for you exactly who you are, and they'll keep nudging, coaxing, poking you until you've changed into that very simple shape."

Is there a richer or more complex story than that?

I like to think that the affection I have for my family is apparent. Well into our adulthoods—teetering on our dotage, most of us—we're still on good terms. We write one another, we talk. We take vacations together. I just can't see the dysfunction in that.

The pieces in this book—both fiction and nonfiction—are the sort I hoped to produce back when I first started writing, at the age of twenty. I didn't know how to get from where I was then to where I am now, but who does? Like everyone else I stumbled along, making mistakes while embarrassing myself and others (sorry everyone I've ever met). I'll always be inclined toward my most recent work, if only because I've had less time to turn on it. When I first started writing essays they were about big, dramatic events, the sort you relate when you meet someone new and are trying to explain to them what made you the person you are. As I get older, I find myself writing about smaller and smaller things. As an exercise it's much more difficult, and thus—for me anyway—much more rewarding. I hope you feel the same. If not I can probably expect to hear from you.

Glen's Homophobia Newsletter Vol. 3, No. 2

Dear Subscriber,

First of all, I'd like to apologize for the lack of both the spring and summer issues of *Glen's Homophobia Newsletter*. I understand that you subscribed with the promise that this was to be a quarterly publication—four seasons' worth of news from the front lines of our constant battle against oppression. That was my plan. It's just that last spring and summer were so overwhelming that I, Glen, just couldn't deal with it all.

I'm hoping you'll understand. Please accept as consolation the fact that this issue is almost twice as long as the others. Keep in mind the fact that it's not easy to work forty hours a week *and* produce a quarterly publication. Also, while I'm at it, I'd like to mention that it would be wonderful if everyone who *read Glen's Homophobia Newsletter* also *subscribed* to *Glen's Homophobia Newsletter*. It seems that many of you are very generous when it comes to lending issues to your friends and family. That is all well and good as everyone should understand the passion with which we as a people are hated beyond belief. But at the same time, it *costs* to put out a newsletter and every dollar helps. It costs to gather data, to Xerox, to staple and mail, let alone the cost of my personal time and energies. So if you don't mind, I'd rather you mention *Glen's Homophobia Newsletter* to everyone you know but tell them they'll have to subscribe for themselves if they want the whole story. Thank you for understanding.

As I stated before, last spring and summer were very difficult for me. In late April Steve Dolger and I broke up and went our separate ways. Steve Dolger (see newsletters volume 2, nos. 1–4 and volume 3, no. 1) turned out to be the most *homophobic* homosexual I've ever had the displeasure of knowing. He lives in constant fear; afraid to make any kind of mature emotional commitment, afraid of growing old and losing what's left of his hair, and afraid to file his state and federal income taxes (which he has not done since 1987). Someday, perhaps someday very soon, Steve Dolger's past will come back to haunt him. We'll see how Steve and his little seventeen-year-old boyfriend feel when it happens!

Steve was very devious and cold during our breakup. I felt the chill of him well through the spring and late months of summer. With deep feelings come deep consequences and I, Glen, spent the last two seasons of my life in what I can only describe as a waking coma—blind to the world around me, deaf to the cries of suffering others, mutely unable to express the stirrings of my wildly shifting emotions.

I just came out of it last Thursday.

What has Glen discovered? I have discovered that living blind to the world around you has its drawbacks but, strangely, it also has its rewards. While I was cut off from the joys of, say, good food and laughter, I was also blind to the overwhelming *homophobia* that is our everlasting cross to bear. I thought that for this edition of the newsletter I might write something along the lines of a *homophobia* Week in Review but this single week has been much too much for me.

Rather, I will recount a single day.

My day of victimization began at seven fifteen a.m. when I held the telephone receiver to my ear and heard Drew Pierson's voice shouting, "Fag, Fag, Fag," over and over and over again. It rings in my ears still. "Fag! I'll kick your ass good and hard the next time I see you. Goddamn you, Fag!" You, reader, are probably asking yourself, "Who is this Drew Pierson and why is he being *so homophobic* toward Glen?"

It all began last Thursday. I stopped into Dave's Kwik Stop on my way home from work and couldn't help but notice the cashier, a bulky, shorthaired boy who had "athletic scholarship" written all over his broad, dullish face and "Drew Pierson: I'm here to help!" written on a nametag pinned to his massive chest. I took a handbasket and bought, I believe, a bag of charcoal briquettes and a quartered fryer. At the register this Drew fellow rang up the items and said, "I'll bet you're going home to grill you some chicken."

I admitted that it was indeed my plan. Drew struck me as being very perceptive and friendly. Most of the Kwik Stop employees are *homophobic* but something about Drew's manner led me to believe that he was different, sensitive and open. That evening, sitting on my patio and staring into the glowing embers nestled in my tiny grill, I thought of Drew Pierson and for the first time in months I felt something akin to a beacon of hope flashing through the darkness of my mind. I, Glen, smiled.

I returned to Dave's Kwik Stop the next evening and bought some luncheon meat, a loaf of bread, potato chips, and a roll of toilet paper.

At the cash register Drew rang up my items and said, 'I'll bet you're going on a picnic in the woods!'

The next evening I had plans to eat dinner at the condominium of my sister and her *homophobic* husband, Vince Covington (see newsletter volume 1, no. 1). On the way to their home I stopped at the Kwik Stop, where I bought a can of snuff. I don't use snuff, wouldn't think of it. I only ordered snuff because it was one of the few items behind the counter and on a lower shelf. Drew, as an employee, is forced to wear an awkward garment—sort of a cross between a vest and a sandwich board. The terrible, synthetic thing ties at the sides and falls practically to the middle of his thigh. I only ordered the snuff so that, as he bent over to fetch it, I might get a more enlightened view of Drew's physique. Regular readers of this newsletter will understand what I am talking about. Drew bent over and squatted on his heels, saying, "Which one? Tuberose? I used to like me some snuff. I'll bet you're going home to relax with some snuff, aren't you?"

The next evening, when I returned for more snuff, Drew explained that he was a fresh man student at Carteret County Community College, where he majors in psychology. I was touched by his naïveté. CCCC might as well print their diplomas on tar paper. One might take a course in diesel mechanics or pipe fitting but under no circumstances should one study psychology at CCCC. That is where certified universities recruit their studies for *abnormal* psychology. CCCC is where the missing links brood and stumble and swing from the outer branches of our educational system.

Drew, bent over, said that he was currently taking a course in dreams. The teacher demands that each student keep a dream notebook, but Drew, exhausted after work, sleeps, he said, "like a gin-soaked log," and wakes remembering nothing.

I told him I've had some interesting dreams lately, because it's true, I have.

Drew said, "Symbolic dreams? Dreams that you could turn around when you're awake and make sense of?"

I said, yes, haunting dreams, meaningful, dense.

He asked then, hunkered down before the snuff, if I would relate my dreams to him. I answered, yes indeed, and he slapped a tin of snuff on the counter and said, "On the house!" I returned home, my heart a bright balloon. Drew might be young, certainly—perhaps no older than, say, Steve Dolger's current boyfriend. He may not be able to hold his own during strenuous intellectual debate, but neither can most people. My buoyant spirit carried me home, where it was immediately deflated by the painful reminder that my evening meal was to consist of an ethnic lasagna pathetically submitted earlier that day by Melinda Delvecchio, a lingering temp haunting the secretarial pool over at the office in which I work. Melinda, stout, inquisitive, and bearded as a pot-bellied pig, has taken quite a shine to me. She is clearly and mistakenly in love with me and presents me, several times a week, with hideous dishes protected with foil. "Someone needs to fatten you up," she says, placing her eager hooves against my stomach. One would think that Melinda Delvecchio's kindness might come as a relief to the grinding *homophobia* I encounter at the office.

One might think that Melinda Delvecchio is thoughtful and generous until they pull back the gleaming foil under which lies her hateful concoction of overcooked pasta stuffed with the synthetic downy fluff used to fill plush toys and cheap cushions. Melinda Delvecchio is no friend of mine—far from it—and, regarding the heated 'lasagna' steaming before me, I made a mental note to have her fired as soon as possible.

That night I dreamt that I was forced to leave my home and move underground into a dark, subterranean chamber with low, muddy ceilings and no furniture. That was bad enough, but to make matters worse I did not live alone but had to share the place with a community of honest-to-God trolls. These were small trolls with full beards and pointy, curled shoes. The trolls were hideously and relentlessly merry. They called me by name, saying, "Glen, so glad you could join us! Look, everybody, Glen's here! Welcome aboard, friend!" They were all so agreeable and satisfied with my company that I woke up sweating at six a.m. and could not return to sleep for fear of them.

I showered twice and shaved my face, passing the time until seven, at which time I phoned Drew at his parents' home. He answered groggy and confused. I identified myself and paused while he went to fetch a pencil and tablet with which to record my story.

Regular readers of *Glen's Homophobia Newsletter* know that I, Glen, honor truth and hold it above all other things. The truth, be it ugly or naked, does not frighten me. The meaner the truth, the harder I, Glen, stare it down. However, on this occasion I decided to make an exception. My dreaming of trolls means absolutely nothing. It's something that came to me in my sleep and is of no real importance. It is our waking dreams, our day dreams that are illuminating. Regular readers of *Glen's Homophobia Newsletter* know that I dream of the day when our people can walk the face of this earth free of the terrible *homophobia* that binds us. What are sleeping dreams but so much garbage? I can't bear to hear other people's dreams unless I myself am in them.

I put all these ideas together in a manageable sort of way and told Drew Pierson that I dreamt I was walking through a forest of angry, vindictive trees.

"Like those hateful trees in *The Wizard of Oz?*" he said. "Those mean trees that threw the apples?"

"Yes," I said, "exactly."

14

"Did any of them hit you?" he asked, concerned.

"A few."

"Ouch! Then what?"

I told him I came upon a clearing where I saw a single tree, younger than the rest but stocky, a husky, good-looking tree that spoke to me, saying, "I'll bet you're tired of being hated, aren't you?"

I could hear Drew scratching away with his pencil and repeating my dictation: "I ... bet ... you're ... tired ... of ... being ... hated ..."

I told Drew that the tree had spoken in a voice exactly like his own, low and firm, yet open and friendly.

"Like my voice, really?" He seemed pleased. "Damn, my voice on a tree. I never thought about a thing like that."

That night I dreamt I was nailed to a cross that was decorated here and there with fragrant tulips. I glanced over at the cross next to me, expecting to see Christ, but instead, nailed there, I saw Don Rickles. We waved to each other and he mouthed the words, "Hang in there."

I called Drew the next morning and told him I once again dreamt I was in a forest clearing. Once again I found myself face-to-face with a husky tree.

Drew asked, "What did the tree say this time?"

I told him the tree said, "Let me out! Let me out! I'm yearning to break free."

"Break free of what?" he asked.

"Chains and limitations," I said. The tree said, "Strip me of my bark, strip me of my bark."

"The tree said that to you personally or was there someone else standing around?"

I told him the tree spoke to me personally and that I had no choice but to do as I was told. I peeled away the bark with my bare hands and out stepped Drew, naked and unashamed.

"Naked in the woods? I was in the woods naked like that? Then what?"

I told Drew I couldn't quite remember what happened next; it was right on the tip of my mind where I couldn't quite grasp it.

Drew said, "I want to know what I was doing naked in the woods is what I want to know."

I said, "Are you naked now?"

"Now?" Drew, apparently uncertain, took a moment before saying, "No. I got my underwear on."

I suggested that if he put the telephone receiver into the pouch of his briefs it might trigger something that would help me recall the rest of my dream.

I heard the phone muffle. When I yelled, "Did you put the phone where I told you to?" I heard a tiny, far-off voice say, "Yes, I sure did. It's there now."

"Jump up and down," I yelled. "Jump."

I heard shifting sounds as Drew's end of the telephone jounced around in his briefs. I heard him yell, "Are you remembering yet?" And then, in the distance, I heard a woman's voice screaming, "Drew Pierson, what in the name of God are you doing with that telephone? Other people have to put their mouth on that thing too, you know. You should be strung up for doing a thing like that, Goddamn you." I heard Drew say that he was doing it in order to help someone remember a dream. Then I heard the words "moron," "shit-for-brains," and the inevitable "fag." As in "Some fag put you up to this, didn't he? God damn you."

Then Drew must have taken the receiver out of his briefs because suddenly I could hear him loud and clear and what I heard was *homophobia* at its worst. "Fag! Fag! I'll kick your ass good and hard the next time I see you. God damn you to hell." The words still echo in my mind.

I urge all my readers to BOYCOTT DAVE'S KWIK STOP. I urge you to phone Drew Pierson anytime day or night and tell him you dreamt you were sitting on his face. Drew Pierson's home(ophobic) telephone number is 787-5008. Call him and raise your voice against *homophobia!*

So that, in a nutshell, was my morning. I pulled myself together and subjected myself to the daily *homophobia* convention that passes as my job. Once there, I was scolded by my devious and *homophobic* department head for accidentally shredding some sort of disputed contract. Later that afternoon I was confronted, once again, by that casserole-wielding mastadon, Melinda Delvecchio, who grew tearful when informed that I would sooner dine on carpet remnants than another of her foil-covered ethnic slurs.

On my way home from the office I made the mistake of stopping at the Food Carnival, where I had no choice but to park in one of the so-called "handicapped" spaces. Once inside the store I had a tiff with the *homophobic* butcher over the dictionary definition of the word *cutlet.* I was completely ignored by the *homophobic* chimpanzee they've hired to run the produce department and I don't even want to talk about the cashier. After collecting my groceries I returned to the parking lot, where I encountered a *homophobe* in a wheelchair, relentlessly bashing my car again and again with the foot pedals of his little chariot. Regular readers of *Glen's Homophobia Newsletter* know that I, Glen, am not a violent man. Far from it. But in this case I had no choice but to make an exception. My daily *homophobia* quota had been exceeded and I, Glen, struck back with brute physical force.

Did it look good? No, it did not.

But I urge you, reader, to understand. Understand my position as it is your own.

Understand and subscribe, subscribe.

Front Row Center with Thaddeus Bristol

Trite Christmas: Scottsfield's young hams offer the blandest of holiday fare

The approach of Christmas signifies three things: bad movies, unforgivable television, and even worse theater. I'm talking bone-crushing theater, the type our ancient ancestors used to oppress their enemies before the invention of the stretching rack. We're talking torture on a par with the Scottsfield Dinner Theater's 1994 revival of *Come Blow Your Horn*, a production that violated every tenet of the Human Rights Accord. To those of you who enjoy the comfort of a nice set of thumbscrews, allow me to recommend any of the crucifying holiday plays and pageants currently eliciting screams of mercy from within the confines of our local elementary and middle schools. I will, no doubt, be taken to task for criticizing the work of children but, as any pathologist will agree, if there's a cancer it's best to treat it as early as possible.

If you happened to stand over four feet tall, the agony awaiting you at Sacred Heart Elementary began the moment you took your seat. These were mean little chairs corralled into a "theater" haunted by the lingering stench of industrial-strength lasagna. My question is not why they chose to stage the production in a poorly disguised cafeteria, but why they chose to stage it at all. "The Story of the First Christmas" is an overrated clunker of a holiday pageant, best left to those looking to cure their chronic insomnia. Although the program listed no director, the apathetic staging suggested the limp, partially paralyzed hand of Sister Mary Elizabeth Bronson, who should have been excommunicated after last season's disastrous Thanksgiving program. Here again the first through third-grade actors graced the stage with an enthusiasm most children reserve for a smallpox vaccination. One could hardly blame them for their lack of vitality, as the stingy, uninspired script consists, not of springy dialogue, but rather of a deadening series of pronouncements.

Mary to Joseph: "I am tired."
Joseph to Mary: "We will rest here for the night."

There's no fire, no give and take, and the audience soon grows weary of this passionless relationship.

In the role of Mary, six-year-old Shannon Burke just barely manages to pass herself off as a virgin. A cloying, preening stage presence, her performance seemed based on nothing but an annoying proclivity toward lifting her skirt and, on rare occasions, opening her eyes. As Joseph, second-grade student Douglas Trazzare needed to be reminded that, although his character did not technically impregnate the virgin mother, he should behave as though he were capable of doing so. Thrown into the mix were a handful of inattentive shepherds and a trio of gift-bearing seven-year-olds who could probably give the Three Stooges a run for their money. As for the lighting, Sacred Heart Elementary chose to rely on nothing more than the flashbulbs ignited by the obnoxious stage mothers and fathers who had created those zombies staggering back and forth across the linoleum-floored dining hall. Under certain circumstances parental pride is understandable but it has no place in the theater, where it tends to encourage a child to believe in a talent that, more often than not, simply fails to exist. In order for a pageant to work, it needs to appeal to everyone, regardless of their relationship to the actors onstage. This production found me on the side of the yawning cafeteria workers.

Pointing to the oversized crate that served as a manger, one particularly insufficient wise man proclaimed, "A child is bored."

Yes, well, so was this adult.

Once again, the sadists at the Jane Snow-Hernandez Middle School have taken up their burning pokers in an attempt to prod *A Christmas Carol* into some form of submission. I might have overlooked the shoddy production values and dry, leaden pacing, but these are sixth-graders we're talking about and they should have known better. There's really no point in adapting this Dickensian stinker unless you're capable of looking beyond the novel's dime-store morality and getting to what little theatrical meat the story has to offer. The point is to eviscerate the gooey center but here it's served up as the entrée, and a foul pudding it is. Most of the blame goes to the director, eleven-year-old Becky Michaels, who seems to have picked up her staging secrets from the school's crossing guard. She tends to clump her actors, moving them only in groups of five or more. A strong proponent of trendy, racially mixed casting, Michaels gives us a black Tiny Tim, leaving the audience to wonder, "What, is this kid supposed to be adopted?" It's a distracting move, wrongheaded and pointless. The role was played by young Lamar Williams, who, if nothing else, managed to sustain a decent limp. The program notes that he recently lost his right foot to diabetes, but was that reason enough to cast him? As Tiny Tim, the boy spends his stage time essentially trawling for sympathy, stealing focus from even the brightly lit Exit sign. Bob Cratchit, played here by the aptly named Benjamin Trite, seems to have picked up his Cockney accent from watching a few videotaped episodes of "Hee-Haw," and Hershel Fleishman's Scrooge was almost as lame as Tiny Tim.

The set was not without its charm but Jodi Lennon's abysmal costumes should hopefully mark the end of a short and unremarkable career. I was gagging from the smell of spray-painted sneakers and if I see one more top hat made from an oatmeal canister, I swear I'm going to pull out a gun.

The problem with both these shows stems partially from their maddening eagerness to please. With smiles stretched tight as bungee cords, these hopeless amateurs pranced and gamboled across our local stages, hiding behind their youth and begging, practically demanding, we forgive their egregious mistakes. The English language was chewed into a paste, missed opportunities came and went, and the sets were changed so slowly you'd think the stagehands were encumbered by full-body casts. While billing themselves as holiday entertainment, none of these productions came close to capturing the spirit of Christmas. This glaring irony seemed to escape the throngs of ticketholders, who ate these undercooked turkeys right down to the bone. Here were audiences that chuckled at every technical snafu and applauded riotously each time a new character wandered out onto the stage. With the close of every curtain they leapt to their feet in one ovation after another, leaving me wedged into my doll-sized chair and wondering, "Is it just them, or am I missing something?"

Christmas Means Giving

For the first twelve years of our marriage Beth and I happily set the neighborhood standard for comfort and luxury. It was an established fact that we were brighter and more successful but the community seemed to accept our superiority without much complaint and life flowed on the way it should. I used to own a hedge polisher, an electric shovel, and three Rolex gas grills that stood side by side in the backyard. One was for chicken, one for beef, and the third I had specially equipped to steam the oriental pancakes we were always so fond of. When the holidays rolled around I used to rent a moving van and drive into the city, snatching up every bright new extravagance that caught my eye. Our twin sons, Taylor and Weston, could always count on the latest electronic toy or piece of sporting equipment. Beth might receive a riding vacuum cleaner or a couple pair of fur-lined jeans and those were just the stocking stuffers! There were disposable boats, ultrasuede basketballs, pewter knapsacks, and solar-powered card shufflers. I'd buy them shoes and clothes and bucketfuls of jewelry from the finest boutiques and department stores. Far be it from me to snoop around for a bargain or discount. I always paid top dollar, thinking that those foot-long price tags really *meant* something about Christmas. After opening our gifts we'd sit down to a sumptuous banquet, feasting on every imaginable variety of meat and pudding. When one of us got full and felt uncomfortable, we'd stick a silver wand down our throats, throw up, and start eating all over again. In effect, we weren't much different from anyone else. Christmas was a season of bounty and, to the outside world, we were just about the most bountiful people anyone could think of. We thought we were happy but that all changed on one crisp Thanksgiving day shortly after the Cottinghams arrived.

If my memory serves me correctly, the Cottinghams were trouble from the very first moment they moved in next door. Doug, Nancy, and their unattractive eight-year-old daughter, Eileen, were exceedingly envious and greedy people. Their place was a little smaller than ours but it made sense, seeing as there were four of us and only three of them. Still though, something about the size of our house so bothered them that they hadn't even unpacked the first suitcase before starting construction on an indoor skating rink and a three-thousand-square-foot pavilion where Doug could show off his collection of pre-Columbian sofa beds. Because we felt like doing so, Beth and I then began construction on an indoor soccer field and a five-thousand-square-foot rotunda where I could comfortably display *my* collection of pre-*pre*-Columbian sofa beds. Doug would tell all the neighbors I'd stolen the idea from him but I'd been thinking about pre-pre-Columbian sofa beds long before the Cottinghams pulled into town. They just had to cause trouble, no matter what the cost. When Beth and I built a seven-screen multiplex theater they had to go and build themselves a *twelve*-screener. This went on and on and, to make a long story short, within a year's time neither one of us had much of a yard. The two houses now butted right up against each other and we blocked out the west-side windows so that we wouldn't have to look into their gaudy fitness center or second-story rifle range.

Despite their competitive nature, Beth and I tried our best to be neighborly and occasionally invite them over for rooftop barbecues and so forth. I'd attempt to make adult conversation, saying something like "I just paid eight thousand dollars for a pair of sandals that don't even fit me." Doug would counter, saying that he himself had just paid ten thousand for a single flip-flop he wouldn't wear even if it *did* fit him. He was always very combative that way. If it cost you seventy thousand dollars to have a cavity filled, you could bet your boots it cost him at least a hundred and twenty-five thousand. I suffered his company for the better part of a year until one November evening when we got into a spat over which family sent out the most meaningful Christmas card. Beth and I normally hired a noted photographer to snap a portrait of the entire family surrounded by the gifts we had received the year before. Inside the card would be the price of these gifts along with the message "Christmas Means Giving." The Cottinghams favored *their* card, which consisted of a Xeroxed copy of Doug and Nancy's stock portfolio. I said that while it is all very well and good to *have* money, their card said nothing about the way they *spent* money. Like our card said, Christmas means giving and even if he were to gussy up his stock report with a couple of press-on candy canes it would still fail to send the proper holiday message. The conversation grew quite heated and some punches were thrown between the wives. We'd all had a few drinks and by the time the Cottinghams left our house it was generally assumed that our friendship was over. I dwelled upon the incident for a day or two and then turned my attention toward the approaching holidays.

We'd just finished another of our gut-busting Thanksgiving dinners and Beth, the boys, and I were watching a bullfight on TV. We could watch whatever we wanted back then because we still had our satellite dish. Juan Carlos Ponce de Velasquez had just been gored something fierce and we were all acting pretty excited about it when the doorbell rang. I figured one of the boys had ordered a pizza and opened the door surprised to find a foul-smelling beggar. He was a thin, barefooted man with pepperoni-sized scabs on his legs and an unkempt beard smeared with several different varieties of jam. I sensed it was the jam we'd thrown into the garbage the night before and one look at our overturned trash can told me I was right. This had me pretty ticked off but before I could say anything about it, the old bum pulled out a coffee mug and started whining for money.

When Beth asked who was at the door I called out, "Code Blue," which was our secret signal that one of us should release the hounds. We had two of them back then, big Dobermans named Butterscotch and Mr. Lewis. Beth tried to summon them from the dining room but, having gorged themselves on turkey and stuffing, it was all they could do to lift their heads and vomit. Seeing as they were laid up, I got down on my hands and knees and bit the guy myself. Maybe it was the bullfight but, for whatever reason, I had a sudden taste for blood. My teeth barely broke the skin but that was all it took to send the old coot hobbling over to the Cottinghams' place. I watched him pound upon their door, knowing full well what would happen when he told competitive Doug Copy Cat that I'd given him one measly bite on the calf. Beth called me into the house for one reason or another and when I returned to the door a few minutes later, I saw Helvetica, the Cottinghams' maid, taking a photograph of Doug, Nancy, and Eileen hand-ing the tramp a one-dollar bill.

I knew something was up and, sure enough, two weeks later I came to find that exact same snapshot on the Cottinghams' Christmas card along with the words "Christmas means giving." That had always been *our* slogan and here he'd stolen it, twisting the message in an attempt to make us appear selfish. It had never been our way to give to others but I started having second thoughts when I noticed the phenom-enal response the Cottinghams received on the basis of their Christmas card. Suddenly they were all anyone was talking about. Walk into any holiday party and you'd hear, "Did you see it? I think it's positively enchanting. Here these people donated money to an absolute stranger! Can you beat that? A whole dollar they gave to this vagrant person with absolutely nothing to his name. If you ask me, those Cottinghams are a couple of very brave and generous people."

Doug would probably say that I unfairly stole his idea when I myself became a generous person but this was not the case. I'd been thinking of being generous long before he showed up on the scene and, besides that, if he could illegally pinch my holiday slogan, why couldn't I casually borrow a concept that had been around for a good ten years? When I first told people that I had given two dollars to the Inner City Headache Fund they turned away as if they didn't believe me. Then I actually *did* give two dollars to the Headache Fund and boy, did things ever change once I started flashing around that canceled check! Generosity can actually make people feel quite uncomfortable if you talk about it enough. I don't mean the bad "boring uncomfortable" but something much richer. If practiced correctly, generosity can induce feelings of shame, inadequacy, and even envy, to name just a few. The most important thing is that you keep some written or visual proof of your donation, otherwise there's really no point in giving to charity. Doug Cottingham would say I took that line from him but I'm pretty sure I read it in a tax manual.

I carried my canceled check to all the important holiday parties but people lost interest shortly after New Year's Eve. The seasons passed and I forgot all about my generosity until the following Thanksgiving, when the old tramp returned to our neighborhood. He must have remembered the previous year's bite to the leg and, as a result, he was just about to pass us by when we called him in for a good dose of benevolence. First we videotaped him eating a palmful of leftover stuffing and then I had Beth snap a picture as I handed the geezer a VCR. It was an old top-loading Betamax but put a new cord on it and I'm sure it would have worked just fine. We watched then as he strapped it on his back and headed next door to continue his begging. The sight of that VCR was all it took for that skunk Doug Cottingham, who stepped into his house and returned to present the old codger with an eight-track tape deck and, oh, once again their maid was on hand to take a picture of it. We then called the tramp over to our house and gave him a year-old blow-dryer. The Cottinghams responded with a toaster oven. Within an hour we had advanced to pool tables and StairMasters. Doug gave him a golf cart and I gave him my satellite dish. This accelerated until any fool could see exactly where it was heading. Handing over the keys to his custom-built motorized travel sauna, Doug Cottingham gave me a look that seemed to say, "Top *that*, Neighbor!" Beth and I had seen that look before and we hated it. I could have easily topped his travel sauna but we were running low on film and thought it best to cut to the chase. Why needlessly escalate when we all knew what was most important? After a brief conference, Beth and I called the tramp back over and asked which he liked better, young boys or young girls. Much to our delight he said that girls were too much of a headache but that he'd had some fun with boys before his last visit to our local state penitentiary. That said, we gave him our ten-year-old sons, Taylor and Weston. Top that, Neighbor! You should have seen the look on Doug Cottingham's face! That year's Christmas card was the most meaningful to date. It pictured our sons' tearful good-bye along with the message "Christmas means giving until it hurts."

We were the toast of the neighborhood that holiday season, back on top where we belonged. Beth and I were *the* couple to have at any cocktail party or informal tree trimming.

"Where are those supergenerous people with that delightful Christmas card?" someone would ask, and the host would point in our direction while the Cottinghams bitterly gritted their teeth. As a last-ditch effort to better their names they donated their horse-faced daughter, Eileen, to a crew of needy pirates but anyone in the know could see it as the desperate gesture it really was. Once again we were the ones everyone wanted to be with and the warm glow of their admiration carried us through the holiday season. We received a second helping of awe early the following summer when the boys were discovered dead in what used to be Doug Cottingham's motorized travel sauna. The neighbors all wanted to send flowers but we said we'd prefer them to make a donation in our name to the National Sauna Advisory Board or the Sex Offenders Defense Fund. This was a good move and soon we had established ourselves as "Christlike." The Cottinghams were, of course, furious and immediately set to work on their tired game of one-upsmanship. It was most likely the only thing they thought about but we didn't lose any sleep over it.

For that year's holiday cards we had settled on the theme "Christmas means giving until it bleeds." Shortly after Thanksgiving Beth and I had visited our local blood bank, where we nearly drained our bodies' precious accounts. Pale and dizzy from our efforts, it was all we could do to lift a hand and wave to one another from our respective gurneys. We recovered in time and were just sealing our envelopes when the postman delivered our neighbors' holiday card, which read "Christmas means giving of yourself." The cover pictured Doug lying outstretched upon an operating table as a team of surgeons busily, studiously, removed his glistening Cottingham lung. Inside the card was a photograph of the organ's recipient, a haggard coal miner holding a sign that read "Douglas Cottingham saved my life."

How dare he! Beth and I had practically invented the theme of medical generosity and it drove us mad, that smug, superior expression seeping from beneath our neighbor's surgical mask. Any long-married couple can, in times of crisis, communicate without speaking. This fact was illustrated as my wife and I wordlessly leapt into action. Throwing down her half-sealed envelope, Beth called the hospital while I contacted a photographer from our car phone. Arrangements were made and before the night was over I had donated both my eyes, a lung, one of my kidneys, and several important veins surrounding my heart. Having an unnatural attachment to her internal organs, Beth surrendered her scalp, her teeth, her right leg, and both breasts. It wasn't until after her surgery that we realized my wife's contributions were nontransferable, but by that time it was too late to sew them back on. She gave the scalp to a startled cancer patient, made a keepsake necklace of her teeth, and brought the leg and breasts to the animal shelter, where they were hand-fed to a litter of starving Border collies. That made the local evening news and once again the Cottinghams were green with envy over our good fortune. Donating organs to humans was one thing, but the community went wild over what Beth had done for those poor abandoned puppies. At each and every holiday party our hosts would beg my wife to shake their dog's hand or pass a blessing over the shell of their ailing tortoise. The coal-mining recipient of Doug Cottingham's lung had died when his cigarette set fire to the sheets and bandages covering his chest and now their name was practically worthless.

We were at the Hepplewhites' Christmas Eve party when I overheard Beth whisper, "That Doug Cottingham couldn't even donate a decent lung!" She laughed then, long and hard, and I placed my hand upon her shoulder, feeling the gentle bite of her keepsake necklace. I was no doubt drawing a good deal of attention myself, but this was Beth's night and I gave it to her freely because I was such a generous person. We were a team, she and I, and while I couldn't see the way people were looking at us, I could feel it just as surely as I sensed the warmth cast off by the Hepplewhites' roaring fire.

There would be other Christmases, but I think Beth and I both knew that this one was special. In a year's time we would give away the house, our money, and what remained of our possessions. After scouting around for the right neighborhood, we would move into a village of cardboard boxes located beneath the Ragsdale Cloverleaf. The Cottinghams, true to their nature, would move into a smaller box next door. The begging would go relatively well during the holiday season but come deep winter things would get hard and we'd be visited by wave after wave of sorrow and disease. Beth would die after a long, sad struggle with tuberculosis but not until after Doug Cottingham and his wife had been killed by pneumonia. I'd try not to let it bother me that they had died first but in truth I would have a very difficult time dealing with it. Whenever my jealousy would get the best of me I would reflect back upon that perfect Christmas Eve at the Hepplewhites'. Shuddering beneath my blanket of damp newspapers, I'd try to recall the comforting sound of Beth's carefree laughter and picture her raw head thrown back in merriment, those bright, gleaming gums reflecting the light of a crystal chandelier. With luck, the memory of our love and generosity would lull me toward a profound and heavy sleep that would last until morning.

The Incomplete Quad

I spent my high-school years staring at the pine trees outside my classroom window and picturing myself on the campus of an Ivy League university, where my wealthy roommate Colgate would leave me notes reading "Meet me on the quad at five." I wasn't sure what a quad was, but I knew that I wanted one desperately. My college friends would own horses and monogrammed shoehorns. I'd spend weekends at my roommate's estate, where his mother would say things like "I've instructed Helvetica to prepare those little pancakes you're so fond of, but she's had a devil of a time locating fresh cape gooseberries." This woman would have really big teeth that she'd reveal every time she threw back her head to laugh at one of my many witticisms. "You're an absolute caution," she'd bray. "Tell me you'll at least consider joining us this Christmas at Bridle Haven; it just wouldn't be the same without you."

I fantasized with the nagging suspicion there was something missing, something I was forgetting. This something turned out to be grades. It was with profound disappointment I discovered it took more than a C average to attend Harvard. *Average*, that was the word that got to me. C and average, the two went hand in hand.

I was sent instead to a state college in western North Carolina where the low brick buildings were marked with plaques reading ERECTED 1974, and my roommate left notes accusing me of stealing his puka shell necklace or remedial English book. I expect someday to open the newspaper and discover the government had used that campus as part of a perverse experiment to study the effects of continuous, high-decibel Pink Floyd albums on the minds of students who could manufacture a bong out of any given object but could not comprehend that it is simply not possible to drive a van to Europe.

I spent my year buckling down and improving my grades in the hope that I might transfer somewhere, anywhere, else. I eventually chose Kent State because people had been killed there. At least they hadn't died of boredom, that was saying something. "Kent State!" everyone said. "Do you think you'll be safe up there?"

I arrived the following September and was assigned to a dormitory largely reserved for handicapped students. It had always been my habit to look away from someone in a wheelchair, but here I had no choice, as they were everywhere. These were people my own age who had jumped into a deceptively shallow pool or underestimated the linebackers of the opposing team. They had driven drunk on prom night or slipped off their parents' roof while cleaning the gutters; one little mistake, and they could never take it back. The paraplegics gathered in the lobby, perfecting their wheelies and discussing their customized cars while the quads purred by in their electric chariots, squinting against the lit cigarettes propped artfully between their lips.

The first quarter I roomed with a fellow named Todd, an amiable Dayton native whose only handicap was having red hair. The quadriplegics had the best drug connections, so we often found ourselves hanging out in their rooms. "The hook-ah's over on the shelf," they'd say. "Right next to the rectal suppositories." Over time I grew accustomed to the sight of a friend's colostomy bag and came to think of Kent State as something of an I.V. League university. The state would pay your board if you roomed with a handicapped student, so second quarter I moved in with Dale, a seventy-five-pound sophomore with muscular dystrophy. I learned to bathe Dale and set him on the toilet. I turned the pages of his books, dialed the telephone, and held the receiver against his mouth as he spoke. I dressed him and combed his hair, fed him and clipped his toenails, but I can't say that we were ever close.

Midway through the term Dale was sent back home to live with his parents, and I moved in with Peg, a fun girl with a degenerative nerve disease. Peg was labeled an "incomplete quad" and liked to joke that she couldn't finish anything. Already we had something in common. She had come to school to escape her parents, who refused her any beverage after six p.m. They complained that at the end of a long day, they were simply too worn out to set her on the toilet. God had chosen her to suffer this disease, and if she had any com-plaints, she should take it up with Him. This was a nasty illness that left its host progressively incapacitated. Peg's limbs were twisted and unreliable and had a mind of their own. A cup of scalding coffee, a lit cigarette, forks and steak knives— objects sprung from her hands with no prior notice. She wore thick glasses strapped to her head and soiled sheepskin booties on her useless, curled feet. Peg's voice was slurred to the point that information operators and pizza-delivery services, think-ing she was drunk, would hang up on her. Unnerved by the sight of her, Peg's professors automatically agreed with everything she had to say. "Good question!" they'd shout. "That's very perceptive of you. Does anyone else have any thoughts on what she just said?" She might ask to use the bathroom, but because no one could understand her, it was always the same answer. "Good point, isn't it class!"

In the cafeteria she was met with frantic congeniality. Rather than embarrass themselves trying to figure out her choice of an entrée, they just went ahead and piled everything on her plate.

A person in a wheelchair often feels invisible. Push a wheelchair and you're invisible as well. Outside of the dorm, the only people to address us would speak as if we were deaf, kneeling beside the chair to shout, 'FATHER TONY IS HAVING A GUITAR MASS THIS SUNDAY. WOULD YOU LIKE TO JOIN US?'

Peg would beckon the speaker close and whisper, 'I collect the teeth from live kittens and use them to make necklaces for Satan.'

'WELL SURE YOU DO,' they'd say. 'THAT'S WHAT OUR FELLOWSHIP IS ALL ABOUT.'

For Peg, being invisible was an old and tiresome story. To me, it definitely had some hidden potential. So began our life of crime.

We started off in grocery stores. Peg had a sack on the back of her wheelchair, which I would fill with thick steaks and frozen lobster tails. There was no need to slink behind pyramids of canned goods, hiding from the manager; we did our stealing right out in the open. Peg carried a canvas bag on her lap and stuffed it with everything she could get her hands on. Canned olives, teriyaki sauce, plastic tubs of pudding—our need had nothing to do with it. The point was to take from an unfair world. We quit going to the cafeteria, preferring to cook our meals in the dormitory kitchen, the butter dripping off our chins. We moved on to bookstores and record shops, guaranteed that no one would say, "I think I see that crippled girl stealing the new Joni Mitchell album." Circumstances prevented us from stealing anything larger than our heads, but anything else was ours for the taking.

For spring break we decided to visit my family in Raleigh. Being invisible has its merits when you're shoplifting but tends to hold a person back while hitchhiking. We parked ourselves beside the interstate, Peg's thumb twitching at odd intervals. The five-hundred-mile trip took us close to three days. It was our story that we were newly married, and were heading south to start a new life for ourselves. Churchy couples would pull over, apologizing that their car was too small to accommodate a wheelchair. They couldn't give us a ride, but would we accept twenty dollars and a bucket of fried chicken?

You bet we would. "There's a hospital in Durham we're hoping might do some good," I'd say, patting Peg on the shoulder. "Here we are, a couple of newlyweds, and then *this* had to happen."

CB radios were activated and station wagons appeared. Waitresses in roadside restaurants would approach our table whispering, "YOUR BILL HAS BEEN TAKEN CARE OF," and pointing to some teary-eyed couple standing beside the cash register. We found it amusing and pictured these Samaritans notifying their pastor to boast, "We saw this crippled girl and her husband and, well, we didn't have much but we did what we could."

Someone would check us into a motel and give us cash for bus fare, making us promise to never hitchhike again. I'd take Peg out of her chair, lay her on the bed, and sprinkle the money down upon her. It was a pale imitation of a movie scene in which crafty con artists shower themselves with hundred-dollar bills. Our version involved smaller denominations and handfuls of change, but still, it made us feel alive.

We were in West Virginia when one of the wheels fell off Peg's chair. It was dusk on a rural state highway without a building in sight when an elderly man in a pickup truck swooped in and carried us all the way to my parents' front door, a trip that was surely out of his way. "Five-four-oh-six North Hills Drive? I'm headed right that way, no trouble at all. Which state did you say that was in?"

We arrived unannounced, surprising the startled members of my family. I'd hoped my parents might feel relaxed in Peg's company, but when they reacted with nervous discomfort, I realized that this was even better. I wanted them to see that I had changed. Far from average, I had become responsible in ways they could never dream of. Peg was *my* charge, *my* toy, and I was the only one who knew how to turn her off and on. "Well," I said, wiping her mouth with a dinner napkin, "I think it's time for *somebody's* bath."

My brother and sisters reacted as though I had brought home a sea lion. They invited their friends to stare from the deck as I laid Peg on a picnic blanket in the backyard. My father repaired the wheelchair, and when Peg thanked him, he left the dinner table and returned handing her a second fork. "She didn't ask for a fork," I said. "She asked for your watch." "My watch?" he said. "The one I'm wearing?" He tapped his fingers against the face for a moment or two. "Well, golly, I guess if it means that much to her, sure, she can have my watch." He handed it over. "And your belt," I said. "She'll need that, too. Hurry up, man, the girl is crippled."

My mother visited her hiding place and returned with a wad of cash for our bus fare back to Ohio. She called me into the kitchen and shoved the money into my hand, whispering, "I don't know what kind of a game you're playing, mister, but you ought to be ashamed of yourself." It was an actual whisper, designed to be heard only by me.

The bus ride back to Ohio was long and cheerless. The second time Peg asked to use the bathroom, I snapped. "You just went three hours ago." I shouted. "Jesus, what's your problem, do I have to take care of everything?" It got on my nerves, the way she depended on me. We'd gone on this trip, she'd had a good time, what *more* did she want? How was it that by the time we left my parents' house, *I* was considered the cripple, not her but *me*, me who had to do everything while she just sat there spilling ashes down the front of her shirt.

My mood deteriorated. We returned to school, where Peg related our adventures to a crowd of friends. I listened in, silently substituting every *we* for an *I*. "We" didn't talk a truck driver out of thirty dollars and a brand-new curling wand, *I* did that, *ME*, how dare she take half the credit. "She is some kind of brave," our classmates would say. "I wouldn't have the courage to do *half* the things that she does—and I can walk!" The spring quarter began but by the second week, I'd stopped attending class, deciding instead to bone up on my drugs and become my own private adventurer. I signed up for sky-diving lessons at the local airfield. The training sessions were deceptively simple, but when the time came for the actual jump, they had to pry my white knuckles off the wing of the plane. I begged and pleaded and all the way down I pictured myself in a wheelchair, hoping that the person assigned to care for me would have none of my qualities.

At the end of the school year I hitchhiked to San Francisco, enchanted with the idea of leading an adult life surrounded by people who could wash their own hair. My friend Veronica got me a room at a residence hotel, and I found work as a bicycle messenger. The streets of my neighborhood were fragrant with eucalyptus trees, and every passing stranger offered the hope that tomorrow just might be the day I was offered a comfortable job or a twelve-room apartment. I was far from my family and often pictured them suffering their vacations without me. They had treated me poorly, but I had come out on top because that was the kind of person I was, headstrong and independent. Me, the winner.

I was cooking spaghetti and ketchup in my electric skillet one night when I heard the pay phone ring outside my room. It was Peg, calling to say she had rolled away from home.

"Good for you," I said. "This is going to be the best thing you've ever done." When I learned she was calling from the San Francisco airport, I modified my statement, saying, "I don't know about this, Peg. Won't your parents be worried about you? What about your education?"

What followed was a lesson that college bears no resemblance to civilian life. Leaving the building involved carrying Peg up and down five flights of stairs before returning for her wheelchair. The landlord charged me a double rate for having a guest in my room, and I lost my job when Peg fell against the bathtub, taking five stitches in her head. This was a big city where people held onto their fried chicken. Nobody cared that we were a young married couple searching for a better life and not even the buses would stop to pick us up. Fed up, Veronica and I decided to head north to pick apples. I told Peg, hoping she might accept the news and return home, but she held fast. Armed with a telephone directory, she placed collect calls to government agencies whose workers held the line when she dropped the phone or took twenty minutes to locate a pen. Volunteers wheeled her to meetings in cluttered ground-floor offices where paraplegics raised their fists in salute to her determination and tenacity. She wound up living alone in a brick apartment building somewhere in Berkeley. An attendant visited every twelve hours to prepare her meals and help her onto the toilet. If a spasm sent her onto the floor, she lay there patiently until help arrived to dress her wounds. When her parents called, she either hung up or cursed them, depending upon her mood. Peg's greatest dream was to live far from her parents and enjoy a satisfying sexual encounter. She sent a postcard detailing the event. There had been three wheelchairs parked around her waterbed, the third belonging to a bisexual paraplegic whose job it was to shift the lovers into position. Within a year her health deteriorated to the point where she could no longer be left alone for twelve-hour stretches. We both wound up crawling back to our parents but continued to keep in touch, her letters progressively harder to read. The last I heard from her was in 1979, shortly before she died. Peg had undergone a religious transformation and was in the process of writing her memoirs, hoping to have them published by the same Christian press that had scored a recent hit with *Joni!*, a book detailing the life of a young quadriplegic who painted woodland creatures by holding the brush between her teeth. She sent me a three-page chapter regarding our hitchhiking trip to North Carolina. "God bless all those wonderful people who helped us along the way!" she wrote. "Each and every day I thank the Lord for their love and kindness."

I wrote back saying that if she remembered correctly, we'd made fun of those people. "We lied to them and mocked them behind their backs, and now you want them blessed? What's happened to you?"

Looking back, I think I can guess what might have happened to her. Following a brief period of hard-won independence she came to appreciate the fact that people aren't foolish as much as they are kind. Peg understood that at a relatively early age. Me, it took years.

Girl Crazy

"Producers of the ABC sitcom *Ellen* are discussing plans to have the main character disclose that she is a lesbian."

—*The Times*

Dear ABC:

Why is it that Ellen can be a lesbian but a six-year-old boy from North Carolina can't kiss a little girl without being suspended for sexual harassment? According to you and Ellen, things would have been just fine had he kissed a *boy!* Just when I think I know what's going on in the world, you switch a show from one time slot to another and then change the characters into homosexuals so nobody can recognize them anymore. You're playing games with our minds and I, for one, don't like it. Mess with Regis and Kathie Lee, and you'll be picking your front teeth out from between my bloody knuckles!

Barb Diesel
High Point, N.C.

Dear ABC:

Kudos for allowing Ellen to reflect the rich cultural diversity of the real America, a place where differences are celebrated and frank discussions of sexuality are common as evening prayer. Don't be fooled or intimidated by the right wing's proposed boycotts. For every rabid fundamentalist, there are ten free-thinking progressives whose viewing habits cannot be altered by fear and hatred. I congratulate you for breaking new ground and feel certain your courageous decision will reward us all. One question, though: How soon after she comes out will Ellen start getting it on with other women? There must be all kinds of college-age girls ready to shed their sweaters and hop into the sack with the stacked and lovely Miss DeGeneres. Stick with the hot stuff and you've got yourself a loyal viewer.

Dimitrius Sappho
New York City

Dear ABC:

Stop the cameras, because I've got a little news flash for you: Not all lesbians own bookstores and drink coffee. As a practicing homosexual for the past eighteen years, I am sick to death of your stereotyping. There are hundreds of thousands of us out here who have never read a book, touched a cash register, or had a sip of coffee, either hot or iced. Caffeine makes me jumpy, and I prefer drinking Hawaiian Punch with just a whisper of vodka. Does that make me a freak? In your attempt to "package" Ellen, you hurt those of us who live outside the little cardboard boxes in which you confine your minority characters. Undoubtedly your network is run by Japanese who think they can squeeze out a few extra yen by stirring up a little controversy. Well, squeeze away, Emperor Mitsubishi. You ain't getting a dime out of me.

Christina Manly
Baltimore, Md.

Dear ABC:

If you are going to turn anyone into a homosexual, I suggest you do it to Hugh Downs on *20/20*. I am a heterosexual man and, as my wife can attest, I have always been a devoted and responsible partner. I have a distinguished war record, three children, and five beautiful grandchildren who are the love of my life. Never have I strayed from my marriage or allowed myself to think sexually of any man other than—You guessed it! Hugh Downs is a fox, and I would love to watch him let loose and cuddle with a few of his guests. I don't know which would be higher—your ratings or *my* blood pressure. (Ha ha.) Seriously, though, if you truly do possess the power to turn people into homosexuals, I'll go to bed praying you have the good sense to choose Hugh Downs rather than some frumpy woman whose show I've never watched.

Name Withheld Upon Request
Santa Fe, N.M.

Dear ABC:

I have read that you are thinking of turning the television character Ellen into a homosexual and am wondering if you plan to make her a slutty lesbian or the type who stays at home and gardens. If you move in favor of the slut, allow me to suggest my former wife as a role model. Is that the right word? I mean that if Ellen wants to be a slutty lesbian you can base her character on my former wife—all she *does* is tell lies and slut around. On our wedding night, I shaved all the hair off my body, because she said it made her nervous. Then, when I was bleeding from razor nicks, guess who chose to sleep on the sofa? Now she's living the slutty high life and I have nothing. If I provide you with my ex-wife's name and address, will you pay me for it? Please have your lawyers contact me as soon as possible. If my mother answers, ask to speak to Timothy. DO NOT LEAVE A MESSAGE WITH MY MOTHER, as I don't want her knowing my business.

Timothy Dykeman
Cleveland, Ohio

Card Wired

"Now even the greeting card industry is getting in on the mass-therapy act [by designing cards] for people who have something delicate to communicate to their partner but somehow cannot find the words—or, more likely, the courage—to say it out loud. Buy enough of these cards and you could virtually hold an entire conversation with your loved one (or not) without opening your mouth." —*The Independent*

May-September Romance / Impotence

To a young Valentine from a venerable husband:
Think of me as a fine champagne, my love,
The grapes crushed long before you were born.
Here's hoping that my impressive label will hold your
    interest
Until I find the strength
To pop my cork.

Locksmiths / Vans and Drinking

Good morning, Valentine!

When you lost your job as a locksmith, I'm afraid I wasn't very understanding. I was wrong, asking you to use your talents to break into my stepmother's van. Call me sentimental, but I'll arrange for your bail as soon as possible. And I'm looking forward to spending a quiet afternoon, just the two of us, with the six-pack we found in my stepmother's van.

Public Disgrace / Chinchillas

When I first told you I planned to resign as Lieutenant
   Governor,
You turned your head,
And I caught the ghost of your perfume.
I'm praying that, come Valentine's Day,
You might agree to leave the house
And visit me here at the treatment center,
Where we can hold hands and discuss my plans
To open a chinchilla ranch.

Former Spouse / Stress / Standup Comedy

Thank you, Valentine,
For understanding my need to maintain a casual sexual
   relationship
With my former wife,
And for replacing the battery in my Taurus on that cold,
   rainy day

When I felt too stressed out.
I appreciate the way you stood by my side during my
    standup comedy "phase,"
And I give you my word:
I'll never again publicly read from your dream journal.
(Though it *is* quite funny!)
I'm not sure why I'm apologizing.
Maybe it's just my way of saying
I still care.

Divorce / Ticket-Stub Collectors

This will be our last Valentine's Day together
So let's make the most of it, shall we?
Oh, I think we can forgo
Chocolate candies and aromatic bouquets,
Candlelit dinners and walks in the rain.
We made a mistake. I did anyway.
I've got a feeling that St. Patrick's Day will find us in the
    company of other, finer lovers.
Me and Josie Tomchuck
And you ... who can say?
Let's take this day to pack your things and call the movers.
Who knows?
Maybe while dividing our collection of ticket stubs
We'll brush shoulders
And exchange a bittersweet smile.

Puncture Wounds

I'm sorry about the puncture wound.

What started off as play became what I'm hoping the courts
   will define as "roughhousing."
I know you need a new kidney.
Under different circumstances, I'd really love to help.
Perhaps this Valentine's Day we can sit quietly for a change.
Maybe you can redraft your will
And withdraw the charges.
Friends?

How to Spend the Budget Surplus

Dear President Clinton:

I read in the Sentinel that, thanks to some belt tightening by the likes of yours truly, we can expect a budget surplus by the year 1999. Seeing as you and your penny-pinching gang of thugs have succeeded in destroying the N.E.A., I strongly urge you to take that budget surplus and use it to sponsor a series of important public art works. The most costly, and I believe, energetic of these projects is my enclosed proposal to carpet the state of New Mexico. This piece calls for the hiring of no less than fourteen thousand Native Americans. Outfitted in government-issue sun visors and kneepads, these people will work nine hours a day for an estimated period of twelve years. The carpet can be bought wholesale through an uncle of mine in Staten Island, and my boyfriend knows where we can get some tacks. Having lost my grant money to tar and feather the Statue of Liberty, I must take the position that you owe not just me but all creative Americans seeking enlightenment through the majesty of art.

Amanda Savage
Brooklyn, N.Y.

Dear President Clinton:

I don't know how much of a surplus you're expecting, but I think the first thing you should do is put some stores on your so-called Washington Mall. My family and I visited last summer and were disappointed to find nothing but grass and statues. Since it's the capital of our country; shouldn't Washington's mall be world-class? You've got a fountain and plenty of room for parking. Let's bring on the food court.

Just a suggestion.

The Taylor Gang
Turf Haven, Mich.

Dear Mr. President:

I hear you're looking for ways to spend our budget surplus and thought my little story might inspire you. When I was young, my father would take half of my weekly allowance and put it into a fish tank for my sister's college education. He did this because he liked her the best and I myself had never expressed any interest in higher education. When, at the age of twenty, my sister left college to become a performance poet, my father returned the balance of my money. It came to two hundred and thirty-eight dollars in change, and I spent it all on records and submarine sandwiches.

Brian Teetsel
Lake Janet, Fla.

Dear President Pothead:

If I remember correctly, the last time we had a surplus, in 1969, you were deseeding a bag of reefer in some cushy college dormitory while I was living in a bamboo cage eating spiders and dung beetles in an effort to stay alive. Sound fair?

Sooner or later, you'll have to lay down your bong and do some serious thinking about this surplus situation. While you are no doubt tempted to spend the money on Thai stick or new Gro Lites for the White House basement, I urge you to take your head out of the clouds and try thinking of someone besides yourself.

Though it probably comes as news to you, wars are fought by men, not by slabs of polished granite. This country deserves a war memorial that resembles a hero, not a retaining wall! As a tax-paying veteran, I demand a monument that looks like me. (See enclosed photograph.) It's time you set aside your roach clip and found yourself a drug-free American sculptor with a degree in art rather than spelling. Do you want to be remembered as the President who rolled the tightest joints or as the statesman who slept around (a lot!) but still gave the American people something we can all appreciate?

Mull it over, Stoney.

Anthony Primo
Cherry Point, Neb.

You Can't Kill the Rooster

When I was young, my father was transferred and our family moved from western New York State to Raleigh, North Carolina. IBM had relocated a great many northerners, and together we made relentless fun of our new neighbors and their poky, backward way of life. Rumors circulated that the locals ran stills out of their toolsheds and referred to their house cats as "good eatin'." Our parents discouraged us from using the titles "ma'am" or "sir" when addressing a teacher or shopkeeper. Tobacco was acceptable in the form of a cigarette, but should any of us experiment with plug or snuff, we would automatically be disinherited. Mountain Dew was forbidden, and our speech was monitored for the slightest hint of a Raleigh accent. Use the word "y'all," and before you knew it, you'd find yourself in a haystack French-kissing an underage goat. Along with grits and hush puppies, the abbreviated form of *you all* was a dangerous step on an insidious path leading straight to the doors of the Baptist church.

We might not have been the wealthiest people in town, but at least we weren't one of *them*.

Our family remained free from outside influence until 1968, when my mother gave birth to my brother, Paul, a North Carolina native who has since grown to become both my father's best ally and worst nightmare. Here was a child who, by the time he had reached the second grade, spoke much like the toothless fishermen casting their nets into Albemarle Sound. This is the grown man who now phones his father to say, "Motherfucker, I ain't seen pussy in so long, I'd throw stones at it."

My brother's voice, like my own, is high-pitched and girlish. Telephone solicitors frequently ask to speak to our husbands or request that we put our mommies on the line. The Raleigh accent is soft and beautifully cadenced, but my brother's is a more complex hybrid, informed by his professional relationships with marble-mouthed, deep-country work crews and his abiding love of hard-core rap music. He talks so fast that even his friends have a hard time understanding him. It's like listening to a foreigner and deciphering only *shit, motherfucker, bitch,* and the single phrase *You can't kill the Rooster.*

"The Rooster" is what Paul calls himself when he's feeling threatened. Asked how he came up with that name, he says only, "Certain motherfuckers think they can fuck with my shit, but you can't kill the Rooster. You might can fuck him up sometimes, but, bitch, nobody kills the motherfucking Rooster. You know what I'm saying?"

It often seems that my brother and I were raised in two completely different households. He's eleven years younger than I am, and by the time he reached high school, the rest of us had all left home. When I was young, we weren't allowed to say "shut up," but once the Rooster hit puberty it had become acceptable to shout, "Shut your motherfucking hole." The drug laws had changed as well. "No smoking pot" became "no smoking pot in the house," before it finally petered out to "please don't smoke any more pot in the living room."

My mother was, for the most part, delighted with my brother and regarded him with the bemused curiosity of a brood hen discovering she has hatched a completely different species. "I think it was very nice of Paul to give me this vase," she once said, arranging a bouquet of wildflowers into the skull-shaped bong my brother had left on the dining-room table. "It's nontraditional, but that's the Rooster's way. He's a free spirit, and we're lucky to have him."

Like most everyone else in our suburban neighborhood, we were raised to meet a certain standard. My father expected me to attend an Ivy League university, where I'd make straight A's, play football, and spend my off-hours strumming guitar with the student jazz combo. My inability to throw a football was exceeded only by my inability to master the guitar. My grades were average at best, and eventually I learned to live with my father's disappointment. Fortunately there were six of us children, and it was easy to get lost in the crowd. My sisters and I managed to sneak beneath the wire of his expectations, but we worried about my brother, who was seen as the family's last hope.

From the age of ten, Paul was being dressed in Brooks Brothers suits and tiny, clip-on rep ties. He endured trumpet lessons, soccer camp, church-sponsored basketball tournaments, and after-school sessions with well-meaning tutors who would politely change the subject when asked about the Rooster's chances of getting into Yale or Princeton. Fast and well-coordinated, Paul enjoyed sports but not enough to take them seriously. School failed to interest him on any level, and the neighbors were greatly relieved when he finally retired his trumpet. His response to our father's impossible and endless demands has, over time, become something of a mantra. Short and sweet, repeated at a fever pitch, it goes simply, "Fuck it," or on one of his more articulate days, "Fuck it, motherfucker. That shit don't mean fuck to me."

My brother politely ma'ams and sirs all strangers but refers to friends and family, his father included, as either "bitch" or "motherfucker." Friends are appalled at the way he speaks to his only remaining parent. The two of them once visited my sister Amy and me in New York City, and we celebrated with a dinner party. When my father complained about his aching feet, the Rooster set down his two-liter bottle of Mountain Dew and removed a fistful of prime rib from his mouth, saying, "Bitch, you need to have them ugly-ass bunions shaved down is what you need to do. But you can't do shit about it tonight, so lighten up, motherfucker."

All eyes went to my father, who chuckled, saying only, "Well, I guess you have a point."

A stranger might reasonably interpret my brother's language as a lack of respect and view my father's response as a form of shameful surrender. This, though, would be missing the subtle beauty of their relationship.

My father is the type who once recited a bawdy limerick, saying, "A woman I know who's quite blunt / had a bear trap installed in her . . . Oh, you know. It's a base, vernacular word for the vagina." He can absolutely kill a joke. When pushed to his limit, this is a man who shouts, "Fudge," a man who curses drivers with a shake of his fist and a hearty "G.D. you!" I've never known him to swear, yet he and my brother seem to have found a common language that eludes the rest of us.

My father likes to talk about money. Spending doesn't interest him in the least, especially as he grows older. He prefers money as a concept and often uses terms such as *annuity* and *fiduciary*, words definitely not listed in the dictionary of mindless entertainment. It puts my ears to sleep, but still, when he talks I pretend to listen to him, if only because it seems like the mature thing to do. When my father talks finance to my brother, Paul will cut him off, saying, "Fuck the stock talk, hoss, I ain't investing in shit." This rarely ends the economics lecture, but my brother wins bonus points for boldly voicing his uninterest, just as my father would do were someone to corner him and talk about Buddhism or the return of the clog. The two of them are unapologetically blunt. It's a quality my father admires so much, he's able to ignore the foul language completely. "That Paul," he says, "now *there's* a guy who knows how to communicate."

When words fail him, the Rooster has been known to communicate with his fists, which, though quick and solid, are no larger than a couple of tangerines. At five foot four, he's shorter than I am, stocky but not exactly intimidating. The year he turned thirty we celebrated Christmas at the home of my older sister Lisa. Paul arrived a few hours late with scraped palms and a black eye. There had been some encounter at a bar, but the details were sketchy.

"Some motherfucker told me to get the fuck out of his motherfucking face, so I said, 'Fuck off, fuckface.'"

"Then what?"

"Then he turned away and I reached up and punched him on the back of his motherfucking neck."

"What happened next?"

"What the fuck do you think happened next, bitch? I ran like hell and the motherfucker caught up with me in the fucking parking lot. He was all beefy, all flexed up and shit. The motherfucker had a taste for blood and he just pummeled my ass."

"When did he stop?"

My brother tapped his fingertips against the tabletop for a

few moments before saying, "I'm guessing he stopped when he was fucking finished."

The physical pain had passed, but it bothered Paul that his face was "all lopsided and shit for the fucking holidays." That said, he retreated to the bathroom with my sister Amy's makeup kit and returned to the table with *two* black eyes, the second drawn on with mascara. This seemed to please him, and he wore his matching bruises for the rest of the evening.

"Did you get a load of that fake black eye?" my father asked. "That guy ought to do makeup for the movies. I'm telling you, the kid's a real artist."

Unlike the rest of us, the Rooster has always enjoyed our father's support and encouragement. With the dream of college officially dead and buried, he sent my brother to technical school, hoping he might develop an interest in computers. Three weeks into the semester, Paul dropped out, and my father, convinced that his son's lawn-mowing skills bordered on genius, set him up in the landscaping business. "I've seen him in action, and what he does is establish a pattern and really tackle it!"

Eventually my brother fell into the floor-sanding business. It's hard work, but he enjoys the satisfaction that comes with a well-finished rec room. He thoughtfully called his company Silly P's Hardwood Floors, Silly P being the name he would have chosen were he a rap star. When my father suggested that the word *silly* might frighten away some of the upper-tier customers, Paul considered changing the name to Silly Fucking P's Hardwood Floors. The work puts him in contact with plumbers and carpenters from such towns as Bunn and Clayton, men who offer dating advice such as "If she's old enough to bleed, she's old enough to breed."

"Old enough to what?" my father asks. "Oh, Paul, those aren't the sort of people you need to be associating with. What are you doing with hayseeds like that? The goal is to better yourself. Meet some intellectuals. Read a book!"

After all these years our father has never understood that we, his children, tend to gravitate toward the very people he's spent his life warning us about. Most of us have left town, but my brother remains in Raleigh. He was there when our mother died and still, years later, continues to help our father grieve: "The past is gone, hoss. What you need now is some motherfucking pussy." While my sisters and I offer our sympathy long-distance, Paul is the one who arrives at our father's house on Thanksgiving day, offering to prepare traditional Greek dishes to the best of his ability. It is a fact that he once made a tray of spanakopita using Pam rather than melted butter. Still, though, at least he tries.

When a hurricane damaged my father's house, my brother rushed over with a gas grill, three coolers full of beer, and an enormous Fuck-It Bucket—a plastic pail filled with jawbreakers and bite-size candy bars. ("When shit brings you down, just say 'fuck it,' and eat yourself some motherfucking candy.") There was no electricity for close to a week. The yard was practically cleared of trees, and rain fell through the dozens of holes punched into the roof. It was a difficult time, but the two of them stuck it out, my brother placing his small, scarred hand on my father's shoulder to say, "Bitch, I'm here to tell you that it's going to be all right. We'll get through this shit, motherfucker, just you wait."

Me Talk Pretty One Day

At the age of forty-one, I am returning to school and have to think of myself as what my French textbook calls "a true debutant." After paying my tuition, I was issued a student ID, which allows me a discounted entry fee at movie theaters, puppet shows, and Festyland, a far-flung amusement park that advertises with billboards picturing a cartoon stegosaurus sitting in a canoe and eating what appears to be a ham sandwich.

I've moved to Paris with hopes of learning the language. My school is an easy ten-minute walk from my apartment, and on the first day of class I arrived early, watching as the returning students greeted one another in the school lobby. Vacations were recounted, and questions were raised concerning mutual friends with names like Kang and Vlatnya. Regardless of their nationalities, everyone spoke in what sounded to me like excellent French. Some accents were better than others, but the students exhibited an ease and confidence I found intimidating.

The first day of class was nerve-racking because I knew I'd be expected to perform. That's the way they do it here—it's everybody into the language pool, sink or swim. The teacher marched in, deeply tanned from a recent vacation, and proceeded to rattle off a series of administrative announcements. I've spent quite a few summers in Normandy, and I took a month-long French class before leaving New York. I'm not completely in the dark, yet I understood only half of what this woman was saying.

"If you have not *meimslsxp* or *lgpdmurct* by this time, then you should not be in this room. Has everyone *apzkiub-jxow?* Everyone? Good, we shall begin." She spread out her lesson plan and sighed, saying, "All right, then, who knows the alphabet?"

It was startling because (a) I hadn't been asked that question in a while and (b) I realized, while laughing, that I myself did *not* know the alphabet. They're the same letters, but in France they're pronounced differently. I know the shape of the alphabet but had no idea what it actually sounded like.

"Ahh." The teacher went to the board and sketched the letter *a.* "Do we have anyone in the room whose first name commences with an *ahh?*"

Two Polish Annas raised their hands, and the teacher instructed them to present themselves by stating their names, nationalities, occupations, and a brief list of things they liked and disliked in this world. The first Anna hailed from an industrial town outside of Warsaw and had front teeth the size of tombstones. She worked as a seamstress, enjoyed quiet times with friends, and hated the mosquito.

"Oh, really," the teacher said. "How very interesting. I thought that everyone loved the mosquito, but here, in front of all the world, you claim to detest him. How is it that we've been blessed with someone as unique and original as you? Tell us, please."

The seamstress did not understand what was being said but knew that this was an occasion for shame. Her rabbity mouth huffed for breath, and she stared down at her lap as though the appropriate comeback were stitched somewhere alongside the zipper of her slacks.

The second Anna learned from the first and claimed to love sunshine and detest lies. It sounded like a translation of one of those Playmate of the Month data sheets, the answers always written in the same loopy handwriting: "Turn-ons: Mom's famous five-alarm chili! Turnoffs: insecurity and guys who come on too strong!!!!"

The two Polish Annas surely had clear notions of what they loved and hated, but like the rest of us, they were limited in terms of vocabulary, and this made them appear less than sophisticated. The teacher forged on, and we learned that Carlos, the Argentine bandonion player, loved wine, music, and, in his words, "making sex with the womens of the world." Next came a beautiful young Yugoslav who identified herself as an optimist, saying that she loved everything that life had to offer.

The teacher licked her lips, revealing a hint of the sadist we would later come to know. She crouched low for her attack, placed her hands on the young woman's desk, and leaned close, saying, "Oh yeah? And do you love your little war?"

While the optimist struggled to defend herself, I scrambled to think of an answer to what had obviously become a trick question. How often is one asked what he loves in this world? More to the point, how often is one asked and then publicly ridiculed for his answer? I recalled my mother, flushed with wine, pounding the tabletop late one night, saying, "Love? I

love a good steak cooked rare. I love my cat, and I love ..."
My sisters and I leaned forward, waiting to hear our names.
"Rennies," our mother said. "I love Rennies."

The teacher killed some time accusing the Yugoslavian
girl of masterminding a program of genocide, and I jotted
frantic notes in the margins of my pad. While I can honestly
say that I love leafing through medical textbooks devoted to
severe dermatological conditions, the hobby is beyond the
reach of my French vocabulary, and acting it out would only
have invited controversy.

When called upon, I delivered an effortless list of things
that I detest: blood sausage, intestinal pâtés, brain pudding.
I'd learned these words the hard way. Having given it some
thought, I then declared my love for IBM typewriters, the
French word for *bruise,* and my electric floor waxer. It was
a short list, but still I managed to mispronounce *IBM* and
assign the wrong gender to both the floor waxer and the
typewriter. The teacher's reaction led me to believe that these
mistakes were capital crimes in the country of France.

"Were you always this *palicmkrexis?*" she asked. "Even a
fiuscrzsa ticiwelmun knows that a typewriter is feminine."

I absorbed as much of her abuse as I could understand,
thinking—but not saying—that I find it ridiculous to assign
a gender to an inanimate object incapable of disrobing and
making an occasional fool of itself. Why refer to Lady Crack
Pipe or Good Sir Dishrag when these things could never live
up to all that their sex implied?

The teacher proceeded to belittle everyone from German
Eva, who hated laziness, to Japanese Yukari, who loved
paintbrushes and soap. Italian, Thai, Dutch, Korean, and
Chinese—we all left class foolishly believing that the worst
was over. She'd shaken us up a little, but surely that was just
an act designed to weed out the deadweight. We didn't know

it then, but the coming months would teach us what it was like to spend time in the presence of a wild animal, something completely unpredictable. Her temperament was not based on a series of good and bad days but, rather, good and bad moments. We soon learned to dodge chalk and protect our heads and stomachs whenever she approached us with a question. She hadn't yet punched anyone, but it seemed wise to protect ourselves against the inevitable.

Though we were forbidden to speak anything but French, the teacher would occasionally use us to practice any of her five fluent languages.

"I hate you," she said to me one afternoon. Her English was flawless. "I really, really hate you." Call me sensitive, but I couldn't help but take it personally.

After being singled out as a lazy *kfdtinvfm,* I took to spending four hours a night on my homework, putting in even more time whenever we were assigned an essay. I suppose I could have gotten by with less, but I was determined to create some sort of identity for myself. We'd have one of those "complete this sentence" exercises, and I'd fool with the thing for hours, invariably settling on something like "A quick run around the lake? I'd love to! Just give me a moment while I strap on my wooden leg." The teacher, through word and action, conveyed the message that if this was my idea of an identity, she wanted nothing to do with it.

My fear and discomfort crept beyond the borders of the classroom and accompanied me out on to the wide boulevards. Stopping for a coffee, asking directions, depositing money in my bank account: these things were out of the question, as they involved having to speak. Before beginning school, there'd been no shutting me up, but now I was convinced that everything I said was wrong. When the phone rang, I ignored it. If someone asked me a question, I pretended to be deaf. I knew my fear was getting the best of me when I started wondering why they don't sell cuts of meat in vending machines.

My only comfort was the knowledge that I was not alone. Huddled in the hallways and making the most of our pathetic French, my fellow students and I engaged in the sort of conversation commonly overheard in refugee camps.

"Sometime me cry alone at night."

"That be common for I, also, but be more strong, you. Much work and someday you talk pretty. People start love you soon. Maybe tomorrow, okay."

Unlike the French class I had taken in New York, here there was no sense of competition. When the teacher poked a shy Korean in the eyelid with a freshly sharpened pencil, we took no comfort in the fact that, unlike Hyeyoon Cho, we all knew the irregular past tense of the verb *to defeat*. In all fairness, the teacher hadn't meant to stab the girl, but neither did she spend much time apologizing, saying only, "Well, you should have been *vkkdyo* more *kdeynfulh*."

Over time it became impossible to believe that any of us would ever improve. Fall arrived and it rained every day, meaning we would now be scolded for the water dripping from our coats and umbrellas. It was mid-October when the teacher singled me out, saying, "Every day spent with you is like having a cesarean section." And it struck me that, for the first time since arriving in France, I could understand every word that someone was saying.

Understanding doesn't mean that you can suddenly speak the language. Far from it. It's a small step, nothing more, yet its rewards are intoxicating and deceptive. The teacher continued her diatribe and I settled back, bathing in the subtle beauty of each new curse and insult.

"You exhaust me with your foolishness and reward my efforts with nothing but pain, do you understand me?"

The world opened up, and it was with great joy that I responded, "I know the thing that you speak exact now. Talk me more, you, plus, please, plus."

Jesus Shaves

"And what does one do on the fourteenth of July? Does one celebrate Bastille Day?"

It was my second month of French class, and the teacher was leading us in an exercise designed to promote the use of *one,* our latest personal pronoun.

"Might one sing on Bastille Day?" she asked. "Might one dance in the streets? Somebody give me an answer."

Printed in our textbooks was a list of major holidays accompanied by a scattered arrangement of photographs depicting French people in the act of celebration. The object of the lesson was to match the holiday with the corresponding picture. It was simple enough but seemed an exercise better suited to the use of the pronoun *they.* I didn't know about the rest of the class, but when Bastille Day eventually rolled around, I planned to stay home and clean my oven.

Normally, when working from the book, it was my habit to tune out my fellow students and scout ahead, concentrating on the question I'd calculated might fall to me, but this afternoon we were veering from the usual format. Questions were answered on a volunteer basis, and I was able to sit back and relax, confident that the same few students would do most of the talking. Today's discussion was dominated by an Italian nanny, two chatty Poles, and a pouty, plump Moroccan woman who had grown up speaking French and had enrolled in the class hoping to improve her spelling. She'd covered these lessons back in the third grade and took every opportunity to demonstrate her superiority. A question would be asked, and she'd race to give the answer, behaving as though this were a game show and, if quick enough, she might go home with a tropical vacation or a side-by-side refrigerator/freezer. A transfer student, by the end of her first day she'd raised her hand so many times that her shoulder had given out. Now she just leaned back and shouted out the answers, her bronzed arms folded across her chest like some great grammar genie.

We'd finished discussing Bastille Day, and the teacher had moved on to Easter, which was represented in our textbooks by a black-and-white photograph of a chocolate bell lying upon a bed of palm fronds.

"And what does one do on Easter? Would anyone like to tell us?"

The Italian nanny was attempting to answer when the Moroccan student interrupted, shouting, "Excuse me, but what's an Easter?"

It would seem that despite having grown up in a Muslim country, she would have heard it mentioned once or twice, but no. "I mean it," she said. "I have no idea what you people are talking about."

The teacher called upon the rest of us to explain.

The Poles led the charge to the best of their ability. "It is," said one, "a party for the little boy of God who call his self

Jesus and ... oh, shit." She faltered and her fellow country-man came to her aid.

"He call his self Jesus and then he die one day on two ... morsels of ... lumber."

The rest of the class jumped in, offering bits of information that would have given the pope an aneurysm.

"He die one day and then he go above of my head to live with your father."

"He weared of himself the long hair and after he die, the first day he come back here for to say hello to the peoples."

"He nice, the Jesus."

"He make the good things, and on the Easter we be sad because somebody makes him dead today."

Part of the problem had to do with vocabulary. Simple nouns such as *cross* and *resurrection* were beyond our grasp, let alone such complicated reflexive phrases as "to give of yourself your only begotten son." Faced with the challenge of explaining the cornerstone of Christianity, we did what any self-respecting group of people might do. We talked about food instead.

"Easter is a party for to eat of the lamb," the Italian nanny explained. "One too may eat of the chocolate."

"And who brings the chocolate?" the teacher asked.

I knew the word, so I raised my hand, saying, "The rabbit of Easter. He bring of the chocolate."

"A rabbit?" The teacher, assuming I'd used the wrong word, positioned her index fingers on top of her head, wriggling them as though they were ears. "You mean one of these? A *rabbit* rabbit?"

"Well, sure," I said. "He come in the night when one sleep on a bed. With a hand he have a basket and foods."

The teacher sighed and shook her head. As far as she was concerned, I had just explained everything that was wrong with my country. "No, no," she said. "Here in France the chocolate is brought by a big bell that flies in from Rome."

I called for a time-out. "But how do the bell know where you live?"

"Well," she said, "how does a rabbit?"

It was a decent point, but at least a rabbit has eyes. That's a start. Rabbits move from place to place, while most bells can only go back and forth—and they can't even do that on their own power. On top of that, the Easter Bunny has character. He's someone you'd like to meet and shake hands with. A bell has all the personality of a cast-iron skillet. It's like saying that come Christmas, a magic dustpan flies in from the North Pole, led by eight flying cinder blocks. Who wants to stay up all night so they can see a bell? And why fly one in from Rome when they've got more bells than they know what to do with right here in Paris? That's the most implausible aspect of the whole story, as there's no way the bells of France would allow a foreign worker to fly in and take their jobs. That Roman bell would be lucky to get work cleaning up after a French bell's dog—and even then he'd need papers. It just didn't add up.

Nothing we said was of any help to the Moroccan student. A dead man with long hair supposedly living with her father, a leg of lamb served with palm fronds and chocolate; equally confused and disgusted, she shrugged her massive shoulders and turned her attention back to the comic book she kept hidden beneath her binder.

I wondered then if, without the language barrier, my classmates and I could have done a better job making sense of Christianity, an idea that sounds pretty far-fetched to begin with.

In communicating any religious belief, the operative word is *faith,* a concept illustrated by our very presence in that classroom. Why bother struggling with the grammar lessons of a six-year-old if each of us didn't believe that, against all reason, we might eventually improve? If I could hope to one day carry on a fluent conversation, it was a relatively short leap to believing that a rabbit might visit my home in the middle of the night, leaving behind a handful of chocolate kisses and a carton of menthol cigarettes. So why stop there? If I could believe in myself, why not give other improbabilities the benefit of the doubt? I told myself that despite her past behavior, my teacher was a kind and loving person who had only my best interests at heart. I accepted the idea that an omniscient God had cast me in his own image and that he watched over me and guided me from one place to the next. The Virgin Birth, the Resurrection, and the countless miracles—my heart expanded to encompass all the wonders and possibilities of the universe.

A bell, though—that's fucked up.

Dog Days

Pepper, Spot, and Leopold
were sent by God, so I've been told,
in hopes we might all comprehend
that every dog is man's best friend!

Hail hyperactive Myrtle,
owned by folks who are infertile.
Her owners boast as she runs wild,
"She's not a spaniel, she's our child!"

Rags, the Shatwells' Irish setter,
doubles as a paper shredder.
His lunch was bills and last year's taxes,
followed by a dozen faxes.

Kimmy, once considered ruthless,
lies in her basket, bald and toothless.
Her youth's long spent so now she passes
all her time releasing gasses.

Petunia May they say was struck
chasing down a garbage truck.
A former purebred Boston terrier,
her family's wond'ring where to bury her.

Most every ev'ning Goldilocks
snacks from Kitty's litter box.
Then on command she gives her missus
lots of little doggy kisses.

Hercules, a Pekingese,
was taken in and dipped for fleas.
Insecticide got in his eyes.
Now he'll be blind until he dies.

The Deavers' errant pit bull, Cass,
bit the postman on the ass.
Her lower teeth destroyed his sphincter.
Now his walk's a bit distincter.

Bitches loved the pug Orestes
till the vet snipped off his testes.
Left with only anal glands,
he's now reduced to shaking hands.

Dachshund Skip from Winnipeg
loves to hump his master's leg.
Every time he gets it up, he
stains Bill's calves with unborn puppy.

A naughty Saint Bernard named Don
finds Polly's Kotex in the john.
He holds the blood steak in his jaws
and mourns her coming menopause.

Each night old Bowser licks his balls,
then falls asleep till nature calls.
He poops a stool then, though it's heinous,
bends back down and licks his anus.

Us and Them

When my family first moved to North Carolina, we lived in a rented house three blocks from the school where I would begin the third grade. My mother made friends with one of the neighbors, but one seemed enough for her. Within a year we would move again and, as she explained, there wasn't much point in getting too close to people we would have to say goodbye to. Our next house was less than a mile away, and the short journey would hardly merit tears or even goodbyes, for that matter. It was more of a "see you later" situation, but still I adopted my mother's attitude, as it allowed me to pretend that not making friends was a conscious choice. I could if I wanted to. It just wasn't the right time.

Back in New York State, we had lived in the country, with no sidewalks or streetlights; you could leave the house and still be alone. But here, when you looked out the window, you saw other houses, and people inside those houses. I hoped that in walking around after dark I might witness a murder, but for the most part our neighbors just sat in their living rooms, watching TV. The only place that seemed truly different was owned by a man named Mr. Tomkey, who did not believe in television. This was told to us by our mother's friend, who dropped by one afternoon with a basketful of okra. The woman did not editorialize—rather, she just presented her information, leaving her listener to make of it what she might. Had my mother said, "That's the craziest thing I've ever heard in my life," I assume that the friend would have agreed, and had she said, "Three cheers for Mr. Tomkey," the friend likely would have agreed as well. It was a kind of test, as was the okra.

To say that you did not believe in television was different from saying that you did not care for it. Belief implied that television had a master plan and that you were against it. It also suggested that you thought too much. When my mother reported that Mr. Tomkey did not believe in television, my father said, "Well, good for him. I don't know that I believe in it, either."

"That's exactly how I feel," my mother said, and then my parents watched the news, and whatever came on after the news.

Word spread that Mr. Tomkey did not own a television, and you began hearing that while this was all very well and good, it was unfair of him to inflict his beliefs upon others, specifically his innocent wife and children. It was speculated that just as the blind man develops a keener sense of hearing, the family must somehow compensate for their loss. "Maybe they read," my mother's friend said. "Maybe they listen to the radio, but you can bet your boots they're doing *something*."

I wanted to know what this something was, and so I began peering through the Tomkeys' windows. During the day I'd stand across the street from their house, acting as though I were waiting for someone, and at night, when the view was better and I had less chance of being discovered, I would creep into their yard and hide in the bushes beside their fence.

Because they had no TV, the Tomkeys were forced to talk during dinner. They had no idea how puny their lives were, and so they were not ashamed that a camera would have found them uninteresting. They did not know what attractive was or what dinner was supposed to look like or even what time people were supposed to eat. Sometimes they wouldn't sit down until eight o'clock, long after everyone else had finished doing the dishes. During the meal, Mr. Tomkey would occasionally pound the table and point at his children with a fork, but the moment he finished, everyone would start laughing. I got the idea that he was imitating someone else, and wondered if he spied on us while we were eating.

When fall arrived and school began, I saw the Tomkey children marching up the hill with paper sacks in their hands. The son was one grade lower than me, and the daughter was one grade higher. We never spoke, but I'd pass them in the halls from time to time and attempt to view the world through their eyes. What must it be like to be so ignorant and alone? Could a normal person even imagine it? Staring at an Elmer Fudd lunch box, I tried to divorce myself from everything I already knew: Elmer's inability to pronounce the letter *r*, his constant pursuit of an intelligent and considerably more famous rabbit. I tried to think of him as just a drawing, but it was impossible to separate him from his celebrity.

One day in class a boy named William began to write the wrong answer on the blackboard, and our teacher flailed her arms, saying, "Warning, Will. Danger, danger." Her voice was synthetic and void of emotion, and we laughed, knowing that she was imitating the robot in a weekly show about a family who lived in outer space. The Tomkeys, though, would have thought she was having a heart attack. It occurred to me that they needed a guide, someone who could accompany them through the course of an average day and point out all the things they were unable to understand. I could have done it on weekends, but friendship would have taken away their mystery and interfered with the good feeling I got from pitying them. So I kept my distance.

In early October the Tomkeys bought a boat, and everyone seemed greatly relieved, especially my mother's friend, who noted that the motor was definitely secondhand. It was reported that Mr. Tomkey's father-in-law owned a house on the lake and had invited the family to use it whenever they liked. This explained why they were gone all weekend, but it did not make their absences any easier to bear. I felt as if my favorite show had been canceled.

Halloween fell on a Saturday that year, and by the time my mother took us to the store, all the good costumes were gone. My sisters dressed as witches and I went as a hobo. I'd looked forward to going in disguise to the Tomkeys' door, but they were off at the lake, and their house was dark. Before leaving, they had left a coffee can full of gumdrops on the front porch, alongside a sign reading don't be greedy. In terms of Halloween candy, individual gumdrops were just about as low as you could get. This was evidenced by the large number of them floating in an adjacent dog bowl. It was disgusting to think that this was what a gumdrop might look like in your stomach, and it was insulting to be told not to take too much of something you didn't really want in the first place. "Who do these Tomkeys think they are?" my sister Lisa said.

The night after Halloween, we were sitting around watching TV when the doorbell rang. Visitors were infrequent at our house, so while my father stayed behind, my mother, sisters, and I ran downstairs in a group, opening the door to discover the entire Tomkey family on our front stoop. The parents looked as they always had, but the son and daughter were dressed in costumes—she as a ballerina and he as some kind of a rodent with terry-cloth ears and a tail made from what looked to be an extension cord. It seemed they had spent the previous evening isolated at the lake and had missed the opportunity to observe Halloween. "So, well, I guess we're trick-or-treating *now*, if that's okay," Mr. Tomkey said.

I attributed their behavior to the fact that they didn't have a TV, but television didn't teach you everything. Asking for candy on Halloween was called trick-or-treating, but asking for candy on November first was called begging, and it made people uncomfortable. This was one of the things you were supposed to learn simply by being alive, and it angered me that the Tomkeys did not understand it.

"Why of course it's not too late," my mother said. "Kids, why don't you ... run and get ... the candy."

"But the candy is gone," my sister Gretchen said. "You gave it away last night."

"Not *that* candy," my mother said. "The other candy. Why don't you run and go get it?"

"You mean *our* candy?" Lisa said. "The candy that we *earned?*"

This was exactly what our mother was talking about, but she didn't want to say this in front of the Tomkeys. In order to spare their feelings, she wanted them to believe that we always kept a bucket of candy lying around the house, just waiting for someone to knock on the door and ask for it. "Go on, now," she said. "Hurry up."

My room was situated right off the foyer, and if the Tomkeys had looked in that direction, they could have seen my bed and the brown paper bag marked MY CANDY. KEEP OUT. I didn't want them to know how much I had, and so I went into my room and shut the door behind me. Then I closed the curtains and emptied my bag onto the bed, searching for whatever was the crummiest. All my life chocolate has made me ill. I don't know if I'm allergic or what, but even the smallest amount leaves me with a blinding headache. Eventually, I learned to stay away from it, but as a child I refused to be left out. The brownies were eaten, and when the pounding began I would blame the grape juice or my mother's cigarette smoke or the tightness of my glasses—anything but the chocolate. My candy bars were poison but they were brand-name, and so I put them in pile no. 1, which definitely would not go to the Tomkeys.

Out in the hallway I could hear my mother straining for something to talk about. "A boat!" she said. "That sounds marvelous. Can you just drive it right into the water?"

"Actually, we have a trailer," Mr. Tomkey said. "So what we do is back it into the lake."

"Oh, a trailer. What kind is it?"

"Well, it's a *boat* trailer," Mr. Tomkey said.

"Right, but is it wooden or, you know . . . I guess what I'm asking is what *style* trailer do you have?"

Behind my mother's words were two messages. The first and most obvious was "Yes, I am talking about boat trailers, but also I am dying." The second, meant only for my sisters and me, was "If you do not immediately step forward with that candy, you will never again experience freedom, happiness, or the possibility of my warm embrace."

I knew that it was just a matter of time before she came into my room and started collecting the candy herself, grabbing indiscriminately, with no regard to my rating system. Had I been thinking straight, I would have hidden the most valuable items in my dresser drawer, but instead, panicked by the thought of her hand on my doorknob, I tore off the wrappers and began cramming the candy bars into my mouth, desperately, like someone in a contest. Most were miniature, which made them easier to accommodate, but still there was only so much room, and it was hard to chew and fit more in at the same time. The headache began immediately, and I chalked it up to tension.

My mother told the Tomkeys she needed to check on something, and then she opened the door and stuck her head inside my room. "What the *hell* are you doing?" she whispered, but my mouth was too full to answer. "I'll just be a moment," she called, and as she closed the door behind her and moved toward my bed, I began breaking the wax lips and candy necklaces pulled from pile no. 2. These were the second-best things I had received, and while it hurt to destroy them, it would have hurt even more to give them away. I had just started to mutilate a miniature box of Red Hots when my mother pried them from my hands, accidentally finishing the job for me. BB-size pellets clattered onto the floor, and as I followed them with my eyes, she snatched up a roll of Necco wafers.

"Not those," I pleaded, but rather than words, my mouth expelled chocolate, chewed chocolate, which fell onto the sleeve of her sweater. "Not those. Not those."

She shook her arm, and the mound of chocolate dropped like a horrible turd upon my bedspread. "You should look at yourself," she said. "I mean, *really* look at yourself."

Along with the Necco wafers she took several Tootsie Pops and half a dozen caramels wrapped in cellophane. I heard her apologize to the Tomkeys for her absence, and then I heard my candy hitting the bottom of their bags.

"What do you say?" Mrs. Tomkey asked.

And the children answered, "Thank you."

*

While I was in trouble for not bringing my candy sooner, my sisters were in more trouble for not bringing theirs at all. We spent the early part of the evening in our rooms, then one by one we eased our way back upstairs, and joined our parents in front of the TV. I was the last to arrive, and took a seat on the floor beside the sofa. The show was a Western, and even if my head had not been throbbing, I doubt I would have had the wherewithal to follow it. A posse of outlaws crested a rocky hilltop, squinting at a flurry of dust advancing from the horizon, and I thought again of the Tomkeys and of how alone and out of place they had looked in their dopey costumes. "What was up with that kid's tail?" I asked.

"Shhhh," my family said.

For months I had protected and watched over these people, but now, with one stupid act, they had turned my pity into something hard and ugly. The shift wasn't gradual, but immediate, and it provoked an uncomfortable feeling of loss. We hadn't been friends, the Tomkeys and I, but still I had given them the gift of my curiosity. Wondering about the Tomkey family had made me feel generous, but now I would have to shift gears and find pleasure in hating them. The only alternative was to do as my mother had instructed and take a good look at myself. This was an old trick, designed to turn one's hatred inward, and while I was determined not to fall for it, it was hard to shake the mental picture snapped by her suggestion: here is a boy sitting on a bed, his mouth smeared with chocolate. He's a human being, but also he's a pig, surrounded by trash and gorging himself so that others may be denied. Were this the only image in the world, you'd be forced to give it your full attention, but fortunately there were others. This stagecoach, for instance, coming round the bend with a cargo of gold. This shiny new Mustang convertible. This teenage girl, her hair a beautiful mane, sipping Pepsi through a straw, one picture after another, on and on until the news, and whatever came on after the news.

Let It Snow

In Binghamton, New York, winter meant snow, and though I was young when we left, I was able to recall great heaps of it, and use that memory as evidence that North Carolina was, at best, a third-rate institution. What little snow there was would usually melt an hour or two after hitting the ground, and there you'd be in your windbreaker and unconvincing mittens, forming a lumpy figure made mostly of mud. Snow Negroes, we called them.

The winter I was in the fifth grade we got lucky. Snow fell, and for the first time in years, it accumulated. School was canceled and two days later we got lucky again. There were eight inches on the ground, and rather than melting, it froze. On the fifth day of our vacation my mother had a little breakdown. Our presence had disrupted the secret life she led while we were at school, and when she could no longer take it she threw us out. It wasn't a gentle request, but something closer to an eviction. "Get the hell out of my house," she said.

We reminded her that it was our house, too, and she opened

the front door and shoved us into the carport. "And stay out!" she shouted.

My sisters and I went down the hill and sledded with other children from the neighborhood. A few hours later we returned home, surprised to find that the door was still locked. "Oh, come on," we said. I rang the bell and when no one answered we went to the window and saw our mother in the kitchen, watching television. Normally she waited until five o'clock to have a drink, but for the past few days she'd been making an exception. Drinking didn't count if you followed a glass of wine with a cup of coffee, and so she had both a goblet and a mug positioned before her on the countertop.

"Hey!" we yelled. "Open the door. It's us." We knocked on the pane, and without looking in our direction, she refilled her goblet and left the room.

"That bitch," my sister Lisa said. We pounded again and again, and when our mother failed to answer we went around back and threw snowballs at her bedroom window. "You are going to be in so much trouble when Dad gets home!" we shouted, and in response my mother pulled the drapes. Dusk approached, and as it grew colder it occurred to us that we could possibly die. It happened, surely. Selfish mothers wanted the house to themselves, and their children were discovered years later, frozen like mastodons in blocks of ice.

My sister Gretchen suggested that we call our father, but none of us knew his number, and he probably wouldn't have done anything anyway. He'd gone to work specifically to escape our mother, and between the weather and her mood, it could be hours or even days before he returned home.

"One of us should get hit by a car," I said. "That would teach the both of them." I pictured Gretchen, her life hanging by a thread as my parents paced the halls of Rex Hospital, wishing they had been more attentive. It was really the perfect solution. With her out of the way, the rest of us would be more valuable and have a bit more room to spread out. "Gretchen, go lie in the street."

"Make Amy do it," she said.

Amy, in turn, pushed it off onto Tiffany, who was the youngest and had no concept of death. "It's like sleeping," we told her. "Only you get a canopy bed."

Poor Tiffany. She'd do just about anything in return for a little affection. All you had to do was call her Tiff and whatever you wanted was yours: her allowance money, her dinner, the contents of her Easter basket. Her eagerness to please was absolute and naked. When we asked her to lie in the middle of the street, her only question was "Where?"

We chose a quiet dip between two hills, a spot where drivers were almost required to skid out of control. She took her place, this six-year-old in a butter-colored coat, and we gathered on the curb to watch. The first car to happen by belonged to a neighbor, a fellow Yankee who had outfitted his tires with chains and stopped a few feet from our sister's body. "Is that a person?" he asked.

"Well, sort of," Lisa said. She explained that we'd been locked out of our house and though the man appeared to accept it as a reasonable explanation, I'm pretty sure it was him who told on us. Another car passed and then we saw our mother, this puffy figure awkwardly negotiating the crest of the hill. She did not own a pair of pants, and her legs were buried to the calves in snow. We wanted to send her home, to kick her out of nature just as she had kicked us out of the house, but it was hard to stay angry at someone that pitiful-looking.

"Are you wearing your *loafers?*" Lisa asked, and in response our mother raised her bare foot. "I *was* wearing loafers," she said. "I mean, really, it was there a second ago."

This was how things went. One moment she was locking us out of our own house and the next we were rooting around in the snow, looking for her left shoe. "Oh, forget about it," she said. "It'll turn up in a few days." Gretchen fitted her cap over my mother's foot. Lisa secured it with her scarf, and surrounding her tightly on all sides, we made our way back home.

The Ship Shape

My mother and I were at the dry cleaner's, standing behind a woman we had never seen. "A nice-looking woman," my mother would later say. "Well put together. Classy." The woman was dressed for the season in a light cotton shift patterned with oversize daisies. Her shoes matched the petals and her purse, which was black-and-yellow-striped, hung over her shoulder, buzzing the flowers like a lazy bumblebee. She handed in her claim check, accepted her garments, and then expressed gratitude for what she considered to be fast and efficient service. "You know," she said, "people talk about Raleigh, but it isn't really true, is it?"

The Korean man nodded, the way you do when you're a foreigner and understand that someone has finished a sentence. He wasn't the owner, just a helper who'd stepped in from the back, and it was clear he had no idea what she was saying.

"My sister and I are visiting from out of town," the woman said, a little louder now, and again the man nodded. "I'd love to stay awhile longer and explore, but my home—well, *one* of my homes—is on the garden tour, so I've got to get back to Williamsburg."

I was eleven years old, yet still the statement seemed strange to me. If she'd hoped to impress the Korean, the woman had obviously wasted her breath, so who was this information for?

"My home—well, *one* of my homes": by the end of the day my mother and I had repeated this line no less than fifty times. The garden tour was unimportant, but the first part of her sentence brought us great pleasure. There was, as indicated by the dash, a pause between the words *home* and *well,* a brief moment in which she'd decided, *Oh, why not?* The following word—*one*—had blown from her mouth as if propelled by a gentle breeze, and this was the difficult part. You had to get it just right, or else the sentence lost its power. Falling somewhere between a self-conscious laugh and a sigh of happy confusion, the *one* afforded her statement a double meaning. To her peers it meant "Look at me, I catch myself coming and going!" and to the less fortunate it was a way of saying, "Don't kid yourself, it's a lot of work having more than one house."

The first dozen times we tried it, our voices sounded pinched and snobbish, but by midafternoon they had softened. We wanted what this woman had. Mocking her made it seem hopelessly unobtainable, and so we reverted to our natural selves.

"My home—well, one of my homes . . ." My mother said it in a rush, as if she were under pressure to be more specific. It was the same way she said, "My daughter—well, one of my daughters," but a second home was more prestigious than a second daughter, and so it didn't really work. I went in the opposite direction, exaggerating the word *one* in a way that was guaranteed to alienate my listener.

"Say it like that and people are going to be jealous," my mother said.

"Well, isn't that what we want?"

"Sort of," she said. "But mainly we want them to be happy for us."

"But why should you be happy for someone who has more than you do?"

"I guess it all depends on the person," she said. "Anyway, I suppose it doesn't matter. We'll get it right eventually. When the day arrives, I'm sure it'll just come to us."

And so we waited.

At some point in the mid to late 1960s, North Carolina began referring to itself as "Variety Vacationland." The words were stamped onto license plates, and a series of television commercials reminded us that, unlike certain of our neighbors, we had both the beach *and* the mountains. There were those who bounced back and forth between one and the other, but most people tended to choose a landscape and stick to it. We ourselves were Beach People, Emerald Isle People, but that was mainly my mother's doing. I don't think our father would have cared whether he took a vacation or not. Being away from home left him anxious and crabby, but our mother loved the ocean. She couldn't swim, but enjoyed standing at the water's edge with a pole in her hand. It wasn't exactly what you'd call fishing, as she caught nothing and expressed neither hope nor disappointment in regard to her efforts. What she thought about while looking at the waves was a complete mystery, yet you could tell that these thoughts pleased her, and that she liked herself better while thinking them.

One year our father waited too late to make our reservations, and we were forced to take something on the sound. It wasn't a cottage but a run-down house, the sort of place where poor people lived. The yard was enclosed by a chain-link fence, and the air was thick with the flies and mosquitoes normally blown away by the ocean breezes. Midway through the vacation a hideous woolly caterpillar fell from a tree and bit my sister Amy on the cheek. Her face swelled and discolored, and within an hour, were it not for her arms and legs, it would have been difficult to recognize her as a human. My mother drove her to the hospital, and when they returned she employed my sister as Exhibit A, pointing as if this were not her daughter but some ugly stranger forced to share our quarters. "*This* is what you get for waiting until the last minute," she said to our father. "No dunes, no waves, just *this*."

From that year on, our mother handled the reservations. We went to Emerald Isle for a week every September and were always oceanfront, a word that suggested a certain degree of entitlement. The oceanfront cottages were on stilts, which made them appear if not large, then at least imposing. Some were painted, some were sided "Cape Cod style" with wooden shingles, and all of them had names, the cleverest being Loafer's Paradise. The owners had cut their sign in the shape of two moccasins resting side by side. The shoes were realistically painted and the letters were bloated and listless, loitering like drunks against the soft faux leather.

"Now *that's* a sign," our father would say, and we would agree. There was The Skinny Dipper, Pelican's Perch, Lazy Daze, The Scotch Bonnet, Loony Dunes, the name of each house followed by the name and hometown of the owner. "The Duncan Clan—Charlotte," "The Graftons—Rocky Mount," "Hal and Jean Starling of Pinehurst"—signs that essentially said, "My home—well, *one* of my homes."

While at the beach we sensed more than ever that our lives were governed by luck. When we had it—when it was sunny—my sisters and I felt as if we were somehow personally responsible. We were a fortunate family, and therefore everyone around us was allowed to swim and dig in the sand.

When it rained, we were unlucky, and stayed indoors to search our souls. "It'll clear after lunch," our mother would say, and we would eat carefully, using the place mats that had brought us luck in the past. When that failed, we would move on to Plan B. "Oh, Mother, you work too hard," we'd say. "Let *us* do the dishes. Let *us* sweep sand off the floor." We spoke like children in a fairy tale, hoping our goodness might lure the sun from its hiding place. "You and Father have been so kind to us. Here, let us massage your shoulders."

If by late afternoon it still hadn't cleared, my sisters and I would drop the act and turn on one another, searching for the spoiler who had brought us this misfortune. Which of us seemed the least dissatisfied? Who had curled up on a mildewed bed with a book and a glass of chocolate milk, behaving as though the rain were not such a bad thing after all? We would find this person, most often my sister Gretchen, and then we would beat her.

The summer I was twelve a tropical storm moved up the coast, leaving a sky the same mottled pewter as Gretchen's subsequent bruises, but the following year we started with luck. My father found a golf course that suited him, and for the first time in memory even he seemed to enjoy himself. Relaxing on the deck with a gin and tonic, surrounded by his toast-colored wife and children, he admitted that this really wasn't so bad. "I've been thinking, to hell with these rental cottages," he said. "What do you say we skip the middleman and just buy a place."

He spoke in the same tone he used when promising ice cream. "Who's up for something sweet?" he'd ask, and we'd pile into the car, passing the Tastee Freeze and driving to the grocery store, where he'd buy a block of pus-colored ice milk reduced for quick sale. Experience had taught us not to trust him, but we wanted a beach house so badly it was impossible not to get caught up in the excitement. Even our mother fell for it.

"Do you really mean this?" she asked.

"Absolutely," he said.

The next day they made an appointment with a real-estate agent in Morehead City. "We'll just be discussing the possibility," my mother said. "It's just a meeting, nothing more." We wanted to join them but they took only Paul, who was two years old and unfit to be left in our company. The morning meeting led to half a dozen viewings, and when they returned, my mother's face was so impassive it seemed almost paralyzed. "It-was-fine," she said. "The-real-estate-agent-was-very-nice." We got the idea that she was under oath to keep something to herself and that the effort was causing her actual physical pain.

"It's all right," my father said. "You can tell them."

"Well, we saw this one place in particular," she told us. "Now, it's nothing to get worked up about, but ..."

"But it's perfect," my father said. "A real beauty, just like your mother here." He came from behind and pinched her on the bottom. She laughed and swatted him with a towel, and we witnessed what we would later come to recognize as the rejuvenating power of real estate. It's what fortunate couples turn to when their sex life has faded and they're too pious for affairs. A second car might bring people together for a week or two, but a second home can revitalize a marriage for up to nine months after the closing.

"Oh, Lou," my mother said. "What am I going to do with you?"

"Whatever you want, baby," he said. "Whatever you want."

It was queer when people repeated their sentences twice, but we were willing to overlook it in exchange for a beach house. My mother was too excited to cook that night, and so we ate dinner at the Sanitary Fish Market in Morehead City. On taking our seats I expected my father to mention inadequate insulation or corroded pipes, the dark undersides of home ownership, but instead he discussed only the positive aspects. "I don't see why we couldn't spend our Thanksgivings here. Hell, we could even come for Christmas. Hang a few lights, get some ornaments, what do you think?"

A waitress passed the table, and without saying please, I demanded another Coke. She went to fetch it, and I settled back in my chair, drunk with the power of a second home. When school began, my classmates would court me, hoping I might invite them for a weekend, and I would make a game of pitting them against one another. This was what a person did when people liked him for all the wrong reasons, and I would grow to be very good at it.

"What do you think, David?" my father asked. I hadn't heard the question but said that it sounded good to me. "I like it," I said. "I like it."

The following afternoon our parents took us to see the house. "Now, I don't want you to get your hopes up too high," my mother said, but it was too late for that. It was a fifteen-minute drive from one end of the island to the other, and along the way we proposed names for what we had come to think of as our cottage. I'd already given it a good deal of thought but waited a few minutes before offering my suggestion.

"Are you ready?" I said. "Our sign will be the silhouette of a ship."

Nobody said anything.

"Get it?" I said. "The shape of a ship. Our house will be called The Ship Shape."

"Well, you'd have to write that on the sign," my father said. "Otherwise, nobody will get it."

"But if you write out the words you'll ruin the joke."

"What about The Nut Hut?" Amy said.

"Hey!" my father said. "Now there's an idea." He laughed, not realizing, I guess, that there already was a Nut Hut. We'd passed it a thousand times.

"How about something with the word *sandpiper* in it," my mother said. "Everybody likes sandpipers, right?"

Normally I would have hated them for not recognizing my suggestion as the best, but this was clearly a special time and I didn't want to ruin it with brooding. Each of us wanted to be the one who came up with the name, and inspiration could be hiding anywhere. When the interior of the car had been exhausted of ideas, we looked out the windows and searched the passing landscape.

Two thin girls braced themselves before crossing the busy road, hopping from foot to foot on the scalding pavement. "The Tar Heel," Lisa called out. "No, The Wait 'n' Sea. Get it? S-E-A."

A car trailing a motorboat pulled up to a gas pump. "The Shell Station!" Gretchen shouted.

Everything we saw was offered as a possible name, and the resulting list of nominees confirmed that once you left the shoreline, Emerald Isle was sorely lacking in natural beauty. "The TV Antenna," my sister Tiffany said. "The Telephone Pole." "The Toothless Black Man Selling Shrimp from the Back of His Van."

"The Cement Mixer." "The Overturned Grocery Cart." "Gulls on a Garbage Can." My mother inspired "The Cigarette Butt Thrown Out the Window" and suggested we look for ideas on the beach rather than on the highway. "I mean, my God, how depressing can you get?" She acted annoyed, but we could tell she was really enjoying it. "Give me something that suits us," she said. "Give me something that will last."

What would ultimately last were these fifteen minutes on the coastal highway, but we didn't know that then. When older, even the crankiest of us would accept them as proof that we were once a happy family: our mother young and healthy, our father the man who could snap his fingers and give us everything we wanted, the whole lot of us competing to name our good fortune.

The house was, as our parents had promised, perfect. This was an older cottage with pine-paneled walls that gave each room the thoughtful quality of a den. Light fell in strips from the louvered shutters, and the furniture, which was included in the sale, reflected the taste of a distinguished sea captain. Once we'd claimed bedrooms and lain awake all night, mentally rearranging the furniture, it would be our father who'd say, "Now hold on a minute, it's not ours *yet*." By the next afternoon he had decided that the golf course wasn't so great after all. Then it rained for two straight days, and he announced that it might be wiser to buy some land, wait a few years, and think about building a place of our own. "I mean, let's be practical." Our mother put on her raincoat. She tied a plastic bag over her head and stood at the water's edge, and for the first time in our lives we knew exactly what she was thinking.

By our final day of vacation our father had decided that instead of building a place on Emerald Isle, we should improve the home we already had. "Maybe add a pool," he said. "What do you kids think about that?" Nobody answered.

By the time he'd finished wheedling it down, the house at the beach had become a bar in the basement. It looked just like a real bar, with tall stools and nooks for wine. There was a sink for washing glasses and an assortment of cartoon napkins illustrating the lighter side of alcoholism. For a week or two my sisters and I tottered at the counter, pretending to be drunks, but then the novelty wore off and we forgot all about it.

On subsequent vacations, both with and without our parents, we would drive by the cottage we had once thought of as our own. Each of us referred to it by a different name, and over time qualifiers became necessary. ("You know, *our* house.") The summer after we didn't buy it, the new owners—or "those people," as we liked to call them—painted The Ship Shape yellow. In the late seventies Amy noted that The Nut Hut had extended the carport and paved the driveway. Lisa was relieved when the Wait 'n' Sea returned to its original color, and Tiffany was incensed when The Toothless Black Man Selling Shrimp from the Back of His Van sported a sign endorsing Jesse Helms in the 1984 senatorial campaign. Four years later my mother called to report that The Sandpiper had been badly damaged by Hurricane Hugo. "It's still there," she said. "But barely." Shortly thereafter, according to Gretchen, The Shell Station was torn down and sold as a vacant lot.

I know that such a story does not quite work to inspire sympathy. ("My home—well, *one* of my homes—fell through.") We had no legitimate claim to self-pity, were ineligible even to hold a grudge, but that didn't stop us from complaining.

In the coming years our father would continue to promise what he couldn't deliver, and in time we grew to think of him as an actor auditioning for the role of a benevolent millionaire. He'd never get the part but liked the way that the words felt in his mouth. "What do you say to a new car?" he'd ask. "Who's up for a cruise to the Greek Isles?" He expected us to respond by playing the part of an enthusiastic family, but we were unwilling to resume our old roles. As if carried by a tide, our mother drifted farther and farther away, first to twin beds and then down the hall to a room decorated with seascapes and baskets of sun-bleached sand dollars. It would have been nice, a place at the beach, but we already had a home. A home with a bar. Besides, had things worked out, you wouldn't have been happy for us. We're not that kind of people.

The Girl Next Door

"Well, that little experiment is over," my mother said. "You tried it, it didn't work out, so what do you say we just move on." She was dressed in her roll-up-the-shirtsleeves outfit: the faded turquoise skirt, a cotton head scarf, and one of the sporty blouses my father had bought in the hope she might take up golf. "We'll start with the kitchen," she said. "That's always the best way, isn't it."

I was moving again. This time because of the neighbors.

"Oh, no," my mother said. "They're not to blame. Let's be honest now." She liked to take my problems back to the source, which was usually me. Like, for instance, when I got food poisoning it wasn't the chef's fault. "*You're* the one who wanted to go Oriental. *You're* the one who ordered the lomain."

"Lo mein. It's two words."

"Oh, he speaks Chinese now! Tell me, Charlie Chan, what's the word for six straight hours of vomiting and diarrhea?"

What she meant was that I'd tried to save money. The cheap

Chinese restaurant, the seventy-five-dollar-a-month apartment: "Cut corners and it'll always come back to bite you in the ass." That was one of her sayings. But if you didn't *have* money how could you *not* cut corners?

"And whose fault is it that you don't have any money? I'm not the one who turned up his nose at a full-time job. I'm not the one who spends his entire paycheck down at the hobby shop."

"I understand that."

"Well, good," she said, and then we began to wrap the breakables.

In my version of the story, the problem began with the child next door, a third-grader who, according to my mother, was bad news right from the start. "Put it together," she'd said when I first called to tell her about it. "Take a step back. Think."

But what was there to think about? She was a nine-year-old girl.

"Oh, they're the worst," my mother said. "What's her name? Brandi? Well, that's cheap, isn't it."

"I'm sorry," I said, "but aren't I talking to someone who named her daughter *Tiffany?*"

"My hands were tied!" she shouted. "The damned Greeks had me against the wall and you know it."

"Whatever you say."

"So this girl," my mother continued—and I knew what she would ask before she even said it. "What does her father do?"

I told her there wasn't a father, at least not one that I knew about, and then I waited as she lit a fresh cigarette. "Let's see," she said. "Nine-year-old girl named after an alcoholic beverage. Single mother in a neighborhood the police won't even go to. What else have you got for me?" She spoke as if

I'd formed these people out of clay, as if it were my fault that the girl was nine years old and her mother couldn't keep a husband. "I don't suppose this woman has a job, does she?"

"She's a bartender."

"Oh, that's splendid," my mother said. "Go on."

The woman worked nights and left her daughter alone from four in the afternoon until two or three in the morning. Both were blond, their hair almost white, with invisible eyebrows and lashes. The mother darkened hers with pencil, but the girl appeared to have none at all. Her face was like the weather in one of those places with no discernible seasons. Every now and then, the circles beneath her eyes would shade to purple. She might show up with a fat lip or a scratch on her neck but her features betrayed nothing.

You had to feel sorry for a girl like that. No father, no eyebrows, and that mother. Our apartments shared a common wall, and every night I'd hear the woman stomping home from work. Most often she was with someone, but whether alone or with company she'd find some excuse to bully her daughter out of bed. Brandi had left a doughnut on the TV or Brandi had forgotten to drain her bathwater. They're important lessons to learn, but there's something to be said for leading by example. I never went into their apartment, but what I saw from the door was pretty rough—not simply messy or chaotic, but hopeless, the lair of a depressed person.

Given her home life, it wasn't surprising that Brandi latched onto me. A normal mother might have wondered what was up—her nine-year-old daughter spending time with a twenty-six-year-old man—but this one didn't seem to care. I was just free stuff to her: a free babysitter, a free cigarette machine, the whole store. I'd hear her through the wall sometimes: "Hey, go ask your friend for a roll of toilet paper." "Go ask your friend to make you a sandwich." If company was coming and she wanted to be alone, she'd kick the girl out. "Why don't you go next door and see what your little playmate is up to?"

Before I moved in, Brandi's mother had used the couple downstairs, but you could tell that the relationship had soured. Next to the grocery carts chained to their porch was a store-bought sign, the no trespassing followed by a hand-written "This means you, Brandi!!!!"

There was a porch on the second floor as well, with one door leading to Brandi's bedroom and another door leading to mine. Technically, the two apartments were supposed to share it, but the entire thing was taken up with their junk, and so I rarely used it.

"I can't wait until you get out of your little slumming phase," my mother had said on first seeing the building. She spoke as if she'd been raised in splendor, but in fact her childhood home had been much worse. The suits she wore, the delicate bridges holding her teeth in place—it was all an invention. "You live in bad neighborhoods so you can feel superior," she'd say, the introduction, always, to a fight. "The point is to move *up* in the world. Even sideways will do in a pinch, but what's the point in moving down?"

As a relative newcomer to the middle class, she worried that her children might slip back into the world of public assistance and bad teeth. The finer things were not yet in our blood, or at least that was the way she saw it. My thrift-shop clothing drove her up the wall, as did the secondhand mattress lying without benefit of box springs upon my hardwood floor. "It's not *ironic*," she'd say. "It's not *ethnic*. It's filthy."

Bedroom suites were fine for people like my parents, but as an artist I preferred to rough it. Poverty lent my little dabblings a much-needed veneer of authenticity, and I imagined myself repaying the debt by gently lifting the lives of those around me, not en masse but one by one, the old-fashioned way. It was, I thought, the least I could do.

I told my mother that I had allowed Brandi into my apartment, and she sighed deeply into her end of the telephone. "And I bet you gave her the grand tour, didn't you? Mr. Show-Off. Mr. Big Shot." We had a huge fight over that one. I didn't call her for two days. Then the phone rang. "Brother," she said. "You have no idea what you're getting yourself into."

A neglected girl comes to your door and what are you supposed to do, turn her away?

"Exactly," my mother said. "Throw her the hell out."

But I couldn't. What my mother defined as boasting, I considered a standard show-and-tell. "This is my stereo system," I'd said to Brandi. "This is the electric skillet I received last Christmas, and here's a little something I picked up in Greece last summer." I thought I was exposing her to the things a regular person might own and appreciate, but all she heard was the possessive. "This is my honorable-mention ribbon," meaning "It belongs to *me*. It's not yours." Every now and then I'd give her a little something, convinced that she'd treasure it forever. A postcard of the Acropolis, prestamped envelopes, packaged towelettes bearing the insignia of Olympic Airlines. "Really?" she'd say. "For me?"

The only thing she owned, the only thing special, was a foot-tall doll in a clear plastic carrying case. It was a dime-store version of one of those Dolls from Many Countries, this one Spanish with a beet red dress and a droopy mantilla on her head. Behind her, printed on cardboard, was the place where she lived: a piñata-lined street snaking up the hill to a dusty bullring. The doll had been given to her by her grandmother, who was forty years old and lived in a trailer beside an army base.

"What is this?" my mother asked. "A skit from *Hee Haw?* Who the hell *are* these people?"

"These people," I said, "are my neighbors, and I'd appreciate it if you wouldn't make fun of them. The grandmother doesn't need it, I don't need it, and I'm pretty sure a nine-year-old-girl doesn't need it, either." I didn't tell her that the grandmother was nicknamed Rascal or that, in the picture Brandi showed me, the woman was wearing cutoff shorts and an ankle bracelet.

"We don't talk to her anymore," Brandi had said when I handed back the picture. "She's out of our life, and we're glad of it." Her voice was dull and robotic, and I got the impression that the line had been fed to her by her mother. She used a similar tone when introducing her doll. "She's not for playing with. She's for display."

Whoever imposed this rule had obviously backed it up with a threat. Brandi would trace her finger along the outside of the box, tempting herself, but never once did I see her lift the lid. It was as if the doll would explode if removed from her natural environment. Her world was the box, and a strange world it was.

"See," Brandi said one day, "she's on her way home to cook up those clams."

She was talking about the castanets dangling from the doll's wrist. It was a funny thought, childish, and I probably should have let it go rather than playing the know-it-all. "If she were an American doll those might be clams," I said. "But instead she's from Spain, and those are called castanets." I wrote the word on a piece of paper. "Castanets, look it up."

"She's not from Spain, she's from Fort Bragg."

"Well, maybe she was *bought* there," I said. "But she's supposed to be Spanish."

"And what's *that* supposed to mean?" It was hard to tell without the eyebrows, but I think she was mad at me.

"It's not *supposed* to mean anything," I said. "It's just true."

"You're full of it. There's no such place."

"Sure there is," I said. "It's right next to France."

"Yeah, right. What's that, a store?"

I couldn't believe I was having this conversation. How could you not know that Spain was a country? Even if you were nine years old, it seems you would have picked it up on TV or something. "Oh, Brandi," I said. "We've got to find you a map."

Because I couldn't do it any other way, we fell into a tight routine. I had a part-time construction job and would return home at exactly 5:30. Five minutes later Brandi would knock on my door, and stand there blinking until I let her in. I was going through a little wood-carving phase at the time, whittling figures whose heads resembled the various tools I worked with during the day: a hammer, a hatchet, a wire brush. Before beginning, I'd arrange some paper and colored pencils on my desk. "Draw your doll," I'd say. "Copy the bullring in her little environment. Express yourself!" I encouraged Brandi to broaden her horizons, but she usually quit after the first few minutes, claiming it was too much work.

Mainly she observed, her eyes shifting between my knife and the Spanish doll parked before her on the desktop. She'd talk about how stupid her teachers were, and then she'd ask what I would do if I had a million dollars. If I'd had a million dollars at that time in my life I probably would have spent every last penny of it on drugs, but I didn't admit it, because I wanted to set a good example. "Let's see," I'd say. "If I had that kind of money, I'd probably give it away."

"Yeah, right. You'd what, just hand it out to people on the street?"

"No, I'd set up a foundation and try to make a difference in people's lives." At this one even the doll was gagging.

When asked what she'd do with a million dollars, Brandi described cars and gowns and heavy bracelets encrusted with gems.

"But what about others? Don't you want to make them happy?"

"No. I want to make them jealous."

"You don't mean that," I'd say.

"Try me."

"Oh, Brandi." I'd make her a glass of chocolate milk and she'd elaborate on her list until 6:55, when friendship period was officially over. If work had gone slowly and there weren't many shavings to sweep up, I might let her stay an extra two minutes, but never longer.

"Why do I have to go right this second?" she asked one evening. "Are you going to work or something?"

"Well, no, not exactly."

"Then what's your hurry?"

I never should have told her. The good part about being an obsessive compulsive is that you're always on time for work. The bad part is that you're on time for everything. Rinsing your coffee cup, taking a bath, walking your clothes to the Laundromat: there's no mystery to your comings and goings, no room for spontaneity. During that time of my life I went to the IHOP every evening, heading over on my bike at exactly seven and returning at exactly nine. I never ate there, just drank coffee, facing the exact same direction in the exact same booth and reading library books for exactly an hour. After this I would ride to the grocery store. Even if I didn't need anything I'd go, because that's what that time was allotted for. If the lines were short, I'd bike home the long way or circle the block a few times, unable to return early, as those five or ten minutes weren't scheduled for apartment time.

"What would happen if you were ten minutes late?" Brandi

asked. My mother often asked the same question—everyone did. "You think the world will fall apart if you walk through that door at nine-o-four?"

They said it jokingly, but the answer was yes, that's exactly what I thought would happen. The world would fall apart. On the nights when another customer occupied my regular IHOP booth, I was shattered. "Is there a problem?" the waitress would ask, and I'd find that I couldn't even speak.

Brandi had been incorporated into my schedule for a little over a month when I started noticing that certain things were missing—things like pencil erasers and these little receipt books I'd picked up in Greece. In searching through my drawers and cabinets, I discovered that other things were missing as well: a box of tacks, a key ring in the form of a peanut.

"I see where this is going," my mother said. "The little sneak unlatched your porch door and wandered over while you were off at the pancake house. That's what happened, isn't it?"

I hated that she figured it out so quickly.

When I confronted Brandi, she broke down immediately. It was as if she'd been dying to confess, had rehearsed it, even. The stammered apology, the plea for mercy. She hugged me around the waist, and when she finally pulled away I felt my shirtfront, expecting to find it wet with tears. It wasn't. I don't know why I did what I did next, or rather, I guess I do. It was all part of my ridiculous plan to set a good example. "You know what we have to do now, don't you?" I sounded firm and fair until I considered the consequences, at which point I faltered. "We've got to go . . . and tell your mother what you just *did?*"

I half hoped that Brandi might talk me out of it, but instead she just shrugged.

"I bet she did," my mother said. "I mean, come on, you

might as well have reported her to the cat. What did you expect that mother to do, needlepoint a sampler with the Ten Commandments? Wake up, Dopey, the woman's a whore."

Of course she was right. Brandi's mother listened with her arms crossed, a good sign until I realized that her anger was directed toward me rather than her daughter. In the far corner of the room a long-haired man cleaned beneath his fingernails with a pair of scissors. He looked my way for a moment and then turned his attention back to the television.

"So she took a pencil eraser," Brandi's mother said. "What do you want me to do, dial nine-one-one?" She made it sound unbelievably petty.

"I just thought you should know what happened," I said.

"Well, lucky me. Now I know."

I returned to my apartment and pressed my ear against the bedroom wall. "Who was that?" the guy asked.

"Oh, just some asshole," Brandi's mother said.

Things cooled down after that. I could forgive Brandi for breaking into my apartment, but I could not forgive her mother. *Just some asshole.* I wanted to go to the place where she worked and burn it down. In relating the story, I found myself employing lines I'd probably heard on public radio. "Children *want* boundaries," I said. "They *need* them." It sounded sketchy to me, but everyone seemed to agree—especially my mother, who suggested that in this particular case, a five-by-eleven cell might work. She wasn't yet placing the entire blame on me, so it was still enjoyable to tell her things, to warm myself in the comforting glow of her outrage.

The next time Brandi knocked I pretended to be out—a ploy that fooled no one. She called my name, figured out where this was headed, and then went home to watch TV. I didn't plan to stay mad forever. A few weeks of the silent treatment and then I figured we'd pick up where we left off. In the meantime,

I occasionally passed her in the front yard, just standing there as if she were waiting for someone normal to pick her up. I'd say, "Hello, how's it going?" and she'd give me this tight little smile, the sort you'd offer if someone you hated was walking around with chocolate stains on the back of his pants.

Back when our neighborhood was prosperous, the building we lived in was a single-family home, and sometimes I liked to imagine it as it once was: with proud rooms and chandeliers, a stately working household serviced by maids and coachmen. I was carrying out the trash one afternoon and came upon what used to be the coal cellar, a grim crawl space now littered with shingles and mildewed cardboard boxes. There were worn-out fuses and balls of electrical wire, and there, in the back, a pile of objects I recognized as my own: things I hadn't noticed were missing—photographs, for instance, and slides of my bad artwork. Moisture had fouled the casings, and when I backed out of the cellar and held them to the sun I saw that the film had been scratched, not by accident but intentionally, with a pin or a razor. "Yur a ashole," one of them read. "Suk my dick why dont you." The spelling was all over the place, the writing tiny and furious, bleeding into the mind-bending designs spewed by mental patients who don't know when to stop. It was the exact effect I'd been striving for in my bland imitation folk art, so not only did I feel violated, I felt jealous. I mean, this girl was the real thing.

There were pages of slides, all of them etched with ugly messages. Photographs, too, were ruined. Here was me as a toddler with the word *shity* scratched into my forehead. Here was my newlywed mother netting crabs with her eyes clawed out. Included in the pile were all of the little presents accepted with such false gratitude, the envelopes and postcards, even the towelettes, everything systematically destroyed.

I gathered it all up and went straight to Brandi's mother. It was two o'clock in the afternoon and she was dressed in one of those thigh-length robes people wear when practicing karate. This was morning for her, and she stood drinking cola from a tall glass mug. "Fuck," she said. "Haven't we been through this?"

"Well, actually, no." My voice was higher than normal, and unstable. "Actually, we *haven't* been through this."

I'd considered myself an outsider in this neighborhood, something like a missionary among the savages, but standing there panting, my hair netted with cobwebs, I got the horrible feeling that I fit right in.

Brandi's mother glanced down at the filthy stack in my hand, frowning, as if these were things I was trying to sell door-to-door. "You know what?" she said. "I don't need this right now. No, you know what? I don't need it, period. Do you think having a baby was easy for me? I don't have nobody helping me out, a husband or day care or whatever, I'm all alone here, understand?"

I tried putting the conversation back on track, but as far as Brandi's mother was concerned, there was no other track. It was all about her. "I work my own hours *and* cover shifts for Kathy fucking Cornelius and on my one day off I've got some faggot hassling me about some shit I don't even *know* about? I don't think so. Not today I don't, so why don't you go find somebody else to dump on."

She slammed the door in my face and I stood in the hallway wondering, *Who is Kathy Cornelius? What just happened?*

In the coming days I ran the conversation over and over in my mind, thinking of all the fierce and sensible things I should have said, things like "Hey, *I'm* not the one who decided to have children" and "It's not *my* problem that you have to cover shifts for Kathy fucking Cornelius."

"It wouldn't have made any difference," my mother said. "A woman like that, the way she sees it she's a victim. Everyone's against her, no matter what."

I was so angry and shaken that I left the apartment and went to stay with my parents on the other side of town. My mom drove me to the IHOP and back, right on schedule, but it wasn't the same. On my bike I was left to my own thoughts, but now I had her lecturing me, both coming and going. "What did you hope to gain by letting that girl into your apartment? And don't tell me you wanted to make a difference in her life, please, I just ate." I got it that night and then again the following morning. "Do you want me to give you a ride back to your little shantytown?" she asked, but I was mad at her, and so I took the bus.

I thought things couldn't get much worse, and then, that evening, they did. I was just returning from the IHOP and was on the landing outside Brandi's door when I heard her whisper, "Faggot." She had her mouth to the keyhole, and her voice was puny and melodic. It was the way I'd always imagined a moth might sound. "Faggot. What's the matter, faggot? What's wrong, huh?"

She laughed as I scrambled into my apartment, and then she ran to the porch and began to broadcast through my bedroom door. "Little faggot, little tattletale. You think you're so smart, but you don't know shit."

"That's it," my mother said. "We've got to get you out of there." There was no talk of going to the police or social services, just "Pack up your things. She won."

"But can't I . . ."

"Oh-ho no," my mother said. "You've got her mad now and there's no turning back. All she has to do is go to the authorities, saying you molested her. Is that what you want? One little phone call and your life is ruined."

"But I didn't do *anything*. I'm gay, remember?"

"That's not going to save you," she said. "Push comes to shove and who do you think they're going to believe, a nine-year-old girl or the full-grown man who gets his jollies carving little creatures out of balsa wood?"

"They're *not* little creatures!" I yelled. "They're tool people!"

"What the hell difference does it make? In the eyes of the law you're just some nut with a knife who sits in the pancake house staring at a goddam stopwatch. You dress that girl in something other than a tube top and prop her up on the witness stand—crying her eyes out—and what do you think is going to happen? Get that mother in on the act and you've got both a criminal trial *and* a civil suit on your hands."

"You watch too much TV."

"Not as much as they do," she said. "I can guaran-goddamtee you that. You think these people can't smell money?"

"But I haven't got any."

"It's not your money they'll be after," she said. "It's mine."

"You mean Dad's." I was smarting over the "little creatures" comment and wanted to hurt her, but it didn't work.

"I mean *our* money," she said. "You think I don't know how these things work? I wasn't just born some middle-aged woman with a nice purse and a decent pair of shoes. My God, the things you don't know. My *God*."

My new apartment was eight blocks away, facing our city's first Episcopal church. My mother paid the deposit and the first month's rent and came with her station wagon to help me pack and move my things. Carrying a box of my featherweight balsa-wood sculptures out onto the landing, her hair gathered beneath a gingham scarf, I wondered how she appeared to Brandi, who was certainly watching through the keyhole.

What did she represent to her? The word *mother* wouldn't do, as I don't really think she understood what it meant. A person who shepherds you along the way and helps you out when you're in trouble—what would she call that thing? A queen? A crutch? A teacher?

I heard a noise from behind the door, and then the little moth voice. "Bitch," Brandi whispered.

I fled back into the apartment, but my mother didn't even pause. "Sister," she said, "you don't know the half of it."

Repeat After Me

Although we'd discussed my upcoming visit to Winston-Salem, my sister and I didn't make exact arrangements until the eve of my arrival, when I phoned from a hotel in Salt Lake City.

"I'll be at work when you arrive," she said, "so I'm thinking I'll just leave the key under the hour ott near the ack toor."

"The what?"

"Hour ott."

I thought she had something in her mouth until I realized she was speaking in code.

"What are you, on a speakerphone at a methadone clinic? Why can't you just tell me where you put the goddam house key?"

Her voice dropped to a whisper. "I just don't know that I trust these things."

"Are you on a cell phone?"

"Of course not," she said. "This is just a regular cordless, but still, you have to be careful."

When I suggested that actually she *didn't* have to be careful, Lisa resumed her normal tone of voice, saying, "Really? But I heard ..."

My sister's the type who religiously watches the fear segments of her local Eyewitness News broadcasts, retaining nothing but the headline. She remembers that applesauce can kill you but forgets that in order to die, you have to inject it directly into your bloodstream. Pronouncements that cellphone conversations may be picked up by strangers mix with the reported rise of both home burglaries and brain tumors, meaning that as far as she's concerned, all telecommunication is potentially life-threatening. If she didn't watch it on the news, she read it in *Consumer Reports* or heard it thirdhand from a friend of a friend of a friend whose ear caught fire while dialing her answering machine. Everything is dangerous all of the time, and if it's not yet been pulled off the shelves, then it's certainly under investigation—so there.

"Okay," I said. "but can you tell me *which* hour ott? The last time I was there you had quite a few of them."

"It's ed," she told me. "Well ... edd*ish*."

I arrived at Lisa's house late the following afternoon, found the key beneath the flowerpot, and let myself in through the back door. A lengthy note on the coffee table explained how I might go about operating everything from the television to the waffle iron, each carefully detailed procedure ending with the line *"Remember to turn off and unplug after use."* At the bottom of page three, a postscript informed me that if the appliance in question had no plug—the dishwasher, for instance—I should make sure it had completed its cycle and was cool to the touch before leaving the room. The note reflected a growing hysteria, its subtext shrieking, *Oh-my-God-he's-going-to-be-alone-in-my-house-for-close-to-an-hour.* She left her work number, her husband's work number, and the number of the next-door neighbor, adding that she didn't know the woman very well, so I probably shouldn't bother her unless it was an emergency. "P.P.S. She's a Baptist, so don't tell her you're gay."

The last time I was alone at my sister's place she was living in a white-brick apartment complex occupied by widows and single, middle-aged working women. This was in the late seventies, when we were supposed to be living in dorms. College hadn't quite worked out the way she'd expected, and after two years in Virginia she'd returned to Raleigh and taken a job at a wineshop. It was a normal-enough life for a twenty-one-year-old, but being a dropout was not what she had planned for herself. Worse than that, it had not been planned *for* her. As children we'd been assigned certain roles—leader, bum, troublemaker, slut—titles that effectively told us who we were. As the oldest, smartest, and bossiest, it was naturally assumed that Lisa would shoot to the top of her field, earning a master's degree in manipulation and eventually taking over a medium-size country. We'd always known her as an authority figure, and while we took a certain joy in watching her fall, it was disorienting to see her with so little confidence. Suddenly she was relying on other people's opinions, following their advice and withering at the slightest criticism.

Do you really think so? Really? She was putty.

My sister needed patience and understanding, but more often than not, I found myself wanting to shake her. If the oldest wasn't who she was supposed to be, then what did it mean for the rest of us?

Lisa had been marked Most Likely to Succeed, and so it confused her to be ringing up gallon jugs of hearty burgundy. I had been branded as lazy and irresponsible, so it felt right when I, too, dropped out of college and wound up living back in Raleigh. After being thrown out of my parents' house, I went to live with Lisa in her white-brick complex. It was a small studio apartment—the adult version of her childhood bedroom—and when I eventually left her with a broken stereo and an unpaid eighty-dollar phone bill, the general consensus was "Well, what did you expect?"

I might reinvent myself to strangers, but to this day, as far as my family is concerned, I'm still the one most likely to set your house on fire. While I accepted my lowered expectations, Lisa fought hard to regain her former title. The wineshop was just a temporary setback, and she left shortly after becoming the manager. Photography interested her, so she taught herself to use a camera, ultimately landing a job in the photo department of a large international drug company, where she took pictures of germs, viruses, and people reacting to germs and viruses. On weekends, for extra money, she photographed weddings, which really wasn't that much of a stretch. Then she got married herself and quit the drug company in order to earn an English degree. When told there was very little call for thirty-page essays on Jane Austen, she got a real estate license. When told the housing market was down, she returned to school to study plants. Her husband, Bob, got a job in Winston-Salem, and so they moved, buying a new three-story house in a quiet suburban neighborhood. It was strange to think of my sister living in such a grown-up place, and I was relieved to find that neither she nor Bob particularly cared for it. The town was nice enough, but the house itself had a way of aging things. Stand outside and you looked, if not young, then at least relatively carefree. Step indoors and you automatically put on twenty years and a 401(k) plan.

My sister's home didn't really lend itself to snooping, and so I spent my hour in the kitchen, making small talk with Henry.

It was the same conversation we'd had the last time I saw him, yet still I found it fascinating. He asked how I was doing, I said I was all right, and then, as if something might have drastically changed within the last few seconds, he asked again.

Of all the elements of my sister's adult life—the house, the husband, the sudden interest in plants—the most unsettling is Henry. Technically he's a blue-fronted Amazon, but to the average layman, he's just a big parrot—the type you might see on the shoulder of a pirate.

"How you doing?" The third time he asked, it sounded as if he really cared. I approached his cage with a detailed answer, and when he lunged for the bars, I screamed like a girl and ran out of the room.

"Henry likes you," my sister said a short while later. She'd just returned from her job at the plant nursery and was sitting at the table, unlacing her sneakers. "See the way he's fanning his tail? He'd never do that for Bob. Would you, Henry?"

Bob had returned from work a few minutes earlier and immediately headed upstairs to spend time with his own bird, a balding green-cheeked conure named José. I'd thought the two pets might enjoy an occasional conversation, but it turns out they can't stand each other.

"Don't even *mention* José in front of Henry," Lisa whispered. Bob's bird squawked from the upstairs study, and the parrot responded with a series of high, piercing barks. It was a trick he'd picked up from Lisa's border collie, Chessie, and what was disturbing was that he sounded *exactly* like a dog. Just as, when speaking English, he sounded exactly like Lisa. It was creepy to hear my sister's voice coming from a beak, but I couldn't say it didn't please me.

"Who's hungry?" she asked.

"Who's hungry?" the voice repeated.

I raised my hand, and she offered Henry a peanut. Watching him take it in his claw, his belly sagging almost to the perch, I could understand what someone might see in a parrot. Here was this strange little fatso living in my sister's kitchen, a sympathetic listener turning again and again to ask, "So, really, how are you?"

I'd asked her the same question and she'd said, "Oh, fine. You know." She's afraid to tell me anything important, knowing I'll only turn around and write about it. In my mind, I'm like a friendly junkman, building things from the little pieces of scrap I find here and there, but my family's started to see things differently. Their personal lives are the so-called pieces of scrap I so casually pick up, and they're sick of it. More and more often their stories begin with the line "You have to swear you will never repeat this." I always promise, but it's generally understood that my word means nothing.

I'd come to Winston-Salem to address the students at a local college, and then again to break some news. Sometimes when you're stoned it's fun to sit around and think of who might play you in the movie version of your life. What makes it fun is that no one is actually going to make a movie of your life. Lisa and I no longer got stoned, so it was all the harder to announce that my book had been optioned, meaning that, in fact, someone was going to make a movie of our lives—not a student, but a real director people had actually heard of.

"A *what?*"

I explained that he was Chinese, and she asked if the movie would be in Chinese.

"No," I said, "he lives in America. In California. He's been here since he was a baby."

"Then what does it matter if he's Chinese?"

"Well," I said, "he's got ... you know, a sensibility."

"Oh brother," she said.

I looked to Henry for support, and he growled at me.

"So now we have to be in a movie?" She picked her sneakers off the floor and tossed them into the laundry room. "Well," she said, "I can tell you right now that you are not dragging my bird into this." The movie was to be based on our pre-parrot years, but the moment she put her foot down I started wondering who we might get to play the role of Henry. "I know what you're thinking," she said. "And the answer is no."

Once, at a dinner party, I met a woman whose parrot had learned to imitate the automatic icemaker on her new refrigerator. "That's what happens when they're left alone," she'd said. It was the most depressing bit of information I'd heard in quite a while, and it stuck with me for weeks. Here was this creature, born to mock its jungle neighbors, and it wound up doing impressions of man-made kitchen appliances. I repeated the story to Lisa, who told me that neglect had nothing to do with it. She then prepared a cappuccino, setting the stage for Henry's pitch-perfect imitation of the milk steamer. "He can do the blender, too," she said.

She opened the cage door, and as we sat down to our coffees, Henry glided down onto the table. "Who wants a kiss?" She stuck out her tongue, and he accepted the tip gingerly between his upper and lower beak. I'd never dream of doing such a thing, not because it's across-the-board disgusting but because he would have bitten the shit out of me. Though Henry might occasionally fan his tail in my direction, it is understood that he is loyal to only one person, which, I think, is another reason my sister is so fond of him.

"Was that a good kiss?" she asked. "Did you like that?"

I expected a yes-or-no answer and was disappointed when he responded with the exact same question: "Did you like that?" Yes, parrots can talk, but unfortunately they have no idea what they're actually saying. When she first got him, Henry spoke the Spanish he'd learned from his captors. Asked if he'd had a good night's sleep, he'd say simply, *"Hola,"* or *"Bueno."* He goes through phases, favoring an often repeated noise or sentence, and then moving on to something else. When our mother died, Henry learned how to cry. He and Lisa would set each other off, and the two of them would go on for hours. A few years later, in the midst of a brief academic setback, she trained him to act as her emotional cheerleader. I'd call and hear him in the background, screaming, "We love you, Lisa!" and "You can do it!" This was replaced, in time, with the far more practical "Where are my keys?"

After finishing our coffees, Lisa and I drove to Greensboro, where I delivered my scheduled lecture. That is to say, I read stories about my family. After the reading, I answered questions about them, thinking all the while how odd it was that these strangers seemed to know so much about my brother and sisters. In order to sleep at night, I have to remove myself from the equation, pretending that the people I love expressly choose to expose themselves. Amy breaks up with a boyfriend and sends out a press release. Paul regularly discusses his bowel movements on daytime talk shows. I'm not the conduit, but just a poor typist stuck in the middle. It's a delusion much harder to maintain when a family member is actually *in* the audience.

The day after the reading, Lisa called in sick and we spent the afternoon running errands. Winston-Salem is a city of plazas—midsize shopping centers, each built around an enormous grocery store. I was looking for cheap cartons of cigarettes, so we drove from plaza to plaza, comparing prices and talking about our sister Gretchen. A year earlier she'd bought a pair of flesh-eating Chinese box turtles with pointed noses and spooky translucent skin. The two of them lived in an outdoor pen and were relatively happy until raccoons dug beneath the wire, chewing the front legs off the female and the rear legs off her husband.

"I may have the order wrong." Lisa said. "But you get the picture."

The couple survived the attack and continued to track the live mice that constituted their diet, propelling themselves forward like a pair of half-stripped Volkswagens.

"The sad part is that it took her two weeks to notice it," Lisa said. "Two weeks!" She shook her head and drove past our exit. "I'm sorry, but I don't know how a responsible pet owner could go that long without noticing a thing like that. It's just not right."

According to Gretchen, the turtles had no memories of their former limbs, but Lisa wasn't buying it. "Oh, come on," she said. "They must at least have phantom pains. I mean, how can a living creature not mind losing its legs? If anything like that happened to Chessie, I honestly don't know how I could live with myself." Her eyes misted and she wiped them with the back of her hand. "My little collie gets a tick and I go crazy."

Lisa's a person who once witnessed a car accident, saying, "I just hope there isn't a dog in the backseat." Human suffering doesn't faze her much, but she'll cry for days over a sick-pet story.

"Did you see that movie about the Cuban guy?" she asked. "It played here for a while but I wouldn't go. Someone told me a dog gets killed in the first fifteen minutes, so I said forget it."

I reminded her that the main character died as well, horribly, of AIDS, and she pulled into the parking lot, saying, "Well, I just hope it wasn't a *real* dog."

*

I wound up buying cigarettes at Tobacco USA, a discount store with the name of a theme park. Lisa had officially quit smoking ten years earlier and might have taken it up again were it not for Chessie, who, according to the vet, was predisposed to lung ailments. "I don't want to give her secondhand emphysema, but I sure wouldn't mind taking some of this weight off. Tell me the truth, do I look fat to you?"

"Not at all."

She turned sideways and examined herself in the front window of Tobacco USA. "You're lying."

"Well, isn't that what you want me to say?"

"Yes," she said. "But I want you to really mean it."

But I *had* meant it. It wasn't the weight I noticed so much as the clothing she wore to cover it up. The loose, baggy pants and oversize shirts falling halfway to her knees: This was the look she'd adopted a few months earlier, after she and her husband had gone to the mountains to visit Bob's parents. Lisa had been sitting beside the fire, and when she scooted her chair toward the center of the room, her father-in-law said, "What's the matter, Lisa? Getting too fat—I mean hot. Getting too hot?"

He tried to cover his mistake, but it was too late. The word had already been seared into my sister's brain.

"Will I have to be fat in the movie?" she asked.

"Of course not," I said. "You'll be just ... like you are."

"Like I am according to who?" she asked. "The Chinese?"

"Well, not *all* of them," I said. "Just one."

Normally, if at home during a weekday, Lisa likes to read nineteenth-century novels, breaking at one to eat lunch and watch a television program called *Matlock*. By the time we finished with my errands, the day's broadcast had already ended, and so we decided to go to the movies—whatever she wanted. She chose the story of a young Englishwoman struggling to remain happy while trying to lose a few extra pounds, but in the end she got her plazas confused, and we arrived at the wrong theater just in time to watch *You Can Count on Me,* the Kenneth Lonergan movie in which an errant brother visits his older sister. Normally, Lisa's the type who talks from one end of the picture to the other. A character will spread mayonnaise onto a chicken sandwich and she'll lean over, whispering, "One time, I was doing that? And the knife fell into the toilet." Then she'll settle back in her seat and I'll spend the next ten minutes wondering why on earth someone would make a chicken sandwich in the bathroom. This movie reflected our lives so eerily that for the first time in recent memory, she was stunned into silence. There was no physical resemblance between us and the main characters— the brother and sister were younger and orphaned—but like us, they'd stumbled to adulthood playing the worn, confining roles assigned to them as children. Every now and then one of them would break free, but for the most part they behaved not as they wanted to but as they were expected to. In brief, a guy shows up at his sister's house and stays for a few weeks until she kicks him out. She's not evil about it, but having him around forces her to think about things she'd rather not, which is essentially what family members do, at least the family members my sister and I know.

On leaving the theater, we shared a long, uncomfortable silence. Between the movie we'd just seen and the movie about to be made, we both felt awkward and self-conscious, as if we were auditioning for the roles of ourselves. I started in with some benign bit of gossip I'd heard concerning the man who'd played the part of the brother but stopped after the first few sentences, saying that, on second thought, it wasn't very interesting. She couldn't think of anything, either, and so we said nothing, each of us imagining a bored audience shifting in their seats.

We stopped for gas on the way home and were parking in front of her house when she turned to relate what I've come to think of as the quintessential Lisa story. "One time," she said, "one time I was out driving?" The incident began with a quick trip to the grocery store and ended, unexpectedly, with a wounded animal stuffed into a pillowcase and held to the tailpipe of her car. Like most of my sister's stories, it provoked a startling mental picture, capturing a moment in time when one's actions seem both unimaginably cruel and completely natural. Details were carefully chosen and the pace built gradually, punctuated by a series of well-timed pauses. "And then ... and then ..." She reached the inevitable conclusion and just as I started to laugh, she put her head against the steering wheel and fell apart. It wasn't the gentle flow of tears you might release when recalling an isolated action or event, but the violent explosion that comes when you realize that all such events are connected, forming an endless chain of guilt and suffering.

I instinctively reached for the notebook I keep in my pocket and she grabbed my hand to stop me. "If you ever," she said, "*ever* repeat that story, I will never talk to you again."

In the movie version of our lives, I would have turned to offer her comfort, reminding her, convincing her that the action she'd described had been kind and just. Because it was. She's incapable of acting otherwise.

In the *real* version of our lives, my immediate goal was simply to change her mind. "Oh, come on," I said. "The story's really funny, and, I mean, it's not like *you're* going to do anything with it."

Your life, your privacy, your occasional sorrow—it's not like you're going to do anything with it. Is this the brother I always was, or the brother I have become?

I'd worried that, in making the movie, the director might get me and my family wrong, but now a worse thought occurred to me: What if he got us right?

Dusk. The camera pans an unremarkable suburban street, moving in on a parked four-door automobile, where a small, evil man turns to his sobbing sister, saying, "What if I use the story but say that it happened to a friend?"

But maybe that's not the end. Maybe before the credits roll, we see this same man getting out of bed in the middle of the night, walking past his sister's room, and continuing downstairs into the kitchen. A switch is thrown, and we notice, in the far corner of the room, a large standing birdcage covered with a tablecloth. He approaches it carefully and removes the cloth, waking a blue-fronted Amazon parrot, its eyes glowing red in the sudden light. Through everything that's gone before this moment, we understand that the man has something important to say. From his own mouth the words are meaningless, and so he pulls up a chair. The clock reads three a.m., then four, then five, as he sits before the brilliant bird, repeating slowly and clearly the words "Forgive me. Forgive me. Forgive me."

Six to Eight Black Men

I've never been much for guidebooks, so when trying to get my bearings in some strange American city, I normally start by asking the cabdriver or hotel clerk some silly question regarding the latest census figures. I say "silly" because I don't really *care* how many people live in Olympia, Washington, or Columbus, Ohio. They're nice-enough places, but the numbers mean nothing to me. My second question might have to do with the average annual rainfall, which, again, doesn't tell me anything about the people who have chosen to call this place home.

What really interests me are the local gun laws. Can I carry a concealed weapon and, if so, under what circumstances? What's the waiting period for a tommy gun? Could I buy a Glock 17 if I were recently divorced or fired from my job? I've learned from experience that it's best to lead into this subject as delicately as possible, especially if you and the local citizen are alone and enclosed in a relatively small area. Bide your time, though, and you can walk away with some excellent stories. I've learned, for example, that the blind can legally hunt in both Texas and Michigan. In Texas they must be accompanied by a sighted companion, but I heard that in Michigan they're allowed to go it alone, which raises the question: How do they find whatever it is they just shot? In addition to that, how do they get it home? Are the Michigan blind allowed to drive as well? I ask about guns not because I want one of my own but because the answers vary so widely from state to state. In a country that's become increasingly homogeneous, I'm reassured by these last charming touches of regionalism.

Firearms aren't really an issue in Europe, so when traveling abroad, my first question usually relates to barnyard animals. "What do your roosters say?" is a good icebreaker, as every country has its own unique interpretation. In Germany, where dogs bark "vow vow" and both the frog and the duck say "quack," the rooster greets the dawn with a hearty "kik-a-riki." Greek roosters crow "kiri-a-kee," and in France they scream "coco-rico," which sounds like one of those horrible premixed cocktails with a pirate on the label. When told that an American rooster says "cock-a-doodle-doo," my hosts look at me with disbelief and pity.

"When do you open your Christmas presents?" is another good conversation starter, as I think it explains a lot about national character. People who traditionally open gifts on Christmas Eve seem a bit more pious and family-oriented than those who wait until Christmas morning. They go to Mass, open presents, eat a late meal, return to church the following morning, and devote the rest of the day to eating another big meal. Gifts are generally reserved for children, and the parents tend not to go overboard. It's nothing I'd want for myself, but I suppose it's fine for those who prefer food and family to things of real value.

In France and Germany gifts are exchanged on Christmas Eve, while in the Netherlands the children open their presents on December 5, in celebration of St. Nicholas Day. It sounded sort of quaint until I spoke to a man named Oscar, who filled me in on a few of the details as we walked from my hotel to the Amsterdam train station.

Unlike the jolly, obese American Santa, Saint Nicholas is painfully thin and dresses not unlike the pope, topping his robes with a tall hat resembling an embroidered tea cozy. The outfit, I was told, is a carryover from his former career, when he served as the bishop of Turkey.

"I'm sorry," I said, "but could you repeat that?"

One doesn't want to be too much of a cultural chauvinist, but this seemed completely wrong to me. For starters, Santa didn't *used to do* anything. He's not retired and, more important, he has nothing to do with Turkey. It's too dangerous there, and the people wouldn't appreciate him. When asked how he got from Turkey to the North Pole, Oscar told me with complete conviction that Saint Nicholas currently resides in Spain, which again is simply not true. Though he could probably live wherever he wanted, Santa chose the North Pole specifically because it is harsh and isolated. No one can spy on him, and he doesn't have to worry about people coming to the door. Anyone can come to the door in Spain, and in that outfit he'd most certainly be recognized. On top of that, aside from a few pleasantries, Santa doesn't speak Spanish. "Hello. How are you? Can I get you some candy?" Fine. He knows enough to get by, but he's not fluent and he certainly doesn't eat tapas.

While our Santa flies in on a sled, the Dutch version arrives by boat and then transfers to a white horse. The event is televised, and great crowds gather at the waterfront to greet him. I'm not sure if there's a set date, but he generally docks in late

November and spends a few weeks hanging out and asking people what they want.

"Is it just him alone?" I asked. "Or does he come with some backup?"

Oscar's English was close to perfect, but he seemed thrown by a term normally reserved for police reinforcement.

"Helpers," I said. "Does he have any elves?"

Maybe I'm overly sensitive, but I couldn't help but feel personally insulted when Oscar denounced the very idea as grotesque and unrealistic. "Elves," he said. "They are just so silly."

The words *silly* and *unrealistic* were redefined when I learned that Saint Nicholas travels with what was consistently described as "six to eight black men." I asked several Dutch people to narrow it down, but none of them could give me an exact number. It was always "six to eight," which seems strange, seeing as they've had hundreds of years to get an accurate head count.

The six to eight black men were characterized as personal slaves until the mid-1950s, when the political climate changed and it was decided that instead of being slaves they were just good friends. I think history has proved that something usually comes *between* slavery and friendship, a period of time marked not by cookies and quiet hours beside the fire but by bloodshed and mutual hostility. They have such violence in the Netherlands, but rather than duking it out amongst themselves, Santa and his former slaves decided to take it out on the public. In the early years if a child was naughty, Saint Nicholas and the six to eight black men would beat him with what Oscar described as "the small branch of a tree."

"A switch?"

"Yes," he said. "That's it. They'd kick him and beat him

with a switch. Then if the youngster was really bad, they'd put him in a sack and take him back to Spain."

"Saint Nicholas would *kick* you?"

"Well, not anymore," Oscar said. "Now he just *pretends* to kick you."

He considered this to be progressive, but in a way I think it's almost more perverse than the original punishment. "I'm going to hurt you but not really." How many times have we fallen for that line? The fake slap invariably makes contact, adding the elements of shock and betrayal to what had previously been plain old-fashioned fear. What kind of a Santa spends his time pretending to kick people before stuffing them into a canvas sack? Then, of course, you've got the six to eight former slaves who could potentially go off at any moment. This, I think, is the greatest difference between us and the Dutch. While a certain segment of our population might be perfectly happy with the arrangement, if you told the average white American that six to eight nameless black men would be sneaking into his house in the middle of the night, he would barricade the doors and arm himself with whatever he could get his hands on.

"*Six to eight,* did you say?"

In the years before central heating, Dutch children would leave their shoes by the fireplace, the promise being that unless they planned to beat you, kick you, or stuff you into a sack, Saint Nicholas and the six to eight black men would fill your clogs with presents. Aside from the threats of violence and kidnapping, it's not much different than hanging your stockings from the mantel. Now that so few people actually have a working fireplace, Dutch children are instructed to leave their shoes beside the radiator, furnace, or space heater. Saint Nicholas and the six to eight black men arrive on horses, which jump from the yard onto the roof. At this point I guess they either jump back down and use the door or stay put and vaporize through the pipes and electrical cords. Oscar wasn't too clear about the particulars, but really, who can blame him? We have the same problem with our Santa. He's supposed to use the chimney, but if you don't have one, he still manages to get in. It's best not to think about it too hard.

While eight flying reindeer are a hard pill to swallow, our Christmas story remains relatively dull. Santa lives with his wife in a remote polar village and spends one night a year traveling around the world. If you're bad, he leaves you coal. If you're good and live in America, he'll give you just about anything you want. We tell our children to be good and send them off to bed, where they lie awake, anticipating their great bounty. A Dutch parent has a decidedly hairier story to relate, telling his children, "Listen, you might want to pack a few of your things together before going to bed. The former bishop of Turkey will be coming tonight along with six to eight black men. They might put some candy in your shoes, they might stuff you into a sack and take you to Spain, or they might just pretend to kick you. We don't know for sure, but we want you to be prepared."

This is the reward for living in the Netherlands. As a child you get to hear this story, and as an adult you get to turn around and repeat it. As an added bonus, the government has thrown in legalized drugs and prostitution—so what's *not* to love about being Dutch?

Oscar finished his story just as we arrived at the station. He was an amiable guy—very good company—but when he offered to wait until my train arrived I begged off, claiming I had some calls to make. Sitting alone in the vast, vibrant terminal, surrounded by thousands of polite, seemingly interesting Dutch people, I couldn't help but feel second-rate. Yes, the Netherlands was a small country, but it had six to eight black men and a really good bedtime story. Being a fairly competitive person, I felt jealous, then bitter. I was edging toward hostile when I remembered the blind hunter tramping off alone into the Michigan forest. He may bag a deer, or he may happily shoot a camper in the stomach. He may find his way back to the car, or he may wander around for a week or two before stumbling through your back door. We don't know for sure, but in pinning that license to his chest, he inspires the sort of narrative that ultimately makes me proud to be an American.

Possession

Finding an apartment is a lot like falling in love," the real estate agent told us. She was a stylish grandmother in severe designer sunglasses. Dyed blond hair, black stockings, a little scarf tied just so around the throat: for three months she drove us around Paris in her sports car, Hugh up front and me folded like a lawn chair into the backseat.

At the end of every ride I'd have to teach myself to walk all over again, but that was just a minor physical complaint. My problem was that I already loved an apartment. The one we had was perfect, and searching for another left me feeling faithless and sneaky, as if I were committing adultery. After a viewing, I'd stand in our living room, looking up at the high, beamed ceiling and trying to explain that the other two-bedroom had meant nothing to me. Hugh took the opposite tack and blamed our apartment for making us cheat. We'd offered, practically begged, to buy it, but the landlord was saving the place for his daughters, two little girls who would eventually grow to evict us. Our lease could be renewed for another fifteen years, but Hugh refused to waste his love on a lost cause. When told our apartment could never truly be ours, he hung up the phone and contacted the real estate grandmother, which is what happens when you cross him: he takes action and moves on.

The place was dead to him, but I kept hoping for a miracle. A riding accident, a playhouse fire: lots of things can happen to little girls.

When looking around, I tried to keep an open mind, but the more places we visited, the more discouraged I became. If the apartment wasn't too small, it was too expensive, too modern, too far from the center of town. I'd know immediately that this was not love, but Hugh was on the rebound and saw potential in everything. He likes a wreck, something he can save, and so he became excited when, at the end of the summer, the grandmother got a listing for what translated to "a nicely situated whorehouse." His feeling grew as we made our way up the stairs and blossomed when the door was unlocked and the smell of stagnant urine drifted into the hall. The former tenants had moved out, leaving clues to both their size and their temperament. Everything from the waist down was either gouged, splintered, or smeared with a sauce of blood and human hair. I found a tooth on the living-room floor, and what looked to be an entire fingernail glued with snot to the inside of the front door. Of course, this was just me: Mr. Bad Mouth. Mr. Negative. While I was searching for the rest of the body, Hugh was racing back and forth between the hole that was a kitchen and the hole that was a bathroom, his eyes glazed and dopey.

We'd shared this expression on first seeing the old apartment, but this time he was on his own, feeling something that I could not. I tried to share his enthusiasm—"Look, faulty wiring!"—but there was a hollowness to it, the sound of someone who was settling for something and trying hard to pretend otherwise. It wasn't a horrible place. The rooms were large and bright, and you certainly couldn't argue with the location. It just didn't knock me out.

"Maybe you're confusing love with pity," I told him, to which he responded, "If that's what you think, I really feel sorry for you."

The grandmother sensed my lack of enthusiasm and wrote it off as a failure of imagination. "Some people can see only what's in front of them," she sighed.

"Hey," I said, "I have"—and I said the dumbest thing—"I have powers."

She pulled the phone from her handbag. "Prove it," she said. "The owner has gotten three offers, and he's not going to wait forever."

If finding an apartment is like falling in love, buying one is like proposing on your first date and agreeing not to see each other until the wedding. We put in our bid, and when it was accepted I pretended to be as happy as Hugh and his bridesmaid, the grandmother. We met with a banker, and a lawyer we addressed as Master LaBruce. I hoped that one of them would put an end to this—deny us a mortgage, unearth a codicil—but everything moved according to schedule. Our master presided over the closing, and the following day the contractor arrived. Renovations began, and still I continued to browse the real estate listings, hoping something better might come along. I worried, not just that we'd chosen the wrong apartment but the wrong neighborhood, the wrong city, the wrong country. "Buyer's remorse," the grandmother said. "But don't worry, it's perfectly natural." *Natural*. A strange word when used by an

eighty-year-old with an unlined face and hair the color of
an American school bus.

Three months after moving in, we took a trip to Amsterdam,
a city often recommended by the phrase "You can get so
fucked-up there." I'd imagined Day-Glo bridges and canals
flowing with bong water, but it was actually closer to a
Brueghel painting than a Mr. Natural cartoon. We loved the
lean brick buildings and the wispy sounds of bicycle tires on
freshly fallen leaves. Our hotel overlooked the Herengracht,
and on checking in, I started to feel that we'd made a terrible
mistake. Why settle in Paris before first exploring the possibility of Amsterdam? What had we been thinking?

On our first afternoon we took a walk and came across the
Anne Frank House, which was a surprise. I'd had the impression she lived in a dump, but it's actually a very beautiful
seventeenth-century building right on the canal. Tree-lined
street, close to shopping and public transportation: in terms
of location, it was perfect. My months of house hunting had
caused me to look at things in a certain way, and on seeing
the crowd gathered at the front door, I did not think, *Ticket
line,* but, *Open house!*

We entered the annex behind the famous bookcase, and
on crossing the threshold, I felt what the grandmother had
likened to being struck by lightning, an absolute certainty that
this was the place for me. That it would be mine. The entire
building would have been impractical and far too expensive,
but the part where Anne Frank and her family had lived, their
triplex, was exactly the right size and adorable, which is something they never tell you. In plays and movies it always appears
drab and old ladyish, but open the curtains and the first words
that come to mind are not "I still believe all people are really
good at heart" but "Who do I have to knock off in order to get

this apartment?" That's not to say that I wouldn't have made a few changes, but the components were all there and easy to see, as they'd removed the furniture and personal possessions that normally make a room seem just that much smaller.

Hugh stopped to examine the movie-star portraits glued to Anne Frank's bedroom wall—a wall that I personally would have knocked down—and I raced on to the bathroom, and then to the water closet with its delft toilet bowl looking for all the world like a big soup tureen. Next it was upstairs to the kitchen, which was eat-in with two windows. I'd get rid of the countertop and of course redo all the plumbing, but first I'd yank out the wood stove and reclaim the fireplace. "That's your focal point, there," I heard the grandmother saying. I thought the room beside the kitchen might be my office, but then I saw the attic, with its charming dormer windows, and the room beside the kitchen became a little leisure nook.

Now it was downstairs for another look at the toilet bowl, then back upstairs to reconsider the kitchen countertop, which, on second thought, I decided to keep. Or maybe not. It was hard to think with all these people coming and going, hogging the stairwell, running their mouths. A woman in a Disneyland sweatshirt stood in the doorway taking pictures of my sink, and I intentionally bumped her arm so that the prints would come out blurry and undesirable. "Hey!" she said.

"Oh, 'Hey' yourself." I was in a fever, and the only thing that mattered was this apartment. It wasn't a celebrity or a historical thing, not like owning one of Maria Callas's eyelashes or a pair of barbecue tongs once brandished by Pope Innocent XIII. Sure, I'd *mention* that I was not the first one in the house to ever keep a diary, but it wasn't the reason I'd fallen in love with the place. At the risk of sounding too koombaya, I felt as if I had finally come home. A cruel trick of fate had kept me away, but now I was back to claim what was rightfully mine.

It was the greatest feeling in the world: excitement and relief coupled with the giddy anticipation of buying stuff, of making everything just right.

I didn't snap out of it until I accidentally passed into the building next door, which has been annexed as part of the museum. Above a display case, written across the wall in huge, unavoidable letters, was this quote by Primo Levi: "A single Anne Frank moves us more than the countless others who suffered just as she did but whose faces have remained in the shadows. Perhaps it is better that way. If we were capable of taking in all the suffering of all those people, we would not be able to live."

He did not specify that we would not be able to live *in her house,* but it was definitely implied, and it effectively squashed any fantasy of ownership. The added tragedy of Anne Frank is that she almost made it, that she died along with her sister just weeks before their camp was liberated. Having already survived two years in hiding, she and her family might have stayed put and lasted out the war were it not for a neighbor, never identified, who turned them in. I looked out the window, wondering who could have done such a thing, and caught my reflection staring back at me. Then, beyond that, across the way, I saw the most beautiful apartment.

Nuit of the Living Dead

I was on the front porch, drowning a mouse in a bucket when this van pulled up, which was strange. On an average day a total of fifteen cars might pass the house, but no one ever stops, not unless they live here. And this was late, three o'clock in the morning. The couple across the street are asleep by nine, and from what I can tell, the people next door turn in an hour or so later. There are no streetlamps in our village in Normandy, so when it's dark, it's really dark. And when it's quiet, you can hear everything.

"Did I tell you about the burglar who got stuck in the chimney?" That was the big story last summer. One time it happened in the village at the bottom of the hill, the pretty one bisected by a river, and another time it took place fifteen miles in the opposite direction. I heard the story from four people, and each time it happened in a different place.

"So this burglar," people said. "He tried the doors and windows and when those wouldn't open, he climbed up onto the roof."

It was always a summer house, a cottage owned by English people whose names no one seemed to remember. The couple left in early September and returned ten months later to find a shoe in their fireplace. "Is this yours?" the wife asked her husband.

The two of them had just arrived. There were beds to be made and closets to air out, so between one thing and another the shoe was forgotten. It was early June, chilly, and as night fell, the husband decided to light a fire.

At this point in the story the tellers were beside themselves, their eyes aglow, as if reflecting the light of a campfire. "Do you honestly expect me to believe this?" I'd say. "I mean, *really.*"

At the beginning of the summer the local paper devoted three columns to a Camembert-eating contest. Competitors were pictured, hands behind their backs, their faces buried in soft, sticky cheese. This on the front page. In an area so hard up for news, I think a death by starvation might command the headlines for, oh, about six years.

"But wait," I'm told. "There's more!"

As the room filled with smoke, the husband stuck a broom up the chimney. Something was blocking the flue, and he poked at it again and again, dislodging the now skeletal burglar, who fell feet first into the flames.

There was always a pause here, a break between the story and the practical questions that would ultimately destroy it. "So who was this burglar?" I'd ask. "Did they identify his body?"

He was a Gypsy, a drifter, and, on two occasions, an Arab. No one remembered exactly where he was from. "But it's true," they said. "You can ask anyone," by which they meant the neighbor who had told them, or the person they themselves had told five minutes earlier.

*

I never believed that a burglar starved to death in a chimney. I don't believe that his skeleton dropped onto the hearth. But I do believe in spooks, especially when Hugh is away and I'm left alone in the country. During the war our house was occupied by Nazis. The former owner died in the bedroom, as did the owner before her, but it's not their ghosts that I worry about. It's silly, I know, but what frightens me is the possibility of zombies, former townspeople wandering about in pus-covered nightgowns. There's a church graveyard a quarter of a mile away, and were its residents to lurch out the gate and take a left, ours would be the third house they would stumble upon. Lying in bed with all the lights on, I draw up contingency plans on the off chance they might come a-callin'. The attic seems a wise hideout, but I'd have to secure the door, which would take time, time you do not have when zombies are steadily working their way through your windows.

I used to lie awake for hours, but now, if Hugh's gone for the night, I'll just stay up and keep myself busy: writing letters, cleaning the oven, replacing missing buttons. I won't put in a load of laundry, because the machine is too loud and would drown out other, more significant noises—namely, the shuffling footsteps of the living dead.

On this particular night, the night the van pulled up, I was in what serves as the combination kitchen/living room, trying to piece together a complex model of the Visible Man. The body was clear plastic, a shell for the organs, which ranged in color from bright red to a dull, liverish purple. We'd bought it as a birthday gift for a thirteen-year-old boy, the son of a friend, who pronounced it *null*, meaning "worthless, unacceptable." The summer before, he'd wanted to be a doctor, but over the next few months he seemed to have changed his mind, deciding instead that he might like to design shoes. I suggested that he at least keep the feet, but when he turned up his nose we gave him twenty euros and decided to keep the model for ourselves. I had just separated the digestive system when I heard a familiar noise coming from overhead, and dropped half the colon onto the floor.

There's a walnut tree in the side yard, and every year Hugh collects the fruit and lays it on the attic floor to dry. Shortly thereafter, the mice come in. I don't know how they climb the stairs, but they do, and the first thing on their list is to take Hugh's walnuts. They're much too big to be carried by mouth, so instead they roll them across the floor, pushing them toward the nests they build in the tight spaces between the walls and the eaves. Once there, they discover that the walnuts won't fit, and while I find this to be comic, Hugh thinks differently and sets the attic with traps I normally spring before the mice can get to them. Were they rats, it would be different, but a couple of mice? "Come on," I say. "What could be cuter?"

Sometimes, when the rolling gets on my nerves, I'll turn on the attic light and make like I'm coming up the stairs. This quiets them for a while, but on this night the trick didn't work. The noise kept up but sounded like something being dragged rather than rolled. A shingle? A heavy piece of toast? Again I turned on the attic light, and when the noise continued I went upstairs and found a mouse caught in one of the traps Hugh had set. The steel bar had come down on his back, and he was pushing himself in a tight circle, not in a death throe, but with a spirit of determination, an effort to work within this new set of boundaries. "I can live with this," he seemed to be saying. "Really. Just give me a chance."

I couldn't leave him that way, so I scooted the trapped mouse into a cardboard box and carried him down onto the front porch. The fresh air, I figured, would do him some good, and once released, he could run down the stairs and into the yard, free from the house that now held such bitter memories. I should have lifted the bar with my fingers, but instead, worried that he might try to bite me, I held the trap down with my foot and attempted to pry it open with the end of a metal ruler. Which was stupid. No sooner had the bar been raised than it snapped back, this time on the mouse's neck. My next three attempts were equally punishing, and when finally freed, he staggered onto the doormat, every imaginable bone broken in at least four different places. Anyone could see that he was not going to get any better. Not even a vet could have fixed this mouse, and so, to put him out of his misery, I decided to drown him.

The first step, and for me the most difficult, was going into the cellar to get the bucket. This involved leaving the well-lit porch, walking around to the side of the house, and entering what is surely the bleakest and most terrifying hole in all of Europe. Low ceiling, stone walls, a dirt floor stamped with paw prints. I never go in without announcing myself. "Hyaa!" I yell. "Hyaa. Hyaa!" It's the sound my father makes when entering his toolshed, the cry of cowboys as they round up dogies, and it suggests a certain degree of authority. Snakes, bats, weasels—it's time to head up and move on out. When retrieving the bucket, I carried a flashlight in each hand, holding them low, like pistols. Then I kicked in the door—"Hyaa! Hyaa!"—grabbed what I was looking for, and ran. I was back on the porch in less than a minute, but it took much longer for my hands to stop shaking.

The problem with drowning an animal—even a crippled one—is that it does not want to cooperate. This mouse had nothing going for him, and yet he struggled, using what, I don't really know. I tried to hold him down with a broom handle but it wasn't the right tool for the job and he kept breaking free and heading back to the surface. A creature that determined, you want to let it have its way, but this was for the best, whether he realized it or not. I'd just managed to pin his tail to the bottom of the bucket when this van drove up and stopped in front of the house. I say "van," but it was more like a miniature bus, with windows and three rows of seats. The headlights were on high, and the road before them appeared black and perfect.

After a moment or two the driver's window rolled down, and a man stuck his head into the pool of light spilling from the porch. "Bonsoir," he called. He said it the way a man in a lifeboat might yell, "Ahoy!" to a passing ship, giving the impression that he was very happy to see me. As he opened the door, a light came on and I could see five people seated behind him, two men and three women, each looking at me with the same expression of relief. All were adults, perhaps in their sixties or early seventies, and all of them had white hair.

The driver referred to a small book he held in his hand. Then he looked back at me and attempted to recite what he had just read. It was French, but just barely, pronounced phonetically, with no understanding of where the accents lay.

"Do you speak English?" I asked.

The man clapped his hands and turned around in his seat. "He speaks English!" The news was greeted with a great deal of excitement and then translated for one of the women, who apparently did not understand the significance. Meanwhile, my mouse had popped back to the surface and was using his good hand to claw at the sides of the bucket.

"We are looking for a particular place," the driver said. "A house we are renting with friends." He spoke loudly and with a slight accent. Dutch, I thought, or maybe Scandinavian.

I asked what town the house was in, and he said that it was not in a town, just a willage.

"A what?"

"A willage," he repeated.

Either he had a speech impediment or the letter *v* did not exist in his native language. Whatever the case, I wanted him to say it again.

"I'm sorry," I said. "But I couldn't quite hear you."

"A *willage*," he said. "Some friends have rented a house in a little willage and we can't seem to find it. We were supposed to be there hours ago, but now we are quite lost. Do you know the area?"

I said that I did, but drew a blank when he called out the name. There are countless small villages in our part of Normandy, clusters of stone buildings hidden by forests or knotted at the end of unpaved roads. Hugh might have known the place the man was looking for, but because I don't drive, I tend not to pay too much attention. "I have a map," the man said. "Do you think you could perhaps look at it?"

He stepped from the van and I saw that he was wearing a white nylon tracksuit, the pants puffy and gathered tight at the ankles. You'd expect to find sneakers attached to such an outfit, but instead he wore a pair of black loafers. The front gate was open, and as he made his way up the stairs, I remembered what it was that I'd been doing, and I thought of how strange it might look. It occurred to me to meet the man halfway, but by this time he had already reached the landing and was offering his hand in a gesture of friendship. We shook, and on hearing the faint, lapping noise, he squinted down into the bucket. "Oh," he said. "I see that you have a little swimming mouse." His tone did not invite explanation, and so I offered none. "My wife and I have a dog," he continued. "But we did not bring it with us. Too much trouble."

I nodded and he held out his map, a Xerox of a Xerox marked with arrows and annotated in a language I did not recognize. "I think I've got something better in the house," I said, and at my invitation, he followed me inside.

An unexpected and unknown visitor allows you to see a familiar place as if for the very first time. I'm thinking of the meter reader rooting through the kitchen at eight a.m., the Jehovah's Witness suddenly standing in your living room. "Here," they seem to say. "Use *my* eyes. The focus is much keener." I had always thought of our main room as cheerful, but walking through the door, I saw that I was mistaken. It wasn't dirty or messy, but like being awake when all decent people are fast asleep, there was something slightly suspicious about it. I looked at the Visible Man spread out on the table. The pieces lay in the shadow of a large taxidermied chicken that seemed to be regarding them, determining which organ might be the most appetizing. The table itself was pleasant to look at—oak and hand-hewn—but the chairs surrounding it were mismatched and in various states of disrepair. On the back of one hung a towel marked with the emblem of the Los Angeles County Coroner's Office. It had been a gift, not bought personally, but still it was there, leading the eye to an adjacent daybed, upon which lay two copies of a sordid true-crime magazine I purportedly buy to help me with my French. The cover of the latest issue pictured a young Belgian woman, a camper beaten to death with a cinder block. Is there a serial killer in *your* region? the headline asked. The second copy was opened to the crossword puzzle I'd attempted earlier in the evening. One of the clues translated to "female sex organ," and in the space provided I had written the word for *vagina*. It was the first time I had ever answered a French crossword puzzle question, and in celebration I had marked the margins with bright exclamation points.

There seemed to be a theme developing, and everything

I saw appeared to substantiate it: the almanac of guns and firearms suddenly prominent on the bookshelf, the meat cleaver lying for no apparent reason upon a photograph of our neighbor's grandchild.

"It's more of a summer home," I said, and the man nodded. He was looking now at the fireplace, which was slightly taller than he was. I tend to see only the solid stone hearth and high oak mantel, but he was examining the meat hooks hanging from the clotted black interior.

"Every other house we passed was dark," he said. "We've been driving I think for hours, just looking for someone who was awake. We saw your lights, the open door ..." His words were familiar from innumerable horror movies, the wayward soul announcing himself to the count, the mad scientist, the werewolf, moments before he changes.

"I hate to bother you, really."

"Oh, it's no bother, I was just drowning a mouse. Come in, please."

"So," the man said, "you say you have a map?"

I had several, and pulled the most detailed from a drawer containing, among other things, a short length of rope and a novelty pen resembling a dismembered finger. Where does all this stuff come from? I asked myself. There's a low cabinet beside the table, and pushing aside the delicate skull of a baby monkey, I spread the map upon the surface, identifying the road outside our house and then the village the man was looking for. It wasn't more than ten miles away. The route was fairly simple, but still I offered him the map, knowing he would feel better if he could refer to it on the road.

"Oh no," he said, "I couldn't," but I insisted, and watched from the porch as he carried it down the stairs and into the idling van. "If you have any problems, you know where I live," I said. "You and your friends can spend the night here if you like. Really, I mean it. I have plenty of beds." The man in the tracksuit waved goodbye, and then he drove down the hill, disappearing behind the neighbor's pitched roof.

The mouse that had fought so hard against my broom handle had lost his second wind and was floating, lifeless now, on the surface of the water. I thought of emptying the bucket into the field behind the house, but without the van, its headlights, and the comforting sound of the engine, the area beyond the porch seemed too menacing. The inside of the house suddenly seemed just as bad, and so I stood there, looking out at what I'd now think of as my willage. When the sun came up I would bury my dead and fill the empty bucket with hydrangeas, a bit of life and color, so perfect for the table. So pleasing to the eye.

Solution to Saturday's Puzzle

On the flight to Raleigh, I sneezed, and the cough drop I'd been sucking on shot from my mouth, ricocheted off my folded tray table, and landed, as I remember it, on the lap of the woman beside me, who was asleep and had her arms folded across her chest. I'm surprised the force didn't wake her—that's how hard it hit—but all she did was flutter her eyelids and let out a tiny sigh, the kind you might hear from a baby.

Under normal circumstances, I'd have had three choices, the first being to do nothing. The woman would wake in her own time and notice what looked like a shiny new button sewn to the crotch of her jeans. This was a small plane, with one seat per row on aisle A, and two seats per row on aisle B. We were on B, so should she go searching for answers I would be the first person on her list. "Is this yours?" she'd ask, and I'd look dumbly into her lap.

"Is what mine?"

Option number two was to reach over and pluck it from

her pants, and number three was to wake her up and turn the tables, saying, "I'm sorry, but I think you have something that belongs to me." Then she'd hand the lozenge back and maybe even apologize, confused into thinking that she'd somehow stolen it.

These circumstances, however, were *not* normal, as before she'd fallen asleep the woman and I had had a fight. I'd known her for only an hour, yet I felt her hatred just as strongly as I felt the stream of cold air blowing into my face—this after she'd repositioned the nozzle above her head, a final fuck-you before settling down for her nap.

The odd thing was that she hadn't looked like trouble. I'd stood behind her while boarding and she was just this woman, forty at most, wearing a T-shirt and cutoff jeans. Her hair was brown and fell to her shoulders, and as we waited she gathered it into a ponytail and fastened it with an elastic band. There was a man beside her who was around the same age and was also wearing shorts, though his were hemmed. He was skimming through a golf magazine, and I guessed correctly that the two of them were embarking on a vacation. While on the gangway, the woman mentioned a rental car and wondered if the beach cottage was far from a grocery store. She was clearly looking forward to her trip, and I found myself hoping that, whichever beach they were going to, the grocery store wouldn't be too far away. It was just one of those things that go through your mind. *Best of luck,* I thought.

Once on board, I realized that the woman and I would be sitting next to each other, which was fine. I took my place on the aisle, and within a minute she excused herself and walked a few rows up to talk to the man with the golf magazine. He was at the front of the cabin, in a single bulkhead seat, and I recall feeling sorry for him, because I hate the bulkhead. Tall people covet it, but I prefer as little leg room as possible. When I'm on a plane or in a movie theater, I like to slouch down as low as I can and rest my knees on the seat back in front of me. In the bulkhead, there is no seat in front of you, just a wall a good three feet away, and I never know what to do with my legs. Another drawback is that you have to put all of your belongings in the overhead compartment, and these are usually full by the time I board. All in all, I'd rather hang from one of the wheels than have to sit up front.

When our departure was announced, the woman returned to her seat but hovered a half foot off the cushion so she could continue her conversation with the man she'd been talking to earlier. I wasn't paying attention to what they were saying, but I believe I heard him refer to her as Becky, a wholesome name that matched her contagious, almost childlike enthusiasm.

The plane took off, and everything was as it should have been until the woman touched my arm and pointed to the man she'd been talking to. "Hey," she said, "see that guy up there?" Then she called out his name—Eric, I think—and the man turned and waved. "That's my husband, see, and I'm wondering if you could maybe swap seats so that me and him can sit together."

"Well, actually—," I said, and, before I could finish, her face hardened, and she interrupted me, saying, "What? You have a *problem* with that?"

"Well," I said, "ordinarily I'd be happy to move, but he's in the bulkhead, and I just hate that seat."

"He's in the *what?*"

"The bulkhead," I explained. "That's what you call that front row."

"Listen," she said, "I'm not asking you to switch because

it's a bad seat. I'm asking you to switch because we're married." She pointed to her wedding ring, and when I leaned in closer to get a better look at it she drew back her hand, saying, "Oh, never mind. Just forget it."

It was as if she had slammed a door in my face, and quite unfairly it seemed to me. I should have left well enough alone, but instead I tried to reason with her. "It's only a ninety-minute flight," I said, suggesting that in the great scheme of things it wasn't that long to be separated from your husband. "I mean, what, is he going to prison the moment we land in Raleigh?"

"No, he's not going to *prison*," she said, and on the last word she lifted her voice, mocking me.

"Look," I told her, "if he was a child I'd do it." And she cut me off, saying, "Whatever." Then she rolled her eyes and glared out the window.

The woman had decided that I was a hardass, one of those guys who refuse under any circumstances to do anyone a favor. But it's not true. I just prefer that the favor be *my* idea, and that it leaves me feeling kind rather than bullied and uncomfortable. *So no. Let her sulk,* I decided.

Eric had stopped waving, and signaled for me to get Becky's attention. "My wife," he mouthed. "Get my wife."

There was no way out, and so I tapped the woman on the shoulder.

"Don't touch me," she said, all dramatic, as if I had thrown a punch.

"Your husband wants you."

"Well, that doesn't give you the right to *touch* me." Becky unbuckled her seat belt, raised herself off the cushion, and spoke to Eric in a loud stage whisper: "I asked him to swap seats, but he won't do it."

He cocked his head, sign language for "How come?" and

she said, much louder than she needed to, "'Cause he's an *asshole,* that's why."

An elderly woman in aisle A turned to look at me, and I pulled a *Times* crossword puzzle from the bag beneath my seat. That always makes you look reasonable, especially on a Saturday, when the words are long and the clues are exceptionally tough. The problem is that you have to concentrate, and all I could think of was this Becky person.

Seventeen across: a fifteen-letter word for enlightenment. "I am not an asshole," I wrote, and it fit.

Five down: six-letter Indian tribe. "You are."

Look at the smart man, breezing through the puzzle, I imagined everyone thinking. He must be a genius. That's why he wouldn't swap seats for that poor married woman. He knows something we don't.

It's pathetic how much significance I attach to the *Times* puzzle, which is easy on Monday and gets progressively harder as the week advances. I'll spend fourteen hours finishing the Friday, and then I'll wave it in someone's face and demand that he acknowledge my superior intelligence. I think it means that I'm smarter than the next guy, but all it really means is that I don't have a life.

As I turned to my puzzle, Becky reached for a paperback novel, the kind with an embossed cover. I strained to see what the title was, and she jerked it closer to the window. Strange how that happens, how you can feel someone's eyes on your book or magazine as surely as you can feel a touch. It only works for the written word, though. I stared at her feet for a good five minutes, and she never jerked those away. After our fight, she'd removed her sneakers, and I saw that her toenails were painted white and that each one was perfectly sculpted.

Eighteen across: "Not impressed." Eleven down: "Whore."
I wasn't even looking at the clues anymore.

When the drink cart came, we fought through the flight attendant.

"What can I offer you folks?" she asked, and Becky threw down her book, saying, "We're not together." It killed her that we might be mistaken for a couple, or even friends, for that matter. "I'm traveling with my husband," she continued. "He's sitting up there. In *the bulkhead.*"

You learned that word from me, I thought. "Well, can I offer—"

"I'll have a Coke," Becky said. "Not much ice."

I was thirsty, too, but more than a drink I wanted the flight attendant to like me. And who would you prefer, the finicky baby who cuts you off and gets all specific about her ice cubes, or the thoughtful, nondemanding gentleman who smiles up from his difficult puzzle, saying, "Nothing for me, thank you"?

Were the plane to lose altitude and the only way to stay aloft was to push one person out the emergency exit, I now felt certain that the flight attendant would select Becky rather than me. I pictured her clinging to the doorframe, her hair blown so hard it was starting to fall out. "But my husband—," she'd cry. Then I would step forward, saying, "Hey, I've been to Raleigh before. Take me instead." Becky would see that I am not the asshole she mistook me for, and in that instant she would lose her grip and be sucked into space.

Two down: "Take that!"

It's always so satisfying when you can twist someone's hatred into guilt—make her realize that she was wrong, too quick to judge, too unwilling to look beyond her own petty concerns. The problem is that it works both ways. I'd taken this woman as the type who arrives late at a movie, then asks me to move behind the tallest person in the theater so that she and her husband can sit together. Everyone has to suffer just because she's sleeping with someone. But what if I was wrong? I pictured her in a dimly lit room, trembling before a portfolio of glowing X-rays. "I give you two weeks at the most," the doctor says. "Why don't you get your toenails done, buy yourself a nice pair of cutoffs, and spend some quality time with your husband. I hear the beaches of North Carolina are pretty this time of year."

I looked at her then, and thought, *No.* If she'd had so much as a stomach ache, she would have mentioned it. Or would she? I kept telling myself that I was within my rights, but I knew it wasn't working when I turned back to my puzzle and started listing the various reasons why I was not an asshole.

Forty across: "I give money to p—" Forty-six down: "—ublic radio."

While groping for Reason number two, I noticed that Becky was not making a list of her own. She was the one who called me a name, who went out of her way to stir up trouble, but it didn't seem to bother her in the least. After finishing her Coke, she folded up the tray table, summoned the flight attendant to take her empty can, and settled back for a nap. It was shortly afterward that I put the throat lozenge in my mouth, and shortly after that that I sneezed, and it shot like a bullet onto the crotch of her shorts.

Nine across: "Fuck!" Thirteen down: "Now what?"

It was then that another option occurred to me. *You know,* I thought. *Maybe I will swap places with her husband.* But I'd waited too long, and now he was asleep as well. My only way out was to nudge this woman awake and make the same offer I sometimes make to Hugh. We'll be arguing, and I'll stop in midsentence and ask if we can just start over. "I'll go outside and when I come back in we'll just pretend this never happened, OK?"

If the fight is huge, he'll wait until I'm in the hall, then bolt the door behind me, but if it's minor he'll go along, and I'll reenter the apartment, saying, "What are you doing home?" Or "Gee, it smells good in here. What's cooking?"—an easy question as he's always got something on the stove. For a while, it feels goofy, but eventually the self-consciousness wears off, and we ease into the roles of two decent people, trapped in a rather dull play. "Is there anything I can do to help?"

"You can set the table if you want."

"All-righty, then!"

I don't know how many times I've set the table in the middle of the afternoon, long before we sit down to eat. But the play would be all the duller without action, and I don't want to do anything really hard, like paint a room. I'm just so grateful that he goes along with it. Other people's lives can be full of screaming and flying plates, but I prefer that my own remains as civil as possible, even if it means faking it every once in a while.

I'd gladly have started over with Becky, but something told me she wouldn't go for it. Even asleep, she broadcast her hostility, each gentle snore sounding like an accusation. *Asshole. Ass-ho-ole.* The landing announcement failed to wake her, and when the flight attendant asked her to fasten her seat belt she did it in a drowse, without looking. The lozenge disappeared beneath the buckle, and this bought me an extra ten minutes, time spent gathering my things, so that I could make for the door the moment we arrived at our gate. I just didn't count on the man in front of me being a little bit quicker and holding me up as he wrestled his duffel bag from the overhead bin. Had it not been for him, I might have been gone by the time Becky unfastened her seat belt, but as it was I was only four rows away, standing, it turned out, right beside the bulkhead.

The name she called me was nothing I hadn't heard before, and nothing that I won't hear again, probably. Eight letters, and the clue might read, "Above the shoulders, he's nothing but crap." Of course, they'd don't put words like that in the *Times* crossword puzzle. If they did, anyone could finish it.

The Understudy

In the spring of 1967, my mother and father went out of town for the weekend and left my four sisters and me in the company of a woman named Mrs. Byrd, who was old and black and worked as a maid for one of our neighbors. She arrived at our house on a Friday afternoon, and, after carrying her suitcase to my parents' bedroom, I gave her a little tour, the way I imagined they did in hotels. "This is your TV, this is your private sundeck, and over here you've got a bathroom—just yours and nobody else's."

Mrs. Byrd put her hand to her cheek. "Somebody pinch me. I'm about to fall out."

She cooed again when I opened a dresser drawer and explained that when it came to coats and so forth we favored a little room called a closet. "There are two of them against the wall there, and you can use the one on the right."

It was, I thought, a dream for her: *your* telephone, *your* massive bed, *your* glass-doored shower stall. All you had to do was leave it a little cleaner than you found it.

A few months later, my parents went away again and left us with Mrs. Robbins, who was also black, and who, like Mrs. Byrd, allowed me to see myself as a miracle worker. Night fell, and I pictured her kneeling on the carpet, her forehead grazing my parents' gold bedspread. "Thank you, Jesus, for these wonderful white people and all that they have given me this fine weekend."

With a regular teenage babysitter, you horsed around, jumped her on her way out of the bathroom, that sort of thing, but with Mrs. Robbins and Mrs. Byrd we were respectful and well behaved, not like ourselves at all. This made our parents' getaway weekend a getaway for us as well—for what was a vacation but a chance to be someone different?

In early September of that same year, my parents joined my aunt Joyce and uncle Dick for a week in the Virgin Islands. Neither Mrs. Byrd nor Mrs. Robbins was available to stay with us, and so my mother found someone named Mrs. Peacock. Exactly *where* she found her would be speculated on for the remainder of our childhoods.

"Has Mom ever been to a women's prison?" my sister Amy would ask.

"Try a *man's* prison," Gretchen would say, as she was never convinced that Mrs. Peacock was a legitimate female. The "Mrs." part was a lie anyway, that much we knew.

"She just says she was married so people will believe in her!!!!" This was one of the insights we recorded in a notebook while she was staying with us. There were pages of them, all written in a desperate scrawl, with lots of exclamation points and underlined words. It was the sort of writing you might do when a ship was going down, the sort that would give your surviving loved ones an actual chill. "If only we'd known," they'd moan. "Oh, for the love of God, if only we had known."

But what was there to know, really? Some fifteen-year-old

offers to watch your kids for the night and, sure, you ask her parents about her, you nose around. But with a grown woman you didn't demand a reference, especially if the woman was white.

Our mother could never remember where she had found Mrs. Peacock. "A newspaper ad," she'd say, or, "I don't know, maybe she sat for someone at the club."

But who at the club would have hired such a creature? In order to become a member you had to meet certain requirements, one of them being that you did not know people like Mrs. Peacock. You did not go to places where she ate or worshipped, and you certainly didn't give her the run of your home.

I smelled trouble the moment her car pulled up, a piece of junk driven by a guy with no shirt on. He looked just old enough to start shaving, and remained seated as the figure beside him pushed open the door and eased her way out. This was Mrs. Peacock, and the first thing I noticed was her hair, which was the color of margarine and fell in waves to the middle of her back. It was the sort of hair you might find on a mermaid, completely wrong for a sixty-year-old woman who was not just heavy but fat, and moved as if each step might be her last.

"Mom!" I called, and, as my mother stepped out of the house, the man with no shirt backed out of the driveway and peeled off down the street.

"Was that your husband?" my mother asked, and Mrs. Peacock looked at the spot where the car had been. "Naw," she said. "That's just Keith."

Not "my nephew Keith" or "Keith, who works at the filling station and is wanted in five states," but "just Keith," as if we had read a book about her life and were expected to remember all the characters.

She'd do this a lot over the coming week, and I would grow to hate her for it. Someone would phone the house, and after hanging up she'd say, "So much for Eugene" or "I told Vicky not to call me here no more."

"Who's Eugene?" we'd ask. "What did Vicky do that was so bad?" And she'd tell us to mind our own business.

She had this attitude, not that she was better than us but that she was as good as us—and that simply was not true. Look at her suitcase, tied shut with rope! Listen to her mumble, not a clear sentence to be had. A polite person would express admiration when given a tour of the house, but aside from a few questions regarding the stovetop Mrs. Peacock said very little and merely shrugged when shown the master bathroom, which had the word "master" in it and was supposed to make you feel powerful and lucky to be alive. *I've seen better,* her look seemed to say, but I didn't for one moment believe it.

The first two times my parents left for vacation, my sisters and I escorted them to the door and said that we would miss them terribly. It was just an act, designed to make us look sensitive and English, but on this occasion we meant it. "Oh, stop being such babies," our mother said. "It's only a week." Then she gave Mrs. Peacock the look meaning "Kids. What are you going to do?"

There was a corresponding look that translated to "You tell me," but Mrs. Peacock didn't need it, for she knew exactly what she was going to do: enslave us. There was no other word for it. An hour after my parents left, she was lying facedown on their bed, dressed in nothing but her slip. Like her skin, it was the color of Vaseline, an uncolor really, which looked even worse with yellow hair. Add to this her great bare legs, which were dimpled at the inner knee and streaked throughout with angry purple veins.

My sisters and I attempted diplomacy. "Isn't there, perhaps, some *work* to be done?"

"You there, the one with the glasses." Mrs. Peacock pointed at my sister Gretchen. "Your mama mentioned they's some sodie pops in the kitchen. Go fetch me one, why don't you."

"Do you mean Coke?" Gretchen asked.

"That'll do," Mrs. Peacock said. "And put it in a mug with ice in it."

While Gretchen got the Coke, I was instructed to close the drapes. It was, to me, an idea that bordered on insanity, and I tried my best to talk her out of it. "The private deck is your room's best feature," I said. "Do you *really* want to block it out while the sun's still shining?"

She did. Then she wanted her suitcase. My sister Amy put it on the bed, and we watched as Mrs. Peacock untied the rope and reached inside, removing a plastic hand attached to a foot-long wand. The business end was no bigger than a monkey's paw, the fingers bent slightly inward, as if they had been frozen in the act of begging. It was a nasty little thing, the nails slick with grease, and over the coming week we were to see a lot of it. To this day, should any of our boyfriends demand a back-scratch, my sisters and I recoil. "Brush yourself against a brick wall," we say. "Hire a nurse, but don't look at me. I've done my time."

No one spoke of carpal tunnel syndrome in the late 1960s, but that doesn't mean it didn't exist. There just wasn't a name for it. Again and again we ran the paw over Mrs. Peacock's back, the fingers leaving white trails and sometimes welts. "Ease up," she'd say, the straps of her slip lowered to her forearms, the side of her face mashed flat against the gold bedspread. "I ain't made of stone, you know."

That much was clear. Stone didn't sweat. Stone didn't stink or break out in a rash, and it certainly didn't sprout little black hairs between its shoulder blades. We drew this last one to Mrs. Peacock's attention, and she responded, saying, "Y'all's got the same damn thing, only they ain't poked out yet."

That one was written down verbatim and read aloud during the daily crisis meetings my sisters and I had taken to holding in the woods behind our house. "Y'all's got the same damn thing, only they ain't poked out yet." It sounded chilling when said in her voice, and even worse when recited normally, without the mumble and the country accent.

"Can't speak English," I wrote in the complaint book. "Can't go two minutes without using the word 'damn.' Can't cook worth a damn hoot."

The last part was not quite true, but it wouldn't have hurt her to expand her repertoire. Sloppy joe, sloppy joe, sloppy joe, held over our heads as if it were steak. Nobody ate unless they earned it, which meant fetching her drinks, brushing her hair, driving the monkey paw into her shoulders until she moaned. Mealtime came and went—her too full of Coke and potato chips to notice until one of us dared to mention it. "If y'all was hungry, why didn't you say nothing? I'm not a mind reader, you know. Not a psychic or some damn thing."

Then she'd slam around the kitchen, her upper arms jiggling as she threw the pan on the burner, pitched in some ground beef, shook ketchup into it.

My sisters and I sat at the table, but Mrs. Peacock ate standing, *like a cow,* we thought, *a cow with a telephone:* "You tell Curtis for me that if he don't run Tanya to R.C.'s hearing, he'll have to answer to both me *and* Gene Junior, and that's no lie."

Her phone calls reminded her that she was away from the action. Events were coming to a head: the drama with Ray, the business between Kim and Lucille, and here she was, stuck in the middle of nowhere. That's how she saw our house: the end of the earth. In a few years' time, I'd be the first to agree with her, but when I was eleven, and you could still smell the fresh pine joists from behind the Sheetrocked walls, I thought there was no finer place to be.

"I'd like to see where *she* lives," I said to my sister Lisa. And then, as punishment, we did see.

This occurred on day five, and was Amy's fault—at least according to Mrs. Peacock. Any sane adult, anyone with children, might have taken the blame upon herself. *Oh, well,* she would have thought. *It was bound to happen sooner or later.* Seven-year-old girl, her arm worn to rubber after hours of back-scratching, carries the monkey paw into the master bathroom, where it drops from her hand and falls to the tile floor. The fingers shatter clean off, leaving nothing—a jagged little fist at the end of a stick.

"Now you done it," Mrs. Peacock said. All of us to bed without supper. And the next morning Keith pulled up, still with no shirt on. He honked in the driveway, and she shouted at him through the closed door to hold his damn horses.

"I don't think he can hear you," Gretchen said, and Mrs. Peacock told her she'd had all the lip she was going to take. She'd had all the lip she was going to take from any of us, and so we were quiet as we piled into the car, Keith telling a convoluted story about him and someone named Sherwood as he sped beyond the Raleigh we knew and into a neighborhood of barking dogs and gravel driveways. The houses looked like something a child might draw, a row of shaky squares with triangles on top. Add a door, add two windows. Think of putting a tree in the front yard, and then decide against it because branches aren't worth the trouble. Mrs. Peacock's place was divided in half, her in the back, and someone named Leslie living in the front. A *man* named Leslie, who wore fatigues and stood by the mailbox play-wrestling with a Doberman pinscher as we drove up. I thought he would scowl at the sight of Mrs. Peacock, but instead he smiled and waved, and she waved in return. Five children wedged into the backseat, children just dying to report that they'd been abducted, but Leslie didn't seem to notice us any more than Keith had.

When the car stopped, Mrs. Peacock turned around in the front seat and announced that she had some work that needed doing.

"Go ahead," we told her. "We'll wait here." "Like fun you will," she said.

We started outdoors, picking up turds deposited by the Doberman, whose name turned out to be Rascal. The front yard was mined with them, but the back, which Mrs. Peacock tended, was surprisingly normal, better than normal, really. There was a small lawn and, along its border, a narrow bed of low-lying flowers—pansies, I think. There were more flowers on the patio outside her door, most of them in plastic pots and kept company by little ceramic creatures: a squirrel with its tail broken off, a smiling toad. I'd thought of Mrs. Peacock as a person for whom the word "cute" did not register, and so it was startling to enter her half of the house and find it filled with dolls. There must have been a hundred of them, all squeezed into a single room. There were dolls sitting on the television, dolls standing with their feet glued to the top of the electric fan, and tons more crowded onto floor-to-ceiling shelves. Strange to me was that she hadn't segregated them according to size or quality. Here was a fashion model in a stylish dress, dwarfed by a cheap bawling baby or a little girl who'd apparently come too close to the hot plate, her hair singed off, her face disfigured into a frown.

"First rule is that nobody touches nothing," Mrs. Peacock said. "Not nobody and not for no reason."

She obviously thought that her home was something

special, a children's paradise, a land of enchantment, but to me it was just overcrowded.

"*And* dark," my sisters would later add. "*And* hot *and* smelly."

Mrs. Peacock had a Dixie cup dispenser mounted to the wall above her dresser. She kept her bedroom slippers beside the bathroom door, and inside each one was a little troll doll, its hair blown back as if by a fierce wind. "See," she told us. "It's like they's riding in boats!"

"Right," we said. "That's really something."

She then pointed out a miniature kitchen set displayed on one of the lower shelves. "The refrigerator broke, so I made me another one out of a matchbox. Get up close, and y'all can look at it."

"You *made* this?" we said, though of course it was obvious. The strike pad gave it away.

Mrs. Peacock was clearly trying to be a good hostess, but I wished she would stop. My opinion of her had already been formed, was written on paper, even, and factoring in her small kindnesses would only muddy the report. Like any normal fifth grader, I preferred my villains to be evil and stay that way, to act like Dracula rather than Frankenstein's monster, who ruined everything by handing that peasant girl a flower. He sort of made up for it by drowning her a few minutes later, but, still, you couldn't look at him the same way again. My sisters and I didn't want to understand Mrs. Peacock. We just wanted to hate her, and so we were relieved when she reached into her closet and withdrew another backscratcher, the good one, apparently. It was no larger than the earlier model, but the hand was slimmer and more clearly defined, that of a lady rather than a monkey. The moment she had it, the hostess act melted away. Off came the man's shirt she'd worn over her slip, and she took up her position on the bed, surrounded by the baby dolls she referred to as "doll babies." Gretchen was given the first shift, and the rest of us were sent outside to pull weeds in the blistering sun.

"Thank God," I said to Lisa. "I was worried for a minute there that we'd have to feel sorry for her."

As children we suspected that Mrs. Peacock was crazy, a catchall term we used for anyone who did not recognize our charms. As adults, though, we narrow it down and wonder if she wasn't clinically depressed. The drastic mood swings, the hours of sleep, a gloom so heavy she was unable to get dressed or wash herself—thus the slip, thus the hair that grew greasier and greasier as the week progressed and left a permanent stain on our parents' gold bedspread.

"I wonder if she'd been institutionalized," Lisa will say. "Maybe she had shock treatments, which is what they did back then, the poor thing."

We'd like to have been that compassionate as children, but we already had our list, and it was unthinkable to disregard it on account of a lousy matchbox. Our parents returned from their vacation, and before they even stepped out of the car we were upon them, a mob, all of us talking at the same time. "She made us go to her shack and pick up turds." "She sent us to bed one night without supper." "She said the master bathroom was ugly, and that you were stupid to have air-conditioning."

"All right," our mother said. "Jesus, calm down."

"She made us scratch her back until our arms almost fell off." "She cooked sloppy joe every night, and when we ran out of buns she told us to eat it on crackers."

We were still at it when Mrs. Peacock stepped from the breakfast nook and out into the carport. She was dressed, for once, and even had shoes on, but it was too late to play normal. In the presence of my mother, who was tanned and pretty, she looked all the more unhealthy, sinister almost, her mouth twisted into a freaky smile.

"She spent the whole week in bed and didn't do laundry until last night."

I guess I expected a violent showdown. How else to explain my disappointment when, instead of slapping Mrs. Peacock across the face, my mother looked her in the eye, and said, "Oh, come on. I don't believe that for a minute." It was the phrase she used when she believed every word of it but was too tired to care.

"But she *abducted* us."

"Well, good for her." Our mother led Mrs. Peacock into the house and left my sisters and me standing in the carport. "Aren't they just horrible?" she said. "Honest to God, I don't know how you put up with them for an entire week."

"You don't know how *she* put up with *us?*"

Slam! went the door, right in our faces, and then our mom sat her guest down in the breakfast nook and offered her a drink.

Framed through the window, they looked like figures on a stage, two characters who seem like opposites and then discover they have a lot in common: a similarly hard upbringing, a fondness for the jugged Burgundies of California, and a mutual disregard for the rowdy matinee audience, pitching their catcalls from beyond the parted curtain.

Town and Country

They looked like people who had just attended a horse show: a stately couple in their late sixties, he in a cashmere blazer and she in a gray tweed jacket, a gem-encrusted shamrock glittering against the rich felt of her lapel. They were my seatmates on the flight from Denver to New York, and as I stood in the aisle to let them in, I felt the shame of the tragically outclassed. The sport coat I had prided myself on now looked clownish, as did my shoes, and the fistful of pine straw I refer to as my hair. "Excuse me," I said, apologizing, basically, for my very existence.

The couple took their seats and, just as I settled in beside them, the man turned to the woman, saying, "I don't want to hear this shit."

I assumed he was continuing an earlier argument, but it turned out he was referring to the Gershwin number the airline had adopted as its theme song. "I can't believe the fucking crap they make you listen to on planes nowadays."

The woman patted her silver hair and agreed, saying that whoever had programmed the music was an asshole.

"A cocksucker," the man corrected her. "A goddamn cocksucking asshole." They weren't loud people and didn't even sound all that angry, really. This was just the way they spoke, the verbal equivalent of their everyday china. Among company, the wife might remark that she felt a slight chill, but here that translated to "I am fucking freezing."

"Me too," her husband said. "It's cold as shit in here." *Shit* is the tofu of cursing and can be molded to whichever condition the speaker desires. Hot as shit. Windy as shit. I myself was confounded as shit, for how had I so misjudged these people? Why, after all these years, do I still believe that expensive clothing signifies anything more than a disposable income, that tweed and cashmere actually bespeak refinement?

When our boxed bistro meals were handed out, the couple really went off. "What is this garbage?" the man asked.

"It's shit," his wife said. "A box of absolute fuck-ing shit." The man took out his reading glasses and briefly examined his plastic-wrapped cookie before tossing it back into the box. "First they make you listen to shit, and then they make you eat it!"

"Well, I'm not fucking eating it," the woman said. "We'll just have to grab something at the airport."

"And pay some son of a bitch fifteen bucks for a sandwich?"

The woman sighed and threw up her hands. "What choice do we have? It's either that or eat what we've got, which is shit."

"Aww, it's all shit," her husband said.

It was as if they'd kidnapped the grandparents from a Ralph Lauren ad and forced them into a David Mamet play—and that, in part, is why the couple so appealed to me: there was something ridiculous and unexpected about them. They made a good team, and I wished that I could spend a week or two invisibly following behind them and seeing the world through their eyes. "Thanksgiving dinner, my ass," I imagined them saying.

It was late afternoon by the time we arrived at LaGuardia. I caught a cab outside the baggage claim and stepped into what smelled like a bad tropical cocktail, this the result of a coconut air freshener that dangled from the rearview mirror. One hates to be a baby about this kind of thing, and so I cracked the window a bit and gave the driver my sister's address in the West Village.

"Yes, sir."

The man was foreign, but I have no idea where he was from. One of those tragic countries, I supposed, a land beset by cobras and typhoons. But that's half the world, really. He had dark skin, more brown than olive, and thick black hair he had treated with oil. The teeth of his comb had left deep troughs that ran down the back of his head and disappeared beneath the frayed collar of his shirt. The cab left the curb, and as he merged into traffic the driver opened the window between the front and back seats and asked me my name. I told him, and he looked at me in the rearview mirror, saying, "You are a good man, David, is that right? Are you good?"

I said I was OK, and he continued. "David is a good name, and New York is a good town. Do you think so?"

"I guess," I said.

The driver smiled shyly, as if I had paid him a compliment, and I wondered what his life was like. One reads things, newspaper profiles and so forth, and gets an idea of the tireless, hardworking immigrant who hits the ground running—or, more often, driving. The man couldn't have been older than thirty-five, and after his shift I imagined that he probably went to school and studied until he couldn't keep his eyes open. A few hours at home with his wife and children, and then it was back to the front seat, and on and on until he earned a diploma and resumed his career as a radiologist. The only thing holding him up was his accent, but that would likely disappear with time and diligence.

I thought of my first few months in Paris and of how frustrating it had been when people spoke quickly or used improper French, and then I answered his question again, speaking as clearly as possible. "I have no opinion on the name David," I said. "But I agree with you regarding the city of New York. It is a very satisfactory place."

He then said something I didn't quite catch, and when I asked him to repeat it, he became agitated and turned in his seat, saying, "What is the problem, David? You cannot hear when a person is talking?"

I told him my ears were stopped up from the plane, though it wasn't true. I could hear him perfectly. I just couldn't understand him.

"I ask you what you do for a profession," he said. "Do you make a lot of moneys? I know by your jacket that you do, David. I know that you are rich."

Suddenly my sport coat looked a lot better. "I get by," I said. "That is to say that I am able to support myself, which is not the same as being rich."

He then asked if I had a girlfriend, and when I told him no he gathered his thick eyebrows and made a little *tsk*ing sound. "Oh, David, you need a woman. Not for love, but for the pussy, which is a necessary thing for a man. Like me, for example. I fuck daily."

"Oh," I said. "And this is ... Tuesday, right?" I'd hoped I might steer him onto another track—the days of the week, maybe—but he was tired of English 101.

"How is it that you do not need pussy?" he asked. "Does not your dick stand up?"

"Excuse me?"

"Sex," he said. "Has no one never told you about it?"

I took the *New York Times* from my carry-on bag and pre-tended to read, an act that apparently explained it all.

"Ohhh," the driver said. "I understand. You do not like pussy. You like the dick. Is that it?" I brought the paper close to my face, and he stuck his arm through the little window and slapped the back of his seat. "David," he said. "David, listen to me when I am talking to you. I asked do you like the dick?"

"I just work," I told him. "I work, and then I go home, and then I work some more." I was trying to set a good example, trying to be the person I'd imagined him to be, but it was a lost cause.

"I fucky-fuck every day," he boasted. "Two women. I have a wife and another girl for the weekend. Two kind of pussy. Are you sure you no like to fucky-fuck?"

If forced to, I can live with the word "pussy," but "fucky-fuck" was making me carsick. "That is not a real word," I told him. "You can say that you *fuck*, but *fucky-fuck* is just non-sense. Nobody talks that way. You will never get ahead with that kind of language."

Traffic thickened because of an accident and, as we slowed to a stop, the driver ran his tongue over his lips. "Fucky-fuck," he repeated. "I fucky-fucky-fucky-fuck."

Had we been in Manhattan, I might have gotten out and found myself another taxi, but we were still on the express-way, so what choice did I have but to stay put and look with envy at the approaching rescue vehicles? Eventually the traffic began moving, and I resigned myself to another twenty minutes of torture.

"So you go to West Village," the driver said. "Very good place for you to live. Lots of boys and boys together. Girls and girls together."

"It is not where I live," I said. "It is the apartment of my sister."

"Tell me how those lesbians have sex? How do they do it?"

I said I didn't know, and he looked at me with the same sad expression he had worn earlier when told that I didn't have a girlfriend. "David." He sighed. "You have never seen a lesbian movie? You should, you know. You need to go home, drink whiskey, and watch one just to see how it is done. See how they get their pussy. See how they fucky-fuck."

And then I snapped, which is unlike me, really. "You know," I said, "I do not think that I am going to take you up on that. In fact, I *know* that I am not going to take you up on that."

"Oh, but you should."

"Why?" I said. "So I can be more like *you?* That's a worthwhile goal, isn't it? I will just get myself a coconut air freshener and drive about town impressing people with the beautiful language I have picked up from pornographic movies. 'Hello, sir, does not your dick stand up?' 'Good afternoon, madam, do you like to fucky-fuck?' It sounds enchanting, but I don't know that I could stand to have such a rewarding existence. I am not worthy, OK, so if it is all right with you, I will not watch any lesbian movies tonight or tomorrow night or any other night, for that matter. Instead I will just work and leave people alone."

I waited for a response, and when none came I settled back in my seat, completely ashamed of myself. The driver's familiarity had been maddening, but what I'd said had been cruel and uncalled for. Mocking him, bringing up his air freshener: I felt as though I had just kicked a kitten—a filthy one, to be sure—but still something small and powerless. Sex is what you boast about when you have no exterior signs of wealth. It's a way of saying, "Look, I might not own a fancy sport coat, or even a carry-on bag, but I do have two women and all the intercourse I can handle." And would it have hurt me to acknowledge his success?

"I think it is wonderful that you are so fulfilled," I said, but rather than responding the driver turned on the radio, which was of course tuned to NPR.

By the time I got to my sister's, it was dark. I poured myself a Scotch and then, like always, Amy brought out a few things she thought I might find interesting. The first was a copy of *The Joy of Sex,* which she'd found at a flea market and planned to leave on the coffee table the next time our father visited. "What do you think he'll say?" she asked. It was the last thing a man would want to find in his daughter's apartment—that was my thought anyway—but then she handed me a magazine called *New Animal Orgy,* which was *truly* the last thing a man would want to find in his daughter's apartment. This was an old issue, dated 1974, and it smelled as if it had spent the past few decades in the dark, not just hidden but locked in a chest and buried underground.

"Isn't that the filthiest thing you've ever seen in your life?" Amy asked, but I found myself too stunned to answer. The magazine was devoted to two major stories—photo essays, I guess you could call them. The first involved a female cyclist who stops to rest beside an abandoned windmill and seduces what the captions refer to as "a stray collie."

"He's not a stray," Amy said. "Look at that coat. You can practically smell the shampoo."

The second story was even sadder and concerned a couple of women named Inga and Bodil, who stimulate a white stallion using first their hands and later their tongues. It was supposedly the luckiest day of the horse's life, but if the sex was really that good you'd think he would stop eating or at least do something different with his eyes. Instead he just went about his business, acting as if the women were not there. On the next page, he's led into the bedroom, where he stands on the carpet and stares dumbly at the objects on the women's dresser: a hairbrush, an aerosol can turned on its side, a framed photo of a girl holding a baby. Above the dresser was a curtainless window, and through it could be seen a field leading to a forest of tall pines.

Amy leaned closer and pointed to the bottom of the picture. "Look at the mud on that carpet," she said, but I was way ahead of her.

"Number one reason *not* to blow a horse in your bedroom," I told her, though it was actually much further down on the list. Number four maybe, the top slots being reserved for the loss of dignity, the invitation to disease, and the off chance that your parents might drop by.

Once again the women stimulate the horse to an erection, and then they begin to pleasure each other—assuming, I guess, that he will enjoy watching. This doesn't mean they were necessarily lesbians—not any more than the collie was a stray—but it gave me pause and forced me to think of the cabdriver. "I am not like you," I had told him. Then, half an hour later, here I was: a glass in one hand and in the other a magazine showing two naked women making out in front of a stallion. Of course, the circumstances were a bit different. I was drinking Scotch instead of whiskey. This was a periodical rather than a video. I was with my sister, and we were just two decent people having a laugh. Weren't we?

In the Waiting Room

Six months after moving to Paris, I gave up on French school and decided to take the easy way out. All I ever said was "Could you repeat that?" And for what? I rarely understood things the second time around, and when I did it was usually something banal, the speaker wondering how I felt about toast, or telling me that the store would close in twenty minutes. All that work for something that didn't really matter, and so I began saying *"D'accord,"* which translates to "I am in agreement," and means, basically, "OK." The word was a key to a magic door, and every time I said it I felt the thrill of possibility.

"D'accord," I told the concierge, and the next thing I knew I was sewing the eye onto a stuffed animal belonging to her granddaughter. *"D'accord,"* I said to the dentist, and she sent me to a periodontist, who took some X-rays and called me into his conference room for a little talk. *"D'accord,"* I said, and a week later I returned to his office, where he sliced my gums from top to bottom and scraped great deposits of plaque

from the roots of my teeth. If I'd had any idea that this was going to happen, I'd never have said *d'accord* to my French publisher, who'd scheduled me the following evening for a television appearance. It was a weekly cultural program, and very popular. I followed the pop star Robbie Williams, and as the producer settled me into my chair I ran my tongue over my stitches. It was like having a mouthful of spiders—spooky, but it gave me something to talk about on TV, and for that I was grateful.

I said *d'accord* to a waiter and received a pig's nose standing erect on a bed of tender greens. I said it to a woman in a department store and walked away drenched in cologne. Every day was an adventure.

When I got a kidney stone, I took the Métro to a hospital and said *"D'accord"* to a cheerful redheaded nurse, who led me to a private room and hooked me up to a Demerol drip. That was undoubtedly the best that *d'accord* got me, and it was followed by the worst. After the stone had passed, I spoke to a doctor, who filled out an appointment card and told me to return the following Monday, when we would do whatever it was I'd just agreed to. *"D'accord,"* I said, and then I supersized it with *"génial,"* which means "great!"

On the day of my appointment, I returned to the hospital, where I signed the register and was led by a slightly less cheerful nurse to a large dressing room. "Strip to your underwear," she told me, and I said, *"D'accord."* As the woman turned to leave, she said something else, and, looking back, I really should have asked her to repeat it, to draw a picture if that's what it took, because once you take your pants off, *d'accord* isn't really OK anymore.

There were three doors in the dressing room, and after removing my clothes I put my ear against each one, trying to determine which was the safest for someone in my condition.

The first was loud, with lots of ringing telephones, so that was out. The second didn't sound much different, and so I chose the third and entered a brightly painted waiting room set with plastic chairs and a glass-topped coffee table stacked high with magazines. A potted plant stood in the corner, and beside it was a second door, which was open and led into a hallway.

I took a seat and had been there for a minute or so when a couple came in and filled two of the unoccupied chairs. The first thing I noticed was that they were fully dressed, and nicely, too—no sneakers or sweat suits for them. The woman wore a nubby gray skirt that fell to her knees and matched the fabric of her husband's sport coat. Their black hair, which was obviously dyed, formed another match, but looked better on her than it did on him—less vain, I supposed.

"Bonjour," I said, and it occurred to me that possibly the nurse had mentioned something about a robe, perhaps the one that had been hanging in the dressing room. I wanted more than anything to go back and get it, but if I did the couple would see my mistake. They'd think I was stupid, so to prove them wrong I decided to remain where I was and pretend that everything was normal. *La la la.*

It's funny the things that run through your mind when you're sitting in your underpants in front of a pair of strangers. Suicide comes up, but just as you embrace it as a viable option you remember that you don't have the proper tools: no belt to wrap around your neck, no pen to drive through your nose or ear and up into your brain. I thought briefly of swallowing my watch, but there was no guarantee I'd choke on it. It's embarrassing, but, given the way I normally eat, it would probably go down fairly easily, strap and all. A clock might be a challenge, but a Timex the size of a fifty-cent piece—no problem.

*

The man with the dyed black hair pulled a pair of glasses from his jacket pocket, and as he unfolded them I recalled a summer evening in my parents' backyard. This was ages ago, a dinner for my sister Gretchen's tenth birthday. My father grilled steaks. My mother set the picnic table with insect-repelling candles, and just as we started to eat she caught me chewing a hunk of beef the size of a coin purse. Gorging always set her off, but on this occasion it bothered her more than usual.

"I hope you choke to death," she said.

I was twelve years old, and paused, thinking, *Did I hear her correctly?*

"That's right, piggy, suffocate."

In that moment, I hoped that I *would* choke to death. The knot of beef would lodge itself in my throat, and for the rest of her life my mother would feel haunted and responsible. Every time she passed a steak house or browsed the meat counter of a grocery store, she would think of me and reflect upon what she had said, the words "hope" and "death" in the same sentence. But, of course, I hadn't choked. Instead, I had lived and grown to adulthood, so that I could sit in this waiting room dressed in nothing but my underpants. *La la la.*

It was around this time that two more people entered. The woman looked to be in her midfifties, and accompanied an elderly man who was, if anything, overdressed: a suit, a sweater, a scarf, *and* an overcoat, which he removed with great difficulty, every button a challenge. *Give it to me,* I thought. *Over here.* But he was deaf to my telepathy and handed his coat to the woman, who folded it over the back of her chair. Our eyes met for a moment—hers widening as they moved from my face to my chest—and then she picked a magazine off the table and handed it to the elderly man, who I now took to be her father. She then selected a magazine of her own, and as she turned the pages I allowed myself to relax a little. She was just a woman reading a copy of *Paris Match*, and I was just the person sitting across from her. True, I had no clothes on, but maybe she wouldn't dwell on that, maybe none of these people would. The old man, the couple with their matching hair: "How was the hospital?" their friends might ask, and they'd answer, "Fine," or "Oh, you know, the same."

"Did you see anything fucked-up?"

"No, not that I can think of."

It sometimes helps to remind myself that not everyone is like me. Not everyone writes things down in a notebook and then transcribes them into a diary. Fewer still will take that diary, clean it up a bit, and read it in front of an audience:

"March 14. Paris. Went with Dad to the hospital, where we sat across from a man in his underpants. They were briefs, not boxers, a little on the gray side, the elastic slack from too many washings. I later said to Father, 'Other people have to use those chairs, too, you know,' and he agreed that it was unsanitary.

"Odd little guy, creepy. Hair on his shoulders. Big idiot smile plastered on his face, just sitting there, mumbling to himself."

How conceited I am to think I might be remembered, especially in a busy hospital where human misery is a matter of course. If any of these people *did* keep a diary, their day's entry would likely have to do with a diagnosis, some piece of news either inconvenient, or life-altering: the liver's not a match, the cancer has spread to the spinal column. Compared with that, a man in his underpants is no more remarkable than a dust-covered plant, or the magazine subscription card lying on the floor beside the table. Then, too, good news or bad, these people would eventually leave the hospital and return to the street, where any number of things might wipe me from their memory.

Perhaps on their way home they'll see a dog with a wooden leg, which I saw myself one afternoon. It was a German shepherd, and his prosthesis looked as though it had been fashioned from a billy club. The network of straps holding the thing in place was a real eye-opener, but stranger still was the noise it made against the floor of the subway car, a dull thud that managed to sound both plaintive and forceful at the same time. Then there was the dog's owner, who looked at the homemade leg and then at me, with an expression reading, Not bad, huh?

Or maybe they'll run into something comparatively small yet no less astonishing. I was walking to the bus stop one morning and came upon a well-dressed woman lying on the sidewalk in front of an office-supply store. A small crowd had formed, and just as I joined it a fire truck pulled up. In America, if someone dropped to the ground, you'd call an ambulance, but in France it's the firemen who do most of the rescuing. There were four of them, and, after checking to see that the woman was OK, one of them returned to the truck and opened the door. I thought he was looking for an aluminum blanket, the type they use for people in shock, but instead he pulled out a goblet. Anywhere else it would have been a cup, made of paper or plastic, but this was glass and had a stem. I guess they carry it around in the front seat, next to the axes or whatever.

The fireman filled the goblet with bottled water, and then he handed it to the woman, who was sitting up now and running her hand over her hair, the way one might when waking from a nap. It was the lead story in my diary that night, but no matter how hard I fiddled with it I felt that something was missing. Had I mentioned that it was autumn? Did the leaves on the sidewalk contribute to my sense of utter delight, or was it just the goblet and the dignity it bespoke: "Yes, you may be on the ground; yes, this drink may be your last—but let's do it right, shall we?"

Everyone has his own standards, but in my opinion a sight like that is at least fifty times better than what I was providing. A goblet will keep you going for years, while a man in his underpants is good for maybe two days, a week at the most. Unless, of course, you *are* the man in his underpants, in which case it will probably stay with you for the rest of your life—not floating on the exact edge of your consciousness, not handy like a phone number, but still within easy reach, like a mouthful of steak, or a dog with a wooden leg. How often you'll think of the cold plastic chair, and of the nurse's face as she passes the room and discovers you with your hands between your knees. Such surprise, such amusement, as she proposes some new adventure, then stands there, waiting for your *"d'accord."*

Undecided

I don't know that it was always this way, but, for as long as I can remember, just as we move into the final weeks of the presidential campaign the focus shifts to the undecided voters. "Who are they?" the news anchors ask. "And how might they determine the outcome of this election?"

Then you'll see this man or woman—someone, I always think, who looks *very happy* to be on TV. "Well, Brian," they say. "I've gone back and forth on the issues and whatnot, but I just can't seem to make up my mind!" Some insist that there's very little difference between candidate A and candidate B. Others claim that they're with A on defense and health care, but are leaning toward B when it comes the economy.

I look at these people and can't quite believe that they exist. *Are they professional actors?* I wonder. *Or are they simply laymen who want a lot of attention?*

To put them in perspective, I think of being on an airplane. The flight attendant comes down the aisle with her food cart and, eventually, parks it beside my seat. "Can I interest you in the chicken?" she asks. "Or would you prefer the human shit with bits of broken glass in it?"

To be undecided in this election is to pause for a moment and then ask how the chicken is cooked.

I mean, really, what's to be confused about?

When doubting that anyone could *not* know whom they're voting for, I inevitably think back to November, 1968. Hubert Humphrey was running against Richard Nixon, and when my mother couldn't choose between them, she had me do it for her. It was crazy. One minute I was eating potato chips in front of the TV, and the next I was at the fire station, waiting with people whose kids I went to school with. When it was our turn, we were led by a woman wearing a sash to one of a half-dozen booths, the curtain of which closed after we entered.

"Go ahead," my mother said. "Flick a switch, any switch."

I looked at the panel in front of me.

"Start on the judges or whatever and we'll be here all day, so just pick a President and make it fast. We've wasted enough time already."

"Which one do you think is best?" I asked.

"I don't have an opinion," she told me. "That's why I'm letting you do it. Come on, now, *vote*."

I put my finger on Hubert Humphrey and then on Richard Nixon, neither of whom meant anything to me. What I most liked about democracy, at least so far, was the booth—its quiet civility, its atmosphere of importance. "Hmm," I said, wondering how long we could stay before someone came and kicked us out.

Ideally, my mother would have waited outside, but as she said, there was no way an unescorted eleven-year-old would be allowed to vote, or even hang out, seeing as the lines were long and the polls were only open for one day. "Will you please hurry it up?" she hissed.

"Wouldn't it be nice to have something like this in our living room?" I asked. "Maybe we could use the same curtains we have on our windows."

"All right, that's it." My mother reached for Humphrey but I beat her to it, and cast our vote for Richard Nixon, who had the same last name as a man at our church. I assumed that the two were related, and only discovered afterwards that I was wrong. Richard Nixon had always been Nixon, while the man at my church had shortened his name from something funnier but considerably more foreign-sounding, Nickapopapopolis, maybe.

"Oh, well," I said.

We drove back home, and when asked by my father whom she had voted for, my mother said that it was none of his business.

"What do you mean, 'none of my business'?" he said. "I told you to vote Republican."

"Well maybe I did and maybe I didn't."

"You're not telling me you voted for *Humphrey*." He said this as if she had done something crazy: dressed like a chicken, or marched through the streets with a pan on her head.

"No," she said. "I'm not telling you that. I'm not telling you anything. It's private—all right? My political opinions are none of your concern."

"What political opinions?" he said. "I'm the one who took you down to register. You didn't even know there *was* an election until I told you."

"Well, thanks for telling me."

She turned to open a can of mushroom soup. This would be poured atop pork chops and noodles and served as our dinner, casserole style. Once we'd taken our seats at the table, my parents would stop fighting directly, and continue their argument through my sisters and me. Lisa might tell a story about her day at school and, if my father said it was interesting, my mother would laugh.

"What's so funny?" he'd say.

"Nothing. It's just that, well, I suppose everyone has a different standard. That's all."

When my father told me that I was holding my fork wrong, my mother would say that I was holding it right, or right in "certain circles."

"We don't know how people eat the world over," she'd say, not to him but to the buffet or the picture window, as if the statement had nothing to do with any of us.

I wasn't looking forward to that kind of evening, so I told my father that I had voted. "She let me," I said. "And I picked Nixon."

"Well at least someone in the family has some brains." He patted me on the shoulder and as my mother turned away I understood that I had chosen the wrong person.

I didn't vote again until 1976, when I was nineteen and legally registered. Because I was at college out of state, I sent my ballot through the mail. The choice that year was between Jimmy Carter and Gerald Ford. I had actually seen Carter in person, way back before the primaries. I liked his humility, but when the time came, I wrote in the name of Jerry Brown, who, it was rumored, liked to smoke pot. This was an issue very close to my heart, too close, obviously, as it amounted to a complete waste of a ballot.

I wonder if, in the end, the undecideds aren't the biggest pessimists of all. Here they could order the airline chicken, but, then again, hmm. "Isn't that adding an extra step?"

they ask themselves. "If it's all going to be chewed up and swallowed, why not cut to the chase, and go with the human shit?"

Ah, though, that's where the broken glass comes in.

The Cat and the Baboon

The cat had a party to attend, and went to the baboon to get herself groomed.

"What kind of party?" the baboon asked, and she massaged the cat's neck in order to relax her, the way she did with all her customers. "Hope it's not that harvest dance down on the riverbank. My sister went last year and said she'd never seen such rowdiness. Said a fight broke out between two possums, and one gal, the wife of one or the other, got pushed onto a stump and knocked out four teeth. And they were pretty ones too, none of this yellowness you find on most things that eat trash."

The cat shuddered. "No," she said. "This is just a little get-together, a few friends. That type of thing."

"Will there be food?" the baboon asked.

"Something," the cat sighed. "I just don't know what."

"'Course it's hard," the baboon said. "Everybody eating different things. You got one who likes leaves and another who can't stand the sight of them. Folks have gotten so picky nowadays, I just lay out some peanuts and figure they either eat them or they don't."

"Now, I wouldn't like a peanut," the cat said. "Not at all."

"Well, I guess you'd just have drinks, then. The trick is knowing when to stop."

"That's never been a problem for me," the cat boasted. "I drink until I'm full, and then I push myself away from the table. Always have."

"Well, you've got sense, then. Not like some of them around here." The baboon picked a flea from the cat's head and stuck it gingerly between her teeth. "Take this wedding I went to—last Saturday, I think it was. Couple of marsh rabbits got married—you probably heard about it."

The cat nodded.

"Now, I like a church service, but this was one of those write-your-own-vows sorts of things. Neither of them had ever picked up a pen in their life, but all of a sudden they're poets, right, like that's all it takes—being in love."

"My husband and I wrote our own vows," the cat said defensively.

"Sure you did," countered the baboon, "but you probably had something to say, not like these marsh rabbits, carrying on that their love was like a tender sapling or some damn thing. And all the while they had this squirrel off to the side, plucking at a harp, I think it was."

"I had a harp player at my wedding," the cat said, "and it was lovely."

"I bet it was, but you probably hired a professional, someone who could really play. This squirrel, I don't think she'd taken a lesson in her life. Just clawed at those strings, almost like she was mad at them."

"Well, I'm sure she tried her best," the cat said.

The baboon nodded and smiled, the way one must in the

service industry. She'd planned to tell a story about a drunken marsh rabbit, the brother of the groom at last week's wedding, but there was no point in it now, not with this client anyway. Whatever she said, the cat disagreed with, and unless she found a patch of common ground she was sure to lose her tip. "You know," she said, cleaning a scab off the cat's neck, "I hate dogs. Simply cannot stand them."

"What makes you bring that up?" the cat asked.

"Just thinking," the baboon said. "Some kind of spaniel mix walked in yesterday, asking for a shampoo, and I sent him packing, said, 'I don't care how much money you have, I'm not making conversation with anyone who licks his own ass.'" And the moment she said it, she realized her mistake.

"Now, what's wrong with that?" the cat protested. "It's good to have a clean anus. Why, I lick mine at least five times a day."

"And I admire you for it," the baboon said, "but you're not a dog."

"Meaning?"

"On a cat it's ... classy," the baboon said. "There's a grace to it, but a dog, you know the way they hunker over, legs going every which way."

"Well, yes," the cat said. "I suppose you have a point."

"Then they slobber and drool all over everything, and what they don't get wet, they chew to pieces."

"That they do." The cat chuckled, and the baboon relaxed and searched her memory for a slanderous dog story. The collie, the German shepherd, the spaniel mix she claimed to have turned away: they were all good friends of hers, and faithful clients, but what would it hurt to pretend otherwise and cross that fine line between licking ass and simply kissing it?

The Motherless Bear

In the three hours before her death, the bear's mother unearthed some acorns buried months earlier by a squirrel. They were damp and worm-eaten, as unappetizing as turds, and, sighing at her rotten luck, she kicked them back into their hole. At around ten she stopped to pull a burr from her left haunch, and then, her daughter would report, "Then she just ... died."

The first few times she said these words, the bear could not believe them. Her mother gone—how could it be! After a day, though, the shock wore off, and she tried to recapture it with an artfully placed pause and an array of amateur theatrical gestures. The faraway look was effective, and eventually she came to master it. "And then," she would say, her eyes fixed on the distant horizon, "then she just ... died."

Seven times she cried, but as the weeks passed this became more difficult, and so she took to covering her face with her paws and doing a jerky thing with her shoulders. "There,

211

there," friends would say, and she would imagine them returning to their families. "I saw that poor motherless bear today, and if she doesn't just break your heart, well, I don't know what will."

Her neighbors brought food, more than enough to get her through the winter, so she stayed awake that year and got very fat. In the spring the others awoke from their hibernations and found her finishing the first of the chokecherries. "Eating helps ease the pain," she explained, the bright juice dripping from her chin. And when they turned away she followed behind them. "Did I mention to you that my mother died? We'd just spent a beautiful morning together, and the next thing I knew—"

"That's no excuse for eating all our choke-cherries," they said, furious.

A few bears listened without interruption, but she could see in their eyes that their pity had turned to something else, boredom at best, and at worst a kind of embarrassment, not for themselves but for her.

The friend who had previously been the most sympathetic, who herself had cried upon first hearing the story, now offered a solution. "Throw yourself into a project," she said. "That's what I did after my grandfather's heart attack, and it worked wonders."

"A project?" the bear said.

"You know," said her friend, "dig yourself a new den or something."

"But I like my den the way it is."

"Then help dig one for somebody else. My ex-husband's aunt lost one of her paws in a trap and spent last winter in a ditch. Help her, why don't you?"

"I hurt my paw once," the bear said. "Broke a nail clean off, and when it finally grew back it looked like a Brazil nut."

She was trying to work the subject back to herself, hoping her friend might forget her suggestion, but it didn't work.

"I'll tell the old gal you'll be by later this afternoon," she said. "It'll make her happy and help you to work off some of that weight you've gained."

The friend ambled off, and the bear glared at her disappearing backside. "Help you work off some of that weight you gained," she mimicked.

Then she overturned a log and ate some ants, low-calorie ones with stripes on their butts. After that, she lay in the sun and was sound asleep when her friend returned and shook her awake, saying, "What's wrong with you?"

"Huh?"

"It's almost dark, and my ex-husband's aunt has been waiting all day."

"Right," said the bear, and she headed up the hill, deciding after a few dozen yards that this was not going to happen. Forget following advice she had never asked for in the first place. Rather than digging a den for a stranger, someone old who was just going to die anyway, she'd leave home and settle on the other side of the mountain. There, she could meet some new bears, strangers who would listen to her story and allow her once again to feel tragic.

The following morning she set out, taking care to avoid the old amputee, who still sat waiting beside her wretched ditch. Beyond a burned-out grove of birch trees there was a stream, and, following it, she came upon a cub who sat waist-deep in the rushing water, swatting at fish with his untrained paws.

"I used to do the same thing when I was your age," called the bear. And the cub looked up and let out a cry of surprise.

"I must have sat in the water all morning, until my mother came over and showed me how to catch fish properly." She waited a beat and then continued. "Of course, that could never happen now, and you know why?"

The cub said nothing.

"It couldn't happen now because my mother is dead," the bear announced. "Happened suddenly, when I least expected it. One moment she was there, and the next she just ... wasn't."

The cub began to whimper.

"You wake up an orphan, your mom's body slowly rotting beside you, and what can you do but soldier on, all alone, with no one to love or protect you."

As the cub began to wail, his mother charged out of the thicket. "What are you, sick?" she shouted. "Get your kicks scaring innocent children, is that it? Go on, now, get the hell out of here."

The bear ran to the opposite shore and into the forest, tripping on logs as she turned to look behind her. What with her weight, she was soon out of breath, so she slowed to a trot after the first hundred yards, her pace gradually degenerating as the morning turned to afternoon and then early evening. Just before dusk she smelled chimney smoke and ambled to the outskirts of a village. Peering through a gap in a thick hedge, she saw a crowd of humans standing with their backs to her. They seemed to be regarding something that stood in a clearing, and when one of them shifted position, she saw that it was a bear, a male, though it took a moment to realize it, as he was wearing a skirt and a tall, cone-shaped hat topped with a satin scarf. The male bear's mouth was muzzled with leather straps and connected to a leash, which was alternately held and yanked by a man in a dirty cape. A boy who was also dressed in a cape carried a drum on a rope around his neck, and as he began to play, the male stood on his hind legs and swayed back and forth to the music.

"Faster," called a soldier at the front of the crowd, and the boy quickened his beat. The male bear struggled to keep up, and when he tripped over the hem of his skirt, the man pulled out a stick and beat him across the face until his nose bled. This made the people laugh, and a few of them threw coins, which the drummer collected before moving on to his next song.

When night fell and the audience went home to their suppers, the man removed the muzzle from the male's snout. Then he put a collar around his neck and attached it by a chain to an iron stake driven deep into the ground. He and the boy retired to a tent, and when she was sure they had fallen asleep, the bear crept out from behind the hedge and approached the chained dancer.

"I don't normally talk to strangers," she said, "but I saw you here and figured, well, I guess there's a first time for everything."

The male was lying in an awkward position. His skirt was gathered around his waist, and she saw that great patches of his legs were without hair and that the skin in these areas was covered with open sores. "I used to talk a lot to my mother," she told him. "She and I were all each other had, and then one morning, out of nowhere, she just ... died. Gone. Before I could say good-bye or anything." Maybe it was the moonlight, maybe the excitement of meeting an entertainer, but for whatever reason, she actually managed a tear—her first in almost six months. It was running slowly down her cheek when the chained male raised his head and spoke. "Can you understand me?" he asked.

The bear nodded, though in fact it was quite difficult.

"That's good," he said. "Most animals can't make out a word I'm saying, and you know why?"

She shook her head.

"It's because I have no teeth," he said. "Not a one of them. The man in the tent took a rock and hammered them out of my head."

"But the muzzle—," the bear said.

"That's just to make me look dangerous."

"Oh," the bear said. "I get it."

"No," he told her, "I don't think you do. See, I have maggots living in my knees. I'm alive, but flies are raising families in my flesh. Okay?"

The bear shivered at the thought of it.

"It's been years since I've eaten solid food. My digestive system is shot, my right foot is broken in three places, and you're coming to me all teary-eyed because your stepmother died?"

"She wasn't a *step*," the bear said.

"Oh, she was too. I can see it in your eyes."

"Well, she was *just like* a real mother," the bear said.

"Yeah, and piss is just like honey if you're hungry enough."

"Maybe males in this part of the country say every ugly thing that enters their heads," the bear said, "but where I'm from—" That was as far as she got before the man and the boy came up from behind and hit her over the head with a padded club. When she came to, it was morning, and the male lay on the ground before her, his throat slit into a meaty smile.

"He wasn't no good to us anyhow," the man said to his assistant. "The knees go, and that's that."

Now the bear travels from village to village. Her jaws are sunken, her gums swollen with the abscesses left by broken teeth, and between the disfigurement and the muzzle, it's nearly impossible to catch what she's saying. Always, though, while tripping and stumbling to the music, she looks out into her audience and tells the story about her mother. Most people laugh and yell for her to lift her skirts, but every so often she'll spot someone weeping and swear they can understand her every word.

The Faithful Setter

Back before I met her, my wife lived on a farm. It was a small operation, organic vegetables, pick-your-own strawberries, and a dozen or so chickens, each and every one of them, to hear her tell it, "an absolute raging asshole." The first time she said this I laughed, as I'd always thought that word was reserved for males. The same goes for "dick," which she uses for females all the time—this raccoon, for example, that sometimes gets into our garbage cans. "Can you believe the nerve of that dick?" she'll say to me, her nose pressed flat against the dining room window. Then she'll bark, "Hey, asshole, go trash somebody else's fucking yard."

I attribute my wife's language to the fact that she's one-quarter spaniel. She says she's only an eighth, but, come on, the ears say it all. That and her mouth.

Still, though, I can't help but love her—forgave her even after she cheated. "They are *too* your children," she'd said, referring to her last litter, a party of four that looked no more like me than that dick of a raccoon. I knew they were fathered

219

by the English bull terrier across the street, but what are you going to do? Everyone's entitled to one mistake, aren't they?

I'd like to tell you that I hated this terrier right from the start, that I'd never, for one moment, trusted him. But what would that say about my wife and me, that our tastes are *that* dissimilar? If you want to know the truth about it, I actually hadn't given the guy much thought. His ugliness I'd noticed, sure—those creepy little eyes. His stupidity was evident as well, but I can't say I'd fashioned a formal "opinion." At least not until this puppy business.

The litter was born, and not one week later the bull terrier bit a kid in the face, practically tore it right off, as a matter of fact. It was the little blond girl who lived in the house next door to him. I was in the backseat of the car, just pulling into the driveway, when the ambulance arrived, and, man, was that ever a scene. The parents were beside themselves.

"Oh well," my wife yawned when I told her about it later that afternoon. "It's not like they can't have more children."

I said, "Come again?"

She said, "That's the way they feel about *us,* so why should we be any different?"

"So we need to stoop to *their* level?" I said. As for the bull terrier, my wife admitted that he was a hothead. She said he had a lousy sense of humor, but she never quite denounced him the way I needed her to. After he was trundled away and put down, she spent the day sulking. "A headache," she said to the kids. "Mommy has a sick headache." She claimed to have one the following day as well. On and on for a week, and all the while she had her eye on the house across the street, the place where her boyfriend had lived.

It wasn't long afterward that the little girl came home from the hospital, her head cocooned in bandages. There were holes for her to look through, and others for her nose and mouth, all of them gunked up with their corresponding fluids: tears, snot, drool. Even if you hated children, you had to feel sorry for her. At least I thought you had to. My wife, though, I could see that she blamed this girl, thinking that were it not for her, the bull terrier would still be alive.

I figured she'd get over him eventually, and in the meantime I'd just settle back and be patient. It helped when our owner put an ad in the paper and got rid of those godforsaken puppies. Oh sure, I cried, but it was more for my wife than for myself. I don't care what you hear about stepparenting, it's just not the same when they're somebody else's kids. Don't get me wrong—I wish them the best. I just don't feel the need to see them again.

Now that it was just the two of us, I hoped that things would return to normal. It was then that our owner took my wife in for a hysterectomy. She was out cold for the operation, saw nothing, felt nothing, went to sleep fertile and woke up a shell, her uterus and whatever else was in there, gone.

I told her that as far as I was concerned, it didn't matter in the least. To this she growled, "Oh, I'm sure it doesn't. I'm sure you're just *fine* with it."

I said, "What are you talking about?"

"You're thinking that this will keep me from cheating on you again. Or that if I do at least nothing will come of it."

It was like she was blaming me for the hysterectomy. I said, "Baby, don't do this."

She didn't talk to me for three days after that. What was going through her mind is anyone's guess. Me, though, I kept thinking about this Weimaraner I met once at the dog run. He had one of those owners who'd get on all fours and try to communicate with him, not just barking but lying on his back, acting submissive and so forth. There are quite a few people like that at the dog run—nuts is what they are—but this guy really took the cake. One morning last fall he went to the hospital and had his tonsils taken out. They weren't raw or swollen or anything, he just wanted them. "In a jar," he supposedly told the doctor. "And don't trim off the fat."

At the end of the day, he returned home, cut the tonsils into pieces with a steak knife, and hand-fed them to this Weimaraner, like, "Here, boy, I love you so much, I want you to have a part of me."

"And?" I said.

"It was a lot like chicken," the Weimaraner told me. So that's what I wondered during the time my wife and I weren't talking. *What did her hysterectomy taste like?* It was crazy, I know, but I couldn't get it out of my mind. Did my thoughts bespeak an urge toward cannibalism? Or did the flesh in question—the fact that it was her uterus—reduce this to a normal sexual fantasy? I would've liked to have discussed it, but the way things stood, I thought it best to keep my mouth shut.

It was right about then, my wife wanting her boyfriend back and me entertaining these insane, dark thoughts, that the bandaged girl reappeared. It seemed there were some complications, an infection or something, and she had to go back to the hospital. We saw her through the living room window, just briefly, getting into the car with her parents. "Little Miss Priss," my wife muttered—the first words out of her mouth in what felt like forever. Then she limped into the den and lay down in front of the TV. This is her way of being alone, as I hate the television. The programs are beside the point. It's the machine itself I can't bear. It stinks to high heaven, so I always stop at the doorway and park myself just this side of the carpet.

"That's right, Mr. Snob," my wife said. She always calls me that when we disagree about something, whether it's a chew toy or the smell of an electrical appliance. "I guess I'm just not as well-bred as you," she'll say. And it's true. She's not. It's also true that she's the one forever bringing it up. It's her own insecurity talking, the tragic self-hatred of a mixed-breed country girl, so I try to let it slide.

My wife mentions my bloodline when she's ticked off, of course, and then again whenever I get sent out on a stud call, which is not the same as cheating, I don't care what you hear. Infidelity involves a choice, while this is arranged by forces beyond my control. "These females don't want me any more than I want them," I tell my wife. "It's not an affair, it's work. It's my job, for God's sake."

She says that if it's a paycheck I'm after, I could just as easily lug around a blind person. "Or better yet, sniff out contraband, you and that selective nose that hates the TV but loves the smell of a book."

"Not *all* books," I tell her. And it's true. I can't stand thrillers.

It was in the midst of our difficulties, my wife's stitches still tender, that I was sent to service a female a few hours west of our home. Normally it's just "hello/good-bye," but the land is beautiful in that part of the world. It's wooded, with lots of hills, so rather than waiting for me to finish, my owner decided to drop me off and spend the rest of the day nosing around in his car. The act itself—it's hard to think of it as sex—lasted no more than a minute. Then this female and I got to talking. She's pure Irish setter, just like me, so we had that in common. Both of us had hookworms when we were young, and both of us, very coincidentally, love the taste and texture of candles. "As long as they're not scented," she said.

"The worst are those cheap *vanilla* candles," I offered.

She agreed, adding that the "cheap" part was redundant. "*All* vanilla-scented candles are cheap."

I told her about a cinnamon-scented candle I'd once chewed on as a puppy, and as she howled her sympathetic disgust, I thought of my wife and of how we would have sounded to her ears. "Arrogant," she'd have called us. "Noses so high in the air you can't smell your own farts." This for the crime of preferring one thing over another.

"You know what else I hate?" I said to the female. "I hate air fresheners, coconut being the worst."

"Well, I don't know," she said. "I think a pretty good case could be built against wild cherry."

"Oh my God, wild cherry!" I said, and I hunched my shoulders, pretending to barf.

From air fresheners, we wandered on to padded toilet seats, novelty mailboxes, and Labradoodles. She'd just started in on light jazz when I suggested we try the breeding thing one more time. "In case the first go didn't work."

"Don't have to ask me twice," she said.

I didn't have to ask at all for round three, and the one after that just seemed to happen on its own. "An aftershock," the female called it. Some might define this as cheating, but I just call it being thorough. Then too I was completely up front about my marital status, practically from the start.

"Your wife?" the female said. "So how did *that* happen?"

I told her we were married by my owner's girlfriend. "Now former girlfriend," I said. "I don't know how binding it is, but I wouldn't want to be with anyone else." And it's true, I wouldn't. Among other things, I like the fact that my wife needs me. Without my guidance, she's sure to finish what her boyfriend started. The child across the street will be mangled even worse, and for what? "This is *not you*," I keep telling her. For now, though, it's as if she's under a spell. I explained this to the female as best as I could, and after I'd finished she cocked her head.

"So your wife was brainwashed by an English bull terrier?"

"Something like that."

"God," she said, "I *hate* English bull terriers."

That was when we had the aftershock.

It was almost dusk when the owner arrived, and he and I headed off for home. The air conditioner was on, but after some whining I got him to lower the window. I had my head out and we'd been on the road for no more than twenty minutes when we came upon a burning building. It was a house, three stories tall, with a low brick wall around it. The owner pulled over, and before he could stop me I jumped over the seat and joined him on the grass. Had my wife been with me, he'd have forced us back into the car, but I'm pretty reliable, even without a leash. Besides, I make him look good, much more interesting than he actually is.

A small crowd had begun to gather, encircling a barefoot woman with sweatpants on. As we moved closer, I saw that she was holding a dachshund, the type with long hair. Everyone watched as she pushed back his ears, repeatedly kissing his forehead while he twisted and begged to be let down. It was only when an old man arrived and gathered the woman in an embrace that the dog broke free. He and I got to talking, and I learned he was the single thing this woman had reached for when she smelled the smoke and realized that her house was on fire. "Which is nice and everything, don't get me wrong," the dachshund said, "but she's got a teenage son in there." He gestured toward a second-floor window with black smoke pouring out of it. "He and his mother were constantly at each other's throats, but he was always nice to me, poor kid."

The dachshund let out a sigh, and as the woman reached down to snatch him back up, I caught a glimpse of the poor guy's future. *I could have saved anything, and I chose you.*

Who wants to live with that kind of pressure?

As I wished him good luck, the firemen arrived. A group of three headed toward the house and were almost there when a part of the roof collapsed. Sparks shot into the darkening sky, and as they sputtered down to earth, I caught the scent of burning flesh and realized how hungry I was. With any luck the owner would stop on our way home and buy us each a hamburger wrapped in paper. Then, smelling of smoke and ketchup, I'd return to my hangdog wife and continue the long business of loving her.

Dentists Without Borders

One thing that puzzled me during the American healthcare debate was all the talk about socialized medicine and how ineffective it's supposed to be. The Canadian plan was likened to genocide, but even worse were the ones in Europe, where patients languished on filthy cots, waiting for aspirin to be invented. I don't know where these people get their ideas, but my experiences in France, where I've lived off and on for the past thirteen years, have all been good. A house call in Paris will run you around fifty dollars. I was tempted to arrange one the last time I had a kidney stone, but waiting even ten minutes seemed out of the question, so instead I took the subway to the nearest hospital. In the center of town, where we're lucky enough to have an apartment, most of my needs are within arm's reach. There's a pharmacy right around the corner, and two blocks farther is the office of my physician, Dr. Médioni.

Twice I've called on a Saturday morning, and, after answering the phone himself, he has told me to come on over. These visits too cost around fifty dollars. The last time I went, I had a red thunder bolt bisecting my left eyeball.

The doctor looked at it for a moment, and then took a seat behind his desk. "I wouldn't worry about it if I were you," he said. "A thing like that, it should be gone in a day or two."

"Well, where did it come from?" I asked. "How did I get it?"

"How do we get most things?" he answered.

"We buy them?"

The time before that, I was lying in bed and found a lump on my right side, just below my rib cage. It was like a deviled egg tucked beneath my skin. *Cancer,* I thought. A phone call and twenty minutes later, I was stretched out on the examining table with my shirt raised.

"Oh, that's nothing," the doctor said. "A little fatty tumor. Dogs get them all the time."

I thought of other things dogs have that I don't want: Dewclaws, for example. Hookworms. "Can I have it removed?"

"I guess you could, but why would you want to?"

He made me feel vain and frivolous for even thinking about it. "You're right," I told him. "I'll just pull my bathing suit up a little higher."

When I asked if the tumor would get any bigger, the doctor gave it a gentle squeeze. "Bigger? Sure, probably."

"Will it get a *lot* bigger?"

"No."

"Why not?" I asked.

And he said, sounding suddenly weary, "I don't know. Why don't trees touch the sky?"

Médioni works from an apartment on the third floor of a handsome nineteenth-century building, and, on leaving, I always think, *Wait a minute. Did I see a diploma on his wall? Could "Doctor" possibly be the man's first name?* He's not indifferent. It's just that I expect a little something more than "It'll go away." The thunderbolt cleared up, just as he said it would, and I've since met dozens of people who have fatty tumors and get along just fine. Maybe, being American, I want bigger names for things. I also expect a bit more gravity. "I've run some tests," I'd like to hear, "and discovered that what you have is called abilateral ganglial abasement, or, in layman's terms, a cartoidal rupture of the venal septrumus. Dogs get these all the time, and most often they die. That's why I'd like us to proceed with the utmost caution."

For my fifty dollars, I want to leave the doctor's office in tears, but instead I walk out feeling like a hypochondriac, which is one of the few things I'm actually not. If my French physician is a little disappointing, my French periodontist more than makes up for it. I have nothing but good things to say about Dr. Guig, who, gumwise, has really brought me back from the abyss. Twice in the course of our decade long relationship, he's performed surgical interventions. Then, last year, he removed four of my lower incisors, drilled down into my jawbone, and cemented in place two posts. First, though, he sat me down and explained the procedure, using lots of big words that allowed me to feel tragic and important. "I'm going to perform the surgery at nine o'clock on Tuesday morning, and it should take, at most, three hours," he said—all of this, as usual, in French. "At six that evening, you'll go to the dentist for your temporary implants, but still I'd like you to blockout that entire day."

I asked my boyfriend, Hugh, when I got home, "Where did he think I was going to go with four missing teeth?"

I see Dr. Guig for surgery and consultations, but the regular, twice-a-year deep cleanings are performed by his associate, a woman named Dr. Barras. What she does in my mouth is unspeakable, and because it causes me to sweat, I've taken to bringing a second set of clothes and changing in the bathroom before I leave for home. "Oh, Monsieur Sedaris," she chuckles. "You are such a child."

A year ago, I arrived and announced that, since my previous visit, I'd been flossing every night. I thought this might elicit some praise—"How dedicated you are, how disciplined!"— but instead she said, "Oh, there's no need."

It was the same when I complained about all the gaps between my teeth. "I had braces when I was young, but maybe I need them again," I told her. An American dentist would have referred me to an orthodontist, but, to Dr. Barras, I was just being hysterical. "You have what we in France call 'good time teeth,'" she said. "Why on earth would you want to change them?"

"Um, because I can floss with the sash to my bathrobe?"

"Hey," she said, "enough with the flossing. You have better ways to spend your evenings."

I guess that's where the good times come in.

Dr. Barras has a sick mother and a long-haired cat named Andy. As I lie there sweating with my trap wide open, she runs her electric hook under my gum line, and catches me up on her life since my last visit. I always leave with a mouthful of blood, yet I always look forward to my next appointment. She and Dr. Guig are *my* people, completely independent of Hugh, and though it's a stretch to label them friends, I think they'd miss me if I died of a fatty tumor.

Something similar is happening with my dentist, Dr. Granat. He didn't fabricate my implants—that was the work of a prosthodontist—but he took the molds and made certain that the teeth fit. This was done during five visits in the winter of 2011. Once a week, I'd show up at the office and climb into his reclining chair. Then I'd sink back with my mouth open.

"*Ça va?*" he'd ask every five minutes or so, meaning, "All right?" And I'd release a little tone. Like a doorbell. "*E-um.*"

Implants come in two stages. The first teeth that get screwed in, the temporaries, are blocky, and the color is off. These condones are more refined and are somehow dyed or painted to match their neighbors. My four false incisors are connected to form a single unit and were secured into place with an actual screwdriver. Because the teeth affect one's bite, the positioning has to be exact, so my dentist would put them in and then remove them to make minor adjustments. Put them in, take them out. Over and over. All the pain was behind me by this point, so I just lay there, trying to be a good patient.

Dr. Granat keeps a small muted television mounted near the ceiling, and each time I come it is tuned to the French travel channel—Voyage, it's called. Once, I watched a group of mountain people decorate a yak. They didn't string lights on it, but everything else seemed fair game: ribbons, bells, silver sheaths for the tips of its horns.

"*Ça va?*"

"*E-um.*"

Another week we were somewhere in Africa, where a family of five dug into the ground and unearthed what looked to be a burrow full of mice. Dr. Granat's assistant came into the room to ask a question, and when I looked back at the screen the mice had been skinned and placed, kebab-like, on sharp sticks. Then came another distraction, and when I looked up again the family in Africa were grilling the mice over a campfire, and eating them with their fingers.

"*Ça va?*" Dr.Granat asked, and I raised my hand, international dental sign language for "There is something vital I need to communicate." He removed his screwdriver from my mouth, and I pointed to the screen. "*Ils ont mangé des souris en brochette,"* I told him, meaning, "They have eaten some mice on skewers."

He looked up at the little TV. *"Ah, oui?"*

A regular viewer of the travel channel, Dr. Granat is surprised by nothing. He's seen it all and is quite the traveler himself. As is Dr. Guig. Dr. Barras hasn't gone anywhere exciting lately, but what with her mother, how can she? With all these dental professionals in my life, you'd think I'd look less like a jack-o'-lantern. You'd think I could bite into an ear of corn, or at least tear meat from a chicken bone, but that won't happen for another few years, not until we tackle my two front teeth and the wobbly second incisors that flank them. "But after that's done I'll still need to come regularly, won't I?" I said to Dr. Guig, almost panicked. "My gum disease isn't cured, is it?"

I've gone from avoiding dentists and periodontists to practically stalking them, not in some quest for a Hollywood smile but because I enjoy their company. I'm happy in their waiting rooms, the coffee tables heaped with *Gala* and *Madame Figaro*. I like their mumbled French, spoken from behind Tyvek masks. None of them ever call me David, no matter how often I invite them to. Rather, I'm Monsieur Sedaris, not my father but the smaller, Continental model. Monsieur Sedaris with the four lower implants. Monsieur Sedaris with the good-time teeth, sweating so fiercely he leaves the office two kilos lighter. That's me, pointing to the bathroom and asking the receptionist if I may use the sandbox, me traipsing down the stairs in a fresh set of clothes, my smile bittersweet and drearied with blood, counting the days until I can come back and return myself to this curious, socialized care.

Memory Laps

I always told myself that when I hit fifty I was going to discover opera, not just casually but full force: studying the
composers, learning Italian, maybe even buying a cape. It
seemed like something an older person could really sink his
teeth into—that's why I put it off for so long. Then I turned
fifty, and, instead of opera, I discovered swimming. Or, rather,
I *rediscovered* swimming. I've known how to do it since I was
ten and took lessons at the Raleigh Country Club. There was
a better place, the Carolina Country Club, but I don't believe
they admitted Yankees. Jews either, if my memory serves me
correctly. The only blacks I recall were employees, and they
were known to everyone, even children, by their first names.

The man behind the bar was Ike. You were eleven-year-old
Mr. Sedaris.

The better country club operated on the principle that
Raleigh mattered, that its old families were fine ones, and
that they needed a place where they could enjoy one another's
company without being pawed at. Had we not found this

laughable, our country club might have felt desperate. Instead, its attitude was *Look at how much money you saved by not being good enough!*

I can't speak for the two clubs' golf courses, but their pools were the same size, and on a hot, windless afternoon you could probably smell them from an equal distance. Chlorine pits is what they were. Chemical baths. In the deep end, my sisters and I would dive for nickels. Toss one in, and by the time we reached it, half of Jefferson's face would be eaten away. Come lunch time, we'd line up at the snack bar, our hair the texture of cotton candy, our small, burning eyes like little cranberries.

My lessons were taken in June 1966, the first year of our membership. By the following summer, I was on the swim team. This sounds like an accomplishment, but I believe that in 1967 anyone could be on the Raleigh Country Club team. All you had to do was show up and wear an orange Speedo.

Before my first practice, I put swimming in the same category as walking and riding a bike: things one did to get from place to place. I never thought of how well I was doing them. It was only in competing that an activity became fraught and self-conscious. More accurately, it was only in competing with boys. I was fine against girls, especially if they were younger than me. Younger than me and physically challenged was even better. Give me a female opponent with a first-grade education and a leg brace, and I would churn that water like a speedboat. When it came to winning, I never split hairs.

Most of my ribbons were for good sportsmanship, a back-handed compliment if ever there was one. As the starting gun was raised, I would look at my competitors twitching at their places. Parents would shout their boozy encouragement from the sidelines, and it would occur to me that one of us would have to lose, that I could do that for these people. For whether

I placed or came in last, all I ultimately felt was relief. The race was over, and now I could go home. Then the next meet would be announced, and it would start again: the sleepless nights, the stomachaches, a crippling and all-encompassing sense of doom. My sisters Lisa and Gretchen were on the team as well, but I don't think it bothered them as much. For me, every meet day was the same. "Mom"— this said with a groan, like someone calling out from beneath a boulder—"I don't feel too good. Maybe we should—"

"Oh no, you don't."

If I had been trying to get out of school, she'd have at least allowed me to plead my case, but then she had no presence at school. At the club she was front and center, laughing it up with Ike at the bar and with the girls in the restaurant beside the putting green. Once summer got going, we'd spend all day at the pool, us swimming and her roasting on one of the deck chairs. Every so often, she'd go into the water to cool off, but she didn't know how to swim and didn't trust us not to drag her under. So she'd sit waist-deep in the kiddie pool, dropping her cigarette ash onto the wet pavement and dissolving it with her finger.

There was a good-size group of women like her, and they were united in their desire to be left alone. Run to your mother with a complaint, and before she could speak one of the others would say, "Oh, come on now. Let's not be a tattletale," or, "You would have lost that tooth anyway. Now get back into the water." I think of them in that terrible heat, no umbrellas, just sunglasses and bottles of tanning oil that left them smelling like coconuts.

The pool was a land of women and children until swim meets, which usually started at six. Then drinks would be ordered and the dads would arrive. For most of the fathers, this was just one more thing they had to turn up for. Their son was likely on his school's football or basketball team. Maybe he played baseball as well. For my dad, though, this was it, and the way I saw it he should have been grateful. Look at all the time my fear of sports was affording him— weekends and evenings free.

In retrospect, I was never an awful swimmer, just average. I'd come in third sometimes, and once or twice, if I was part of a relay team, we'd place first, though I could hardly take credit. Occasionally, we'd have intraclub races, us against us, and in those, as in the larger meets, the star was a boy named Greg Sakas, who was my size but a few years younger, with pale yellow hair and legs no thicker than jumper cables. "God, that Greg Sakas, did you see him go?" my father said on the way home from my first meet. "Man alive, that kid is *faaaantastic.*"

In the beginning, it didn't bother me. Greg wasn't stuckup. His father was decent enough, and everyone adored his mother. She was one of the few moms who could get away with wearing a bikini, a chocolate-colored one that, as the summer advanced, made it look as if she were naked. "That son of yours is really something," I heard my father say to her after the second meet. "You ought to bring a movie camera out here and film him."

On the way home, he repeated the conversation to my mother. "I said to her, 'Send the footage to a professional swimming coach, and he'll be champing at the bit! Your boy is the real thing. Olympic material, I'm telling you. He's got speed, personality, the whole package.'"

Okay, I thought. *You can shut up about Greg Sakas now.*

We had a station wagon at the time, and my sister Gretchen and I were in what we called the "way back"—the spot where groceries usually went. When she was a baby, a dog bit her face and left her with a scar that was almost invisible until she got a tan. Then it looked like someone had chalked the number 1 four times on her cheek and put a strike mark through them.

"It's the kids swimming *against* him I feel sorry for," my father continued. "Those clowns didn't stand a chance. And did you hear what he said when they handed him his blue ribbon? Who the hell knew Greg Sakas could be so funny? Good-looking too. Just an all-around four-star individual."

When she was young, my sister was what we called chunky, and the longer my dad carried on about Greg the better it seemed to draw attention to it. "Hey," I called. "Gretchen's in a sunbeam. Does anybody else smell bacon frying?"

My sister looked at me like, *Weren't we friends just two minutes ago? Where is this coming from?*

"Maybe Mom should put her on a diet," I said. "That way she won't be so fat."

"Actually, that's not a bad idea," my father said.

My mother, newly pregnant and feeling somewhat chunky herself, put her two cents in, and I settled back, triumphant. This was the advantage of having a large family. You didn't want to focus attention on Lisa—Miss Perfect —but there were three, and later four, others to go after, all younger and all with their particular faults: buckteeth, failing grades. It was like shooting fish in a barrel. Even if I wound up getting punished, it was still a way of changing the channel, switching in this case from *The Greg Show* to *The David Show,* which was today sponsored by Gretchen's weight problem. Meanwhile, my sisters had their own channels to change, and when it got to be too much, when our parents could no longer take it, they'd open the car door and throw us out. The spot they favored—had actually blackened with their tire treads— was at the bottom of a steep hill. The distance home wasn't all that great, a half mile, maybe, but it seemed twice as long when it was hot or raining, or, worse yet, during a thunderstorm. "Aw, it's just heat lightning," our father would say. "That's not going to kill anybody. Now get the hell out of my car."

Neighbors would pass, and when they honked I'd remember that I was in my Speedo. Then I'd wrap my towel like a skirt around my waist and remind my sisters that this was not girl-ish but *Egyptian*, thank you very much.

Drawing attention to Gretchen's weight was the sort of behavior my mother referred to as "stirring the turd," and I did it a lot that summer. *Dad wants Greg Sakas to be his son instead of me,* I thought, and in response I made myself the kind of kid that nobody could like.

"What on earth has gotten into you?" my mother kept asking.

I wanted to tell her, but more than that I wanted her to notice it on her own. *How can you not?* I kept wondering. *It's all he ever talks about.*

The next swim meet was a replay of the first two. Coming home, I was once again in the "wayback"—anything to put some distance between me and my father. "I'll tell you what—that Greg is magic. Success is written all over his face, and when it happens I'm going to say, 'Hey, buddy, remember me? I'm the one who first realized how special you are.'"

He talked as if he actually knew stuff about swimming, like he was a talent scout for Poseidon or something. "The butterfly's his strong suit, but let's not discount his crawl or, hell, even his breaststroke, for that matter. Seeing that kid in the water is like seeing a shark!"

His talk was supposedly directed at my mother, who'd stare out the window and sometimes sigh, "Oh gosh, Lou. I don't know." She never said anything to keep the conversation going, so I could only believe that he was saying these things for my benefit. Why else would he be speaking so loudly, and catching my eye in the rearview mirror?

One week, while riding home, I took my sister Amy's Barbie doll, tied her feet to the end of my beach towel, and lowered her out the way-back window, dragging her behind us as we drove along. Every so often I'd reel her back in and look at the damage—the way the asphalt had worn the hair off one side of her head, whittled her ski-jump nose down to nothing. *What*, I wondered, *was Greg up to at that exact moment?* Did *his* father like him as much as mine did? He was an only child, so chances were he got the star treatment at home as well as at the club. I lowered the doll back out the window and let go of the towel. The car behind us honked, and I ducked down low and gave the driver the finger.

By mid-July, I was begging to quit the team, but my parents wouldn't allow it. "Oh, you're a good swimmer," my mother said. "Not the best, maybe, but so what? Who wants to be the best at something you do in a bathing suit?"

In the winter, my Greek grandmother was hit by a truck and moved from New York State to live with us. Bringing her to the club would have depressed people. The mournful black dresses, the long gray hair pinned into an Old Country bun, she was the human equivalent of a storm cloud. I thought she'd put a crimp in our upcoming pool schedule, but when Memorial Day arrived, it was business as usual. "She's a big girl," my mother said. "Let her stay home by herself."

"Well, shouldn't we be back by five, just in case she falls down the stairs or something?" I didn't want her to ruin my summer—just to keep me off the swim team. "I could come home and sit with her."

"The hell you will," my mother said. "A nice steep fall is just what I'm hoping for."

I thought the birth of my brother, Paul, might limit our pool hours as well, but, again, no luck. It can't have been healthy for a six-month-old in that hot sun. Maybe that's why he never cried. He was in shock—the only baby I'd ever seen with a tan line. "Cute kid," Greg said one afternoon, and I worried that he might win over Paul and my mother the way he had my father.

The summer of '68 was even worse than the one before it. The club started serving a once-a-week prime-rib dinner, dress up—which meant my blue wool sports coat. Sweating over my fruit cocktail, I'd watch my father make his rounds, stopping at the Sakases' table and laying his hand on Greg's shoulder the way he'd never once put it on mine. There weren't many people I truly hated back then—thirty, maybe forty-five at most—and Greg was at the top of my list. The killer was that it wasn't even my idea. I was being *forced* to hate him, or, rather, forced to hate myself for not being him. It's not as if the two of us were all that different, really: same size, similar build. Greg wasn't exceptional-looking. He was certainly no scholar. I was starting to see that he wasn't all that great a swimmer either. Fast enough, sure, but far too choppy. I brought this to my father's attention, and he attributed my observation to sour grapes: "Maybe you should work on your own stroke before you start criticizing everyone else's."

Things will be better when the summer is over, I kept thinking. We continued going to the club for prime rib, but Greg wasn't always there, and without the swimming there wasn't as much for my dad to carry on about. When fall arrived, he got behind a boy in my Scout troop. But my father didn't really understand what went on in Scouts. The most difficult thing we did that year was wrap potatoes in tin-foil, and I could wrap a potato just as well as the next guy. Then one night while watching *The Andy Williams Show,* he came upon Donny Osmond.

"I just saw this kid on TV, and I mean to tell you, he absolutely knocked my socks off. The singing, the dancing—this boy's going to be huge, you mark my words."

"You didn't discover him," I said the following evening at dinner. "If someone's on *The Andy Williams Show,* it means they were *already* discovered. Stop trying to take credit."

"Well, someone's testy, aren't they?" My father lifted his drink off the table. "I wonder when Donny will be on again."

"It's the Osmond *Brothers,*" I said. "Girls at school talk about them all the time. It's not a solo act—they're a group."

"Not without him, they're not. Donny's the thunderbolt. Take him out of the picture, and they're nothing."

The next time they were on *The Andy Williams Show,* my father flushed me out of my room and forced me to watch.

"Isn't he fantastic? Just look at that kid! God Almighty, can you believe it?"

Competing against celebrities, people who were not in any sense "real," was a losing game. I knew this as well as I knew my name and troop number, but the more my father carried on about Donny Osmond, the more threatened and insignificant I felt. The thing was that he didn't even like that kind of music. "Well, normally, no," he said, when I brought it up. "Something about Donny, though, makes me like it." He paused. "And the hell of it is he's even younger than you are."

"A year younger."

"Well, that's still younger."

I'd never know if my father did this to hurt me or to spur me on, but on both fronts he was wildly successful. I remember being at the club in the summer of '69, the day that men walked on the moon. Someone put a TV on the lifeguard chair, and we all gathered around, me thinking that at least today something was bigger than Donny Osmond and Greg Sakas, who was actually now a little shorter than I was.

That Labor Day, at the season's final intraclub meet, I beat Greg in the butterfly. "Were you watching? Did you see that? I won!"

"Maybe you did, but it was only by a hair," my father said on our way home that evening. "Besides, that was, what—one time out of fifty? I don't really see that you've got anything to brag about."

That's when I thought, *Okay, so that's how it is.* My dad was like the Marine Corps, only instead of tearing you to pieces and then putting you back together, he just did the first part and called it a day. Now it seems cruel, abusive even, but this all happened before the invention of self-esteem, which, frankly, I think is a little overrated.

I'm sure my father said plenty of normal things to me when I was growing up, but what stuck, probably because he said it, like, ten thousand times, was "Everything you touch turns to crap." His other catchphrase was "You know what you are? A big fat zero."

I'll show you, I remember thinking. Proving him wrong was what got me out of bed every morning, and when I failed it's what got me back on my feet. I remember calling in the summer of 2008 to tell him my book was number one on the *Times* bestseller list.

"Well, it's not number one on the *Wall Street Journal* list," he said.

"That's not really the list that book people turn to," I told him.

"The hell it isn't," he said. "I turn to it."

"And you're a book person?"

"I read. Sure."

I recalled the copy of *Putt to Win* gathering dust on the backseat of his car. "Of course you read," I said.

Number one on the *Times* list doesn't mean that your book is good—just that a lot of people bought it that week, people who were tricked, maybe, or were never too bright to begin with. It's not like winning the Nobel Prize in Literature, but still, if it's your kid, aren't you supposed to be happy and supportive?

Of course, it complicates things when a lot of that book is about you and what a buffoon you can be. Number one in this particular case meant that a whole lot of people just read about my father sitting around in his underpants and hitting people over the head with spoons. So maybe he had a right to be less than enthusiastic.

When I told him I'd started swimming again, my dad said, "Attaboy." This is the phrase he uses whenever I do something he thinks was his idea.

"I'm going back to college."

"Attaboy."

"I'm thinking of getting my teeth fixed."

"Attaboy."

"On second thought ... ," I always want to say.

It's not my father's approval that troubles me but my child-like hope that maybe this time it will last. He likes that I've started swimming again, so maybe he'll also like the house I bought ("Boy, they sure saw you coming") or the sports coat I picked up on my last trip to Japan ("You look like a god damn clown").

Greg Sakas would have got the same treatment eventually, as would any of the other would-be sons my father pitted me against throughout my adolescence. Once they got used to the sweet taste of his approval, he'd have no choice but to snatch it away, not because of anything they did but because it is in his nature. The guy sees a spark and just can't help but stomp it out.

I was in Las Vegas not long ago and looked up to see Donny Osmond smiling down at me from a billboard only slightly smaller than the sky. *"You,"* I whispered.

In the hotel pool a few hours later, I thought of him as I swam my laps. Then I thought of Greg and was carried right back to the Raleigh Country Club. Labor Day, 1969. A big crowd for the intraclub meet, the air smelling of chlorine and smoke from the barbecue pit. The crummy part of swimming is that while you're doing it you can't really see much: the bottom of the pool, certainly, a smudged and fleeting bit of the outside world as you turn your head to breathe. But you can't pick things out— a man's face, for example, watching from the sidelines when, for the first time in your life, you pull ahead and win.

Think Differenter

Of the many expressions we Americans tend to overuse, I think the most irritating is "Blind people are human too." They are, I guess, but saying so makes you sound preachy and involved, like all your best friends are blind—which they're probably not. I, personally, don't know any blind people, though the guy I used to buy my newspapers from had pretty bad cataracts. His left eye had a patch over it, and the right one reminded me of the sky in a werewolf movie, this pale blue moon obscured by drifting clouds. Still, though, he could see well enough to spot a Canadian quarter. "Oh no you don't," he said to me the last time I bought something. Then he actually grabbed my hand!

I pulled it back. "Well, excuusssse me." Then I said, "I think it's a-boat time I take my business elsewhere." Normally I say "about," but I wanted him to think I was Canadian, which could have been true if I was born a couple hundred miles to the north. The son of a bitch half-blind person. I'm through defending the likes of him.

Number two on my irritating expression list is "I'll never forget the time ..." People say this to me, and I think, *Yawn. Am I ever in for a boring story.* Take this Fourth of July party, the one thrown every year at the apartment complex I live at. I went last summer, and it was me, this guy Teddy from two doors down, and a woman from the ground floor all standing around the pool. The fireworks had ended, and all of a sudden, out of nowhere, Teddy looks down into the water. "I'll never forget the time my five-year-old daughter drowned," he told us, all mournful, as if it happened that week and not an entire year ago.

The woman from the ground floor put her hand on his shoulder. "Oh my God," she said. "That is the saddest thing I ever heard in my life."

I, meanwhile, was standing there thinking that you should never say never, especially in regard to what you'll remember. People get older, and you'd be surprised by what they forget. Like, for example, a few weeks back I called my mother to wish her a happy birthday, her eightieth. "I bet you wish that Dad was still alive," I said. "That way the two of you could celebrate together."

"But he *is* still alive," she told me.

"He is?"

"Well, of course," she said. "Who do you think answered the phone?"

Here I am, just turned fifty, and I forgot that my father isn't dead yet! In my defense, though, he's pretty close to it. Healthy enough for the moment, but he doesn't do any of the stuff he used to do, like give me money or teach me to ride bikes.

There are things you forget naturally—computer passwords, your father's continuing relationship with life—and then there are things you can't forget but wish you could.

Once, for instance, when I was in the third grade, I saw our dog Pepper chew the head off a baby rabbit. I mean right off too, the way I'd pop the lid from an aspirin bottle. That, I can recall just like it was yesterday, while my first child being born—total blank. I know I was in the delivery room. I even remember what I was listening to on my Walkman, but as for the actual kid coming out—nothing. I can't even tell you if it was a boy or a girl, but that's natural for a first marriage.

The Walkman, though, I'll never forget its weight and the way it fit into my jacket pocket. Now, of course, it would be like carrying around a brick, but at the time it was hard to imagine anything more modern. When the first iPod came out, I recall thinking that it would never last. Isn't that funny? It's what old kooks thought when the car was invented, only now the kook was me! I held on to my Walkman until the iPod shuffle was introduced, at which point I caved in and bought one.

I got remarried as well, but it only lasted until the iPod nano, which the child from that marriage—a boy, I'm pretty sure—threw into the toilet along with my wallet and my car keys. Instead of fishing it all out and getting my hands dirty, I left that wife and kid and moved to where I live now, the apartment complex I mentioned earlier. I thought of replacing my nano, but instead I waited a while and got an iPhone, which I specifically use not to call either of my ex-wives or the children they tricked me into having. It's a strain on the eyes, but I also read the paper on it, so take that, newsagent—I'm the half-blind one now, and you're out of a job!

The iPhone 2 led to the 3, but I didn't get the 4 or 5 because I'm holding out for the 7, which, I've heard on good authority, can also be used as a Taser. This will mean I'll have just one less thing to carry around. And isn't that technology's job? To lighten our burden? To broaden our horizons? To make it possible to talk to your attorney and listen to a Styx album and check the obituaries in the town where your parents continue to live and videotape a race riot and send a text message and stun someone into submission all at the same time?

Doing it all while driving is illegal where I live, so I'm moving to a place where freedom still means something. I'm not telling you where it is, because I want it to remain unspoiled. I'll just say it's one of the few states left where the mentally ill can legally own firearms. They used to be limited to muskets, but now they can carry or conceal everything a normal person can. If you don't think a mental patient has the right to bring a sawed-off shotgun to the church where his ex-girlfriend is getting married, you're part of the problem. The truth is that crazy people—who are really just regular people but more misunderstood—have as much of a right to protect themselves as we do.

Live with liberty, and your imagination can soar. If I had been born in the state I'm moving to, there's no telling who I might be by now—an oral surgeon, maybe, or perhaps the ruler of the whole U.S. countryside. Other kings would pay me tribute with livestock and precious gems, but deep inside I don't think I'd be any different from who I am today: just a guy with a phone, waiting for the day when he can buy an even better one.

Loggerheads

The thing about Hawaii, at least the part that is geared toward tourists, is that it's exactly what it promises to be. Step off the plane, and someone places a lei around your neck, as if it were something you had earned—an Olympic medal for sitting on your ass. Raise a hand above your shoulder and, no matter where you are, a drink will appear: something served in a hollowed-out pineapple, or perhaps in a coconut that's been sawed in half. *Just like in the time before glasses!* you think.

Volcanic craters, waterfalls, and those immaculate beaches—shocking things when you're coming from Europe. At the spot Hugh and I go to in Normandy you'll find, in place of sand, speckled stones the size of potatoes.

The water runs from glacial to heart attack and is tinted the color of iced tea. Then there's all the stuff floating in it: not man-made garbage but sea garbage—scum and bits of plant life, all of it murky and rotten-smelling.

The beaches in Hawaii look as if they've been bleached; that's how white the sand is. The water is warm—even in winter—and so clear you can see not just your toes but the corns cleaving, barnacle-like, to the sides of them. On Maui, one November, Hugh and I went swimming, and turned to find a gigantic sea turtle coming up between us. As gentle as a cow, she was, and with a cow's dopey, almost lovesick expression on her face. That, to me, was worth the entire trip, worth my entire life, practically. For to witness majesty, to find yourself literally touched by it—isn't that what we've all been waiting for?

I had a similar experience a few years later, and again with Hugh. We were in Japan, walking through a national forest in a snowstorm, when a monkey the height of a bar stool brushed against us. His fur was a dull silver, the color of dishwater, but he had this beet-red face, set in a serious, almost solemn expression. We saw it full-on when he turned to briefly look at us. Then he shrugged and ambled off over a footbridge.

"Jesus Christ!" I said. Because it was all too much: the forest, the snowstorm, and now this. Monkeys are an attraction in that part of the country. We expected to see them at some point, but I thought they'd be fenced in. As with the sea turtle, part of the thrill was the feeling of being accepted, which is to say, not feared. It allowed you to think that you and this creature had a special relationship, a juvenile thought but one that brings with it a definite comfort. *Well, monkeys like me,* I'd find myself thinking during the next few months, whenever I felt lonely or unappreciated. Just as, in the months following our trip to Hawaii, I thought of the sea turtle. With her, though, my feelings were a bit more complicated, and instead of believing that we had bonded, I'd wonder that she could ever have forgiven me.

The thing between me and sea turtles started in the late '60s, and involved my best friend from grade school, a boy I'll call Shaun, who lived down the street from me in Raleigh. What brought us together was a love of nature, or, more specifically, of catching things and unintentionally killing them. We started when I was in the fourth grade, which would have made me ten, I guess. It's different for everyone, but at that age, though I couldn't have said that I was gay, I knew that I was not like the other boys in my class or my Scout troop. While they welcomed male company, I shrank from it, dreaded it, feeling like someone forever trying to pass, someone who would eventually be found out, and expelled from polite society. *Is this how a normal boy would swing his arms?* I'd ask myself, standing before the full-length mirror in my parents' bedroom. *Is this how he'd laugh? Is this what he would find funny?*

It was like doing an English accent. The more concentrated the attempt, the more self-conscious and unconvincing I became.

With Shaun, though, I could almost be myself. This didn't mean that we were alike, only that he wasn't paying that much attention. Childhood, for him, seemed something to be endured, passed through like a tiresome stretch of road. Ahead of this was the good stuff, and looking at him from time to time, at the way he had of staring off, of boring a hole into the horizon, you got the sense that he could not only imagine it but actually see it: this great grown-up life, waiting on the other side of sixteen.

Apart from an interest in wildlife, the two of us shared an identity as transplants. My family was from the North, and the Taylors were from the Midwest. Shaun's father, Hank, was a psychiatrist and sometimes gave his boys and me tests, the type for which there were, he assured us, "no wrong answers." He and his wife were younger than my parents, and they seemed it, not just in their dress but in their eclectic tastes—records by Donovan and Moby Grape shelved among the Schubert. Their house had real hardcover books in it, and you often saw them lying open on the sofa, the words still warm from being read.

In a neighborhood of stay-at-home moms, Shaun's mother worked. A public-health nurse, she was the one you went to if you woke up with yellow eyes or jammed a piece of caramel corn too far into your ear. "Oh, you're fine," Jean would say, for that was what she wanted us to call her, not Mrs. Taylor. With her high cheek bones and ever so slightly turned-down mouth, she brought to mind a young Katharine Hepburn. Other mothers might be pretty, might, in their twenties or early thirties, *pause* at beauty, but Jean was clearly parked there for a lifetime. You'd see her in her flower bed, gardening gloves hanging from the waistband of her slacks like someone clawing to get out, and you just had to wish she was your mom instead.

The Taylor children had inherited their mother's good looks, especially Shaun. Even as a kid he seemed at home in his skin—never cute, just handsome, blond hair like a curtain drawn over half his face. The eye that looked out the uncurtained side was cornflower blue, and excelled at spotting wounded or vulnerable animals. While the other boys in our neighborhood played touch football in the street, Shaun and I searched the woods behind our houses. I drew the line at snakes, but any thing else was brought home and imprisoned in our ten-gallon aquariums. Lizards, toads, baby birds: they all got the same diet—raw hamburger meat—and, with few exceptions, they all died within a week or two.

"Menu-wise, it might not hurt you to branch out a little," my mother once said, in reference to my captive luna moth. It was the size of a paperback novel, a beautiful mint green, but not much interested in ground chuck. "Maybe you could feed it some, I don't know, flowers or something."

Like she knew.

The best-caught creature belonged to Shaun's younger brother, Chris, who'd found an injured flying squirrel and kept him, uncaged, in his bedroom. The thing was no bigger than an ordinary hamster, and when he glided from the top bunk to the dresser, his body flattened out, making him look like an empty hand puppet. The only problem was the squirrel's disposition, his one-track mind. You wanted him to cuddle or ride sentry on your shoulder, but he refused to relax. *I've got to get out of here,* you could sense him thinking, as he clawed, desperate and wild-eyed, at the windowpane, or tried to squeeze himself underneath the door. He made it out eventually, and though we all hoped he'd return for meals, become a kind of part-time pet, he never did.

Not long after the squirrel broke free, Jean took her boys and me for a weekend on the North Carolina coast. It was mid-October, the start of the sixth grade, and the water was too chilly to swim in. On the Sunday we were to head back home, Shaun and I got up at dawn and took a walk with our nets. We were hunting for ghost crabs, when in the distance we made out these creatures moving blockily, like windup toys on an unsteady surface. On closer inspection we saw that they were baby sea turtles, dozens of them, digging out from under the sand and stumbling toward the ocean.

An adult might have carried them into the surf, or held at bay the predatory gulls, but we were twelve, so while I scooped the baby turtles into a pile, Shaun ran back and got the trash cans from our hotel room. We might have walked off with the whole lot, but they seemed pretty miserable, jumbled atop one another. Thus, in the end, we took just ten, which meant five apiece.

*

The great thing about the sea turtles, as opposed to, say, flying squirrels, was that they would grow exponentially—meaning, what, fifty, a hundred times their original size? When we got them, each called to mind a plastic coin purse, the oval sort handed out by banks and car dealerships. Then there were the flippers and, of course, the heads, which were bald and beaky, like a newly hatched bird's. Since the death of a traumatized mole pried from the mouth of our cat, Samantha, my aquarium had sat empty and was therefore ready for some new tenants. I filled it with a jug of ocean water I'd brought from the beach, then threw in a conch shell and a couple of sand dollars to make it more homey. The turtles swam the short distance from one end of the tank to the other, and then they batted at the glass with their flippers, unable to understand that this was it—the end of the road. What they needed, it seemed, was something to eat.

"Mom, do we have any raw hamburger?"

Looking back, you'd think that someone would have said something—sea turtles, for God's sake!—but maybe they weren't endangered yet. Animal cruelty hadn't been invented either. The thought that a non-human being had *physical* feelings, let alone the wherewithal to lose hope, was outlandish and alien, like thinking that paper had relatives. Then too, when it comes to eliciting empathy, it's the back of the line for reptiles and amphibians, creatures with, face it, not much in the way of a personality. Even giving them names didn't help, as playing with Shelly was no different from playing with Pokyhontus; "playing," in this case, amounting to placing them on my desk and watching them toddle over the edge.

It was good to know that in the house down the street Shaun's turtles weren't faring much better. The hamburger meat we'd put in our aquariums went uneaten, and within a short time it spoiled and started stinking up our rooms. I emptied my tank, and in the absence of more seawater, I made my own with plain old tap water and salt.

"I'm not sure that that's going to work," my mother said. She was standing in my doorway with a cigarette in one hand and an ashtray in the other. Recent experiments with a home-frosting kit had dried out and broken her already brittle hair. What was left she'd covered with a scarf, a turquoise one, that looked great when she had a tan but not so great when she didn't. "Doesn't ocean water have nutrients in it or something?"

"I dunno."

She looked at the turtles unhappily dragging themselves across my bedspread. "Well, if you want to find out, I'm taking Lisa to the library this Saturday."

I'd hoped to spend my weekend outside, but then it rained and my father hogged the TV for one of his football games. It was either go to the library or stay home and die of boredom, so I got into the car, groaning at the unfairness of it all. My mother dropped my sister and me downtown, and then she went to do some shopping, promising to return in a few hours.

It wasn't much to look at, our public library. I'd later learn that it used to be a department store, which made sense: the floor-to-ceiling windows were right for mannequins, and you could easily imagine dress shirts where the encyclopedias were, wigs in place of the magazines. I remember that in the basement there were two restrooms, one marked "Men" and the other marked "Gentlemen." Inside each was a toilet, a sink, and a paper towel dispenser, meaning that whichever you chose you got pretty much the same treatment. Thus it came down to how you saw yourself: as regular or fancy. On the day I went to research turtles, I saw myself as fancy, so I opened the door marked "Gentlemen." What happened next happened very quickly: Two men, both of them black, turned their heads in my direction. One was standing with his pants and underwear pulled down past his knees, and as he bent to yank them up, the other man, who'd been kneeling before him and who also had his pants lowered, covered his face with his hand and let out a little cry.

"Oh," I told them, "I'm sorry."

I backed, shaken, out of the room, and just as the door had closed behind me, it swung open again. Then the pair spilled out, that flying-squirrel look in their eyes. The stairs were at the end of a short hall, and they took them two at a time, the slower man turning his head, just briefly, and looking at me as if I held a gun. When I saw that he was afraid of me, I felt powerful. Then I wondered how I might use that power.

My first instinct was to tell on them—not because I wanted the two punished but because I would have liked the attention. "Are you all right?" the librarian would have asked. "And these were Negroes, you say? Quick, somebody, get this young man a glass of water or, better yet, a Coke. Would you like a Coke while we wait for the police?"

And in my feeblest voice I would have said, "Yes."

Then again, it could so easily backfire. The men were doing something indecent, and recognizing it as such meant that I had an eye for it. That I too was suspect. And wasn't I?

In the end I told no one. Not even Lisa.

"So did you find out what kind of turtles they are?" my mother asked as we climbed back into the car.

"Sea turtles," I told her. "Well, we *know* that."

"No, I mean, that's what they're called, 'sea turtles.'"

"And what do they eat?"

I looked out the rain-streaked window. "Hamburger." My mother sighed. "Have it your way."

*

It took a few weeks for my first turtle to die. The water in the tank had again grown murky with spoiled, uneaten beef, but there was something else as well, something I couldn't begin to identify. The smell that developed in the days after Halloween, this deep, swampy funk, was enough to make your throat close up. It was as if the turtles' very souls were rotting, yet still they gathered in the corner of their tank, determined to find the sea. At night I would hear their flippers against the glass, and think about the Negroes in the Gentlemen's room, wondering what would become of them—what, by extension, would become of me? Would I too have to live on the run? Afraid of even a twelve-year-old?

One Friday in early November my father paid a rare visit to my room. In his hand was a glass of gin, his standard after-work cocktail, mixed with a little water and garnished with a lemon peel. I liked the drink's medicinal smell, but today it was overpowered by the aquarium. He regarded it briefly and, wincing at the stench, removed two tickets from his jacket pocket. "They're for a game," he told me.

"A game?"

"Football," he said. "I thought we could go tomorrow afternoon."

"But tomorrow I have to write a report."

"Write it on Sunday."

I'd never expressed any interest in football. Never played it with the kids on the street, never watched it on TV, never touched the helmet I'd received the previous Christmas. "Why not take Lisa?" I asked.

"Because you're my son, that's why."

I looked at the holocaust taking place in my aquarium. "Do I have to?"

If I were to go to a game today, I'd certainly find something to enjoy: the food, the noise, the fans marked up with paint.

It would be an experience. At the time, though, it threw me into a panic. *Which team am I supposed to care about?* I asked myself as we settled into our seats. *How should I react if somebody scores a point?* The thing about sports, at least for guys, is that nobody ever defines the rules, not even in gym class. Asking what a penalty means is like asking who Jesus was. It's one of those things you're just supposed to know, and if you don't, there's something seriously wrong with you.

Two of the popular boys from my school were standing against a railing a few rows ahead of us, and when I stupidly pointed them out to my father, he told me to go say hello.

How to explain that looking at them, even from this distance, was pushing it. Addressing them, it followed, was completely out of the question. People had their places, and to not understand that, to act in violation of it, demoted you from a nature nut to something even lower, a complete untouchable, basically. "That's all right," I said. "They don't really know who I am."

"Aw, baloney. Go over and talk to them."

"No, really."

"Do you want me to drag you over there?"

As I dug in, I thought of the turtles. All they'd ever wanted was to live in the ocean—that was it, their entire wishlist, and instead I'd decided they'd be better off in my bedroom. Just as my dad had decided that I'd be better off at the football game. If I could have returned them to the beach, I would have, though I knew it was already too late. In another few days they would start going blind. Then their shells would soften, and they'd just sort of melt away, like soap.

"Are you going over there or aren't you?" my dad said.

When the last turtle died and was pitched into the woods behind my house, Shaun and I took up bowling, the only sport

I was ever half decent at. The Western Lanes was a good distance away, and when our parents wouldn't drive us, we rode our bikes, me with a transistor radio attached by rubber bands to my handlebars. We were just thinking of buying our own bowling shoes when Shaun's mother and father separated. Hank took an apartment in one of the new complexes, and a few months later, not yet forty years old, he died.

"Died of what?" I asked.

"His heart stopped beating" was the answer Shaun gave me.

"Well, sure," I said, "but doesn't *every* dead person's heart stop beating? There must have been something else going on."

"His heart stopped beating."

Following the funeral there was a reception at the Taylors' house. Shaun and I spent most of it on the deck off his living room, him firing his BB gun into the woods with that telescopic look in his eye. After informing me that his father's heart had stopped beating, he never said another word about him. I never saw Shaun cry, or buckle at the knees, or do any of the things that I would have done. Dramawise it was the chance of a lifetime, but he wasn't having any of it. From the living room, I could hear my father talking to Jean. "What with Hank gone, the boys are going to need a positive male influence in their lives," he said. "That being the case, I'll be happy to, well, happy to—"

"Ignore them," my mother cut in. "Just like he does with his own damn kids."

And Jean laughed. "Oh, Sharon."

Eighteen years passed before I learned what had really happened to Shaun's father. By then I was living in Chicago. My parents were still in Raleigh, and several times a week I'd talk to my mother on the phone. I don't remember how the subject came up, but after she told me I was stunned.

"Did Shaun know?" I asked.

"I'm sure he did," my mother said, and although I hadn't seen or spoken to him since high school, I couldn't help but feel a little betrayed. If you can't tell your best friend that your dad essentially drank himself to death, who *can* you tell? It's a lot to hold in at that age, but then I guess we all had our secrets.

It was after talking to my mom on the phone that I finally went to the library and looked up those turtles: "loggerheads" is what they were called. When mature, they can measure three and a half feet long. A female might reach four hundred pounds, and, of all the eggs she lays in a lifetime, only one in a thousand will make it to adulthood. Pretty slim odds when, by "making it," you mean simply surviving.

Before the reception ended that day, Shaun handed his BB gun to me. My father was watching from the living room window and interceded just as I raised it to my shoulder.

"Oh no, you don't. You're going to put somebody's eye out."

"Somebody like a bird?" I said. "We're firing into the woods, not into the house."

"I don't give a damn where you're aiming."

I handed the rifle back to Shaun, and as he brushed the hair from his eyes and peered down the scope, I tried to see what I imagined he did: a life on the other side of this, something better, perhaps even majestic, waiting for us to grow into it.

If I Ruled the World

If I ruled the world, the first thing I'd do is concede all power to the *real* King, who, in case you don't happen to know, is named Jesus Christ. A lot of people have managed to forget this lately, so the second thing I'd do is remind them of it. Not only would I bring back mandatory prayer in school, but I'd also institute it at work. Then in skating rinks and airports. Wherever people live or do business, they shall know His name. Christ's picture will go on all our money, and if you had your checks specially printed with sailboats or shamrocks on them, too bad for you because from here on out, the only images allowed will be of Him, or maybe of me reminding you of how important He is.

T-shirts with crosses and apostles on them will be allowed, but none of this nonsense you see nowadays, this one my neighbor has, for example. "Certified Sex Instructor," it says. He claims he only wears it while mowing the lawn, but in the summer that's once a week, which in my book is once a week too often. I mean, please, he's seventy-two!

Jesus and I are going to take that T-shirt, and all the ones like it, and use them as rags for washing people's mouths out. I normally don't believe in rough stuff, but what about those who simply refuse to learn? "Look," I'll say to Jesus, "enough is enough. I suggest we nail some boards together and have ourselves an old-fashioned crucifixion." It's bound to stir up a few bad memories, but having been gone for all that time, He probably won't know how bad things have gotten. "Just turn on the radio," I'll tell Him. "It's the thing next to my ferret cage with all the knobs on it."

Jesus will tune in to our local so-called music station, and within two minutes He'll know what I'm talking about— music so rude it'll make His ears blister. And the TV! I turned mine on the other morning and came upon a man who used to be a woman. Had a little mustache, a potbelly and everything. Changed her name from Mary Louise to Vince and sat back with a satisfied smile on her face, figuring she'd licked the system. And maybe she did last year when they did the operation, but Jesus is the system now, and we'll just have to hear what He has to say about it.

The creature on TV—I can't say male or female without bringing on a stomachache—said that when it was a woman it was attracted to men and that it still is. This means that now, on top of everything else, it's a homosexual. As if we didn't have enough already, some doctor had to go and *make* one!

Well, to hell with him—quite literally—and to hell with all the other gays too. And the abortionists, and the people who have had abortions, even if they were raped or the baby had three heads and delivering it was going to tear the mother to pieces. "That was YOUR baby," I'm going to say to Jesus. "Now, are you going to just sit there and watch it get thrown onto some trashheap?"

And Jesus will say, "No, Cassie Hasselback, I am not!"

He and I are going to work really well together. "What's next on the agenda?" He'll ask, and I'll point Him to the Muslims and vegans who believe their God is the real one. The same goes for the Buddhists and whoever it is that thinks cows and monkeys have special powers. Then we'll move on to the comedians, with their "F this" and "GD that." I'll crucify the Democrats, the Communists, and a good 97 percent of the college students. Don't laugh, Tim Cobblestone, because you're next! Think you can let your cat foul my flower beds and get away with it? Well, think again! And Curtis Devlin, who turned down my application for a home-improvement loan; and Carlotta Buffington, who only got her job because she's paralyzed on one side; and even my grandson Kenyan Bullock. He just turned five, but no matter what Trisha says, this is not a phase—the child is evil, and it's best to stop him now before any real damage is done. And all the other evil people and whores and liars who want to take away our freedom or raise my taxes, they shall know our fury, Jesus's and mine, and burn forever.

Easy, Tiger

On a recent flight from Tokyo to Beijing, at around the time that my lunch tray was taken away, I remembered that I needed to learn Mandarin. "Goddamnit," I whispered. "I knew I forgot something."

Normally, when landing in a foreign country, I'm prepared to say, at the very least, "Hello," and "I'm sorry." This trip, though, was a two-parter, and I'd used my month of prep time to bone up on my Japanese. For this, I returned to the Pimsleur audio program I'd relied on for my previous two visits. I'd used its Italian version as well and had noted that they followed the same basic pattern. In the first thirty-minute lesson, a man approaches a strange woman, asking, in Italian or Japanese or whichever language you've signed up for, if she understands English. The two jabber away for twenty seconds or so, and then an American instructor chimes in and breaks it all down. "Say, 'Excuse me,'" he tells you. "Ask, 'Are you an American?'" The conversations grow more complicated as you progress, and the phrases are regularly repeated so that you don't forget them.

265

Not all the sentences I've learned with Pimsleur are suited to my way of life. I don't drive, for example, so "Which is the road to go to Yokohama?" never did me any good. The same is true of "As for gas, is it expensive?" though I have got some mileage out of "Fill her up, please," which I use in restaurants when getting a second cup of tea.

Thanks to Japanese I and II, I'm able to buy train tickets, count to nine hundred and ninety-nine thousand, and say, whenever someone is giving me change, "Now you are giving me change." I can manage in a restaurant, take a cab, and even make small talk with the driver. "Do you have children?" I ask. "Will you take a vacation this year?" "Where to?" When he turns it around, as Japanese cabdrivers are inclined to do, I tell him that I have three children, a big boy and two little girls. If Pimsleur included "I am a middle-aged homosexual and thus make do with a niece I never see and a very small godson," I'd say that. In the meantime, I work with what I have.

Pimsleur's a big help when it comes to pronunciation.

The actors are native speakers, and they don't slow down for your benefit. The drawbacks are that they never explain anything or teach you to think for yourself. Instead of being provided with building blocks that would allow you to construct a sentence of your own, you're left with using the hundreds or thousands of sentences that you have memorized. That means waiting for a particular situation to arise in order to comment on it; either that, or becoming one of those weird non-sequitur people, the kind who, when asked a question about paint color, answer, "There is a bank in front of the train station," or, "Mrs. Yamada Ito has been playing tennis for fifteen years."

I hadn't downloaded a Pimsleur program for China, so on the flight to Beijing I turned to my Lonely Planet phrase book, knowing it was hopeless. Mandarin is closer to singing than it is to talking, and even though the words were written phonetically, I couldn't begin to get the hang of them. The book was slim and palm-size, divided into short chapters: "Banking," "Shopping," "Border Crossing." The one titled "Romance" included the following: "Would you like a drink?" "You're a fantastic dancer." "You look like some cousin of mine." The latter would work only if you were Asian, but even then it's a little creepy, the implication being "the cousin I have always wanted to undress and ejaculate on."

In the subchapter "Getting Closer," one learns to say, "I like you very much." "You're great." "Do you want a massage?" On the following page, things heat up. "I want you." "I want to make love to you." "How about going to bed?" And, a line that might have been written especially for me, "Don't worry, I'll do it myself."

Oddly, the writers haven't included "Leave the light on," a must if you want to actually *say* any of these things. One pictures the vacationer naked on a bed and squinting into his or her little book to moan, "Oh yeah!" "Easy, tiger," "Faster," "Harder," "Slower," "Softer." "That was … amazing/weird/ wild." "Can I stay over?"

In the following subchapter, it all falls apart: "Are you seeing someone else?" "He/she is just a friend." "You're just using me for sex." "I don't think it's working out." And, finally, "I never want to see you again."

Hugh and I returned from China, and a few days later I started preparing for a trip to Germany. The first time I went, in 1999, I couldn't bring myself to say so much as *"Guten Morgen."* The sounds felt false coming out of my mouth, so instead I spent my time speaking English apologetically. Not that the apologies were needed. In Paris, yes, but in Berlin people's attitude is "Thank you for allowing me to practice my perfect English." And I do mean perfect. "Are you from Minnesota?" I kept asking.

In the beginning, I was put off by the harshness of German. Someone would order a piece of cake, and it sounded as if it were an actual order, like, "Cut the cake and lie facedown in that ditch between the cobbler and the little girl." I'm guessing this comes from having watched too many Second World War movies. Then I remembered the umpteen Fassbinder films I sat through in the '80s, and German began to sound conflicted instead of heartless. I went back twice in 2000, and over time the language grew on me. It's like English, but sideways.

I've made at least ten separate trips by now and have gone from one end of the country to the other. People taught me all sorts of words, but the only ones that stuck were *"Kaiserschnitt,"* which means "cesarean section," and *"Lebensabschnittspartner."* This doesn't translate to "lover" or "life partner" but, rather, to "the person I am with today," the implication being that things change, and you are keeping yourself open.

For this latest trip, I wanted to do better, so I downloaded all thirty lessons of Pimsleur German I, which again start off with "Excuse me, do you understand English?" As with the Japanese and the Italian versions, the program taught me to count and to tell time. Again I learned "The girl is already big" and "How are you?" (*"Wie geht es Ihnen?"*)

In Japanese and Italian, the response to the final question is "I'm fine, and you?" In German it's answered with a sigh and a slight pause, followed by "Not so good."

I mentioned this to my German friend Tilo, who said that of course that was the response. "We can't get it through our heads that people are asking only to be polite," he said.

In Japanese I, lesson 17, the actress who plays the wife says,

"Kaimono ga shitai n desu ga!" ("I want to go shopping, but there's a problem and you need to guess what it is.") The exercise is about numbers, so the husband asks how much money she has. She gives him a figure, and he offers to increase it incrementally.

Similarly, in the German version, the wife announces that she wants to buy something: *"Ich möchte noch etwas kaufen."* Her husband asks how much money she has, and after she answers, he responds coldly, "I'm not giving you any more. You have enough."

There's no discord in Pimsleur's Japan, but its Germany is a moody and often savage place. In one of the exercises, you're encouraged to argue with a bellhop who tries to cheat you out of your change and who ends up sneering, "You don't understand German."

"Oh, but I do," you learn to say. "I *do* understand German."

It's a program full of odd sentence combinations. "We don't live here. We want mineral water" implies that if the couple *did* live in this particular town they'd be getting drunk like everyone else. Another standout is *"Der Wein ist zu teuer und Sie sprechen zu schnell."* ("The wine is too expensive and you talk too fast.") The response to this would be "Anything else, Herr Asshole?" But of course they don't teach you that.

On our last trip to Tokyo, Hugh and I rented an apartment in a nondescript neighborhood a few subway stops from Shinjuku Station. A representative from the real estate agency met us at the front door, and when I spoke to him in Japanese, he told me I needed to buy myself some manga. "Read those and you'll learn how people actually talk," he said. "You, you're a little too polite."

I know what he was getting at, but I really don't see this as much of a problem, especially if you're a foreigner and any perceived rudeness can turn someone not just against you but against your entire country. Here Pimsleur has it all over the phrase books of my youth, where the Ugly American was still alive and kicking people. "I didn't order this!" he raged in Greek and Spanish. "Think you can cheat me, do you?" "Go away or I'll call the police."

Now for the traveling American there's less of a need for phrase books. Not only do we expect everyone to speak our language; we expect everyone to be fluent. I rarely hear an American vacationer say to a waiter or shopkeeper in Europe, "Your English is so good." Rather, we act as if it were part of his job, like carrying a tray or making change. In this respect, the phrase books and audio programs are an almost charming throwback, a suggestion that *the traveler* put himself out there, that *he* open himself to criticism and not the person who's just trying to scrape by selling meatballs in Bumfucchio, Italy.

One of the things I like about Tokyo is the constant reinforcement one gets for trying. "You are very skilled at Japanese," everyone keeps telling me. I know people are just being polite, but it spurs me on, just as I hoped to be spurred on in Germany. To this end, I've added a second audio program, one by a man named Michel Thomas, who works with a couple of students, a male and a female. At the start, he explains that German and English are closely related and thus have a lot in common. In one language, the verb is "to come," and in the other it's *"kommen."* English "to give" is German *"geben."* Boston's "That is good" is Berlin's *"Das ist gut."* It's an excellent way to start and leaves the listener thinking, *Hey, Ich kann dodis.*

Unlike the nameless instructor in Pimsleur, Herr Thomas explains things—the fact, for example, that if there are two verbs in a German sentence, one of them comes at the end. He doesn't give you phrases to memorize. In fact, he actively discourages study. "How would you say, 'Give it to me?'" he asks the female student. She and I correctly answer, and then he turns to the male. "Now try 'I would like for you to give it to me.'"

Ten minutes later, we've graduated to "I can't give it to you today, because I cannot find it." To people who speak nothing but English, this might seem easy enough, but anyone else will appreciate how difficult it is: negatives, multiple uses of "it," and the hell that breaks loose following the German "because." The thrill is that you're actually figuring it out on your own. You're engaging with another language, not just parroting it.

Walking through the grocery store with Pimsleur *und* Thomas on my iPod, I picture myself pulling up to my Munich hotel with my friend Ulrike, who's only ever known me to say "cesarean section" and "the person I am with until someone better comes along."

"Bleiben wir hier heute Abend?" I plan to say. *"Wie viele Nächte? Zwei? Das ist teuer, nicht wahr?"*

She's a wonderful woman, Ulrike, and if that's all I get out of this—seeing the shock register on her face as I natter on—it'll be well worth my month of study.

Perhaps that evening after dinner, I'll turn on the TV in my hotel room. And maybe, if I'm lucky, I'll understand one out of every two hundred words. The trick, ultimately, is to not let that discourage me, to think, *Oh well. That's more than I understood the last time I watched TV in Germany.* That was a few years back, in Stuttgart. There was a television mounted on a perch in my room, and I turned it on to find a couple having sex. This wasn't on pay-per-view but just regular Sunday night TV. And I mean these two were really going at it. If I'd had the Lonely Planet guide to German, I might have recognized "Please don't stop!" "That was amazing/weird." With Herr Thomas, I could understand "I just gave it to you" and, with Pimsleur, "I would like to come now."

I watched this couple for a minute or two, and then I advanced to the next channel, which was snowed out unless you paid for it. *What could they possibly be doing here that they weren't doing for free on the other station?* I asked myself. *Turning each other inside out?*

And isn't that the joy of foreign travel—there's always something to scratch your head over. You don't have to be fluent in order to wonder. Rather, you can sit there with your mouth open, not exactly dumb, just speechless.

Laugh, Kookaburra

I've been to Australia twice so far, but according to my father, I've never actually seen it. He made this observation at the home of my cousin Joan, whom he and I visited just before Christmas one year, and it came on the heels of an equally aggressive comment. "Well," he said, "David's a better *reader* than he is a writer." This from someone who hasn't opened a book since *Dave Stockton's Putt to Win,* in 1996. He's never been to Australia either. Never even come close.

"No matter," he told me. "In order to see the country, you have to see the country*side,* and you've only been to Sydney."

"And Melbourne. And Brisbane," I said. "And I have too gone into the country."

"Like hell you have."

"All right," I said. "Let's get Hugh on the phone. He'll tell you. He'll even send you pictures."

Joan and her family live in Binghamton, New York. They don't see my father and me that often, so it was pretty lousy to sit at their table, he and I bickering like an old married couple. Ashamed by the bad impression we were making, I dropped the countryside business, and as my dad moved on to other people's shortcomings, I thought back to the previous summer and my daylong flight from London to Sydney. I was in Australia on business, and because someone else was paying for the ticket and it would be possible to stop in Japan on the way home, Hugh joined me. This is not to put Australia down, but we'd already gone once before. Then too, spend that much time on a plane, and you're entitled to a whole new world when you step off at the other end—the planet Mercury, say, or at the very least Mexico City. For an American, though, Australia seems pretty familiar: same wide streets, same office towers. It's Canada in a thong, or that's the initial impression.

I hate to admit it, but my dad was right about the country-side. Hugh and I didn't see much of it, but we wouldn't have seen anything were it not for a woman named Pat, who was born in Melbourne and has lived there for most of her life. We'd met her a few years earlier, in Paris, where she'd come to spend a mid-July vacation. Over drinks in our living room, her face dewed with sweat, she taught us the term "shout," as in, "I'm shouting lunch." This means that you're treating and that you don't want any lip about it. "You can also say, 'It's my shout,' or, 'I'll shout the next round,'" she told us.

We kept in touch after her visit, and when my work was done and I was given a day and a half to spend as I liked, Pat offered herself as a guide. On that first afternoon, she showed us around Melbourne and shouted coffee. The follow-ing morning she picked us up at our hotel and drove us into what she called "the bush." I expected a wasteland of dust and human bones, but in fact it was nothing like that. When Australians say "the bush," they mean the woods. The forest.

First, though, we had to get out of Melbourne and drive beyond the seemingly endless suburbs. It was August, the dead of winter, and so we had the windows rolled up. The homes we passed were made of wood, many with high fences around the backyards. They didn't look exactly like American houses, but I couldn't quite identify the difference. *Is it the roofs?* I wondered. *The siding?* Pat was driving, and as we passed the turn off for a shopping center, she invited us to picture a four-burner stove.

"Gas or electric?" Hugh asked, and she said that it didn't matter.

This was not a real stove but a symbolic one, used to prove a point at a management seminar she'd once attended. "One burner represents your family, one is your friends, the third is your health, and the fourth is your work." The gist, she said, was that in order to be successful, you have to cut off one of your burners. And in order to be *really* successful, you have to cut off two.

Pat has her own business, a good one that's allowing her to retire at fifty-five. She owns three houses and two cars, but even without the stuff, she seems like a genuinely happy person. And that alone constitutes success.

I asked which two burners she had cut off, and she said that the first to go had been family. After that she switched off her health. "How about you?"

I thought for a moment and said that I'd cut off my friends. "It's nothing to be proud of, but after meeting Hugh I quit making an effort."

"And what else?" she asked. "Health, I guess."

Hugh's answer was work. "And?"

"Just work," he said.

I asked Pat why she'd cut off her family, and with no trace of bitterness, she talked about her parents, both severe alcoholics. They drank away their jobs and credit, and because they were broke, they moved a lot, most often in the middle of the night. This made it hard to have a pet, though for a short time, Pat and her sister managed to own a sheep. It was an old, beat-up ram they named Mr. Preston. "He was lovely and good-natured, until my father sent him off to be shorn," Pat said. "When he returned there were bald patches and horrible, deep cuts, like stab wounds in his skin. Then we moved to an apartment and had to get rid of him." She looked at her hands on the steering wheel. "Poor old Mr. Preston. I hadn't thought about him in years."

It was around this time that we finally entered the bush. Hugh pointed out the window at a still lump of dirty fur lying beside a fallen tree, and Pat caroled, "Roadkill!" Then she pulled over so we could take a closer look. Since leaving Melbourne, we'd been climbing higher into the foothills. The temperature had dropped, and there were graying patches of snow on the ground. I had on a sweater and a jacket, but they weren't quite enough, and I shivered as we walked toward the body and saw that it was a . . . what, exactly? "A teenage kangaroo?"

"A wallaby," Pat corrected me.

The thing had been struck but not run over. It hadn't decomposed or been disfigured, and I was surprised by the shoddiness of its coat. It was as if you'd bred a rabbit with a mule. Then there was the tail, which reminded me of a lance.

"Hugh," I called, "come here and look at the wallaby."

It's his belief that in marveling at a dead animal on the roadside, you may as well have killed it yourself—not accidentally but on purpose, cackling, most likely, as you ran it down. Therefore he stayed in the car.

"It's your loss," I called, and a great cloud of steam issued from my mouth.

Our destination that afternoon was a place called Daylesford, which looked, when we arrived, more like a movie set than an actual working town. The buildings on the main street were two stories tall and made of wood, like buildings in the Old West but brightly painted. Here was the shop selling hand-made soaps shaped like petits fours. Here was the fudgery, the jammery, your source for moisturizer. If Dodge City had been founded and maintained by homosexuals, this is what it might have looked like. "The spas are fantastic," Pat said, and she parked the car in front of a puppet shop. From there we walked down a slight hill, passing a flock of sulfur-crested cockatoos just milling about, pulling worms from the front lawn of a bed-and-breakfast. This was the moment when familiarity slipped away and Australia seemed not just distant, but impossibly foreign. "Will you look at that," I said.

It was Pat who had made the lunch reservation. The restaurant was attached to a hotel, and on arriving we were seated beside a picture window. The view was of a wooden deck and, immediately beyond it, a small lake. On a sunny day it was probably blinding, but the winter sky was like brushed aluminum. The water beneath it had the same dull sheen, and its surface reflected nothing.

Even before the menus were handed out, you could see what sort of a place this was. Order the pork and it might resemble a rough-hewn raft, stranded by tides on a narrow beach of polenta. Fish might come with shredded turnips or a pabulum of coddled fruit. The younger an ingredient, the more highly it was valued, thus the baby chicken, the baby spinach, the newborn asparagus, each pale stalk as slender as a fang.

As always in a fancy restaurant, I asked Hugh to order for me. "Whatever you think," I told him. "Just so long as there's no chocolate in it."

He and Pat weighed our options, and I watched the hostess seat a party of eight. Bringing up the rear was a woman in her midthirties, pretty, and with a baby on her shoulder. Its back was covered with a shawl, but to judge from the size it looked extremely young—a month old, tops.

Keep it away from the chef, I thought.

A short while later, I noticed that the child hadn't shifted position. Its mother was running her hand over its back, almost as if she were feeling for a switch, and when the top of the shawl fell away, I saw that this was not a baby, but a baby doll.

"Psssst," I whispered, and when Pat raised her eyes, I directed them to the other side of the room.

"Is that normal in Australia?" I asked.

"Maybe it's a grieving thing," she offered. "Maybe she lost a baby in childbirth and this is helping her to work through it."

There's a definite line between looking and staring, and after I was caught crossing it, I turned toward the window. On the highest rail of the deck was a wooden platform, and standing upon it, looking directly into my eyes, was what I knew to be a kookaburra. This thing was as big as a seagull but squatter, squarer, and all done up in earth tones, the complete spectrum from beige to dark walnut. When seen full on, the feathers atop his head looked like brush-cut hair, and that gave him a brutish, almost conservative look. If owls were the professors of the avian kingdom, then kookaburras, I thought, might well be the gym teachers.

When the waitress arrived, I pointed out the window and asked her a half dozen questions, all of them fear-based. "Oh," she said, "that bird's not going to hurt anybody." She took our orders and then she must have spoken to one of the waiters. He was a tall fellow, college age, and he approached our table with a covered bowl in his hands. I assumed it was an appetizer, but it seemed instead that it was for the kookaburra. "Would you like to step outside and feed him?" he asked.

I wanted to say that between the wallaby and the baby doll,

I was already overstimulated, but how often in life do you get such an offer? That's how I found myself on the deck, holding a bowl of raw duck meat cut into slender strips. At the sight of it, the bird stood up and flew on to my arm, which buckled slightly beneath his weight.

"Don't be afraid," the waiter said, and he talked to the kookaburra in a soothing, respectful voice, the way you might to a child with a switchblade in his hand. For that's what this thing's beak was—a serious weapon. I held a strip of raw duck, and after yanking it from my fingers, the bird flew back to the railing. Then he took the meat and began slamming it against his wooden platform. *Whap, whap, whap.* Over and over, as if he were tenderizing it.

"This is what he'd do in the wild with snakes and lizards and such," the waiter said. "He thinks it's still alive, see. He thinks he's killing it."

The kookaburra must have slammed the meat against the wooden platform a good ten times. Only then did he swallow it, and look up, expectantly, for more.

I took another strip from the bowl, and the action repeated itself. *Whap, whap, whap.* On or about his third helping, I got used to the feel of a bird on my arm and started thinking about other things, beginning with the word "kookaburra." I first heard it in the fifth grade, when our music teacher went on an Australian kick. She taught us to sing "Waltzing Matilda," "Tie Me Kangaroo Down, Sport," and what we called simply "Kookaburra." I'd never heard such craziness in my life. The first song, for instance, included the words "jumbuck," "billabong," "swagman," and "tuckerbag," none of which were ever explained. The more nonsensical the lyric, the harder it was to remember, and that, most likely, is why I retained the song about the kookaburra—it was less abstract than the others. I recall that after school that day, I taught it to my sister Amy, who must have been in the first grade at the time. We sang it in the car, we sang it at the table, and then, one night, we sang it in her bed, the two of us lying side by side and rocking back and forth.

We'd been at it for half an hour when the door flung open. "What the hell is going on?" It was our father, one hand resting teapot-style on his hip, and the other—what would be the spout—formed into a fist. He was dressed in his standard around-the-house outfit, which is to say, his underpants. No matter the season he wore them without a shirt or socks, the way a toddler might pad about in a diaper. For as long as any of us could remember, this was the way it went: he returned home from work and stepped out of his slacks, sighing with relief, as if they were oppressive, like high heels. All said, my father looked good in his underpants. Silhouetted in the doorway, he resembled a wrestler. Maybe not one in tip-top condition, but he was closer than any of the other dads on our street. "It's one o'clock in the morning, for God's sake. David, get to your room."

I knew that it was at best ten thirty. Still, though, there was no point in arguing. Down in the basement, I went to my room and he resumed his position in front of the TV. Within a few minutes he was snoring, and I crept back upstairs to join Amy for another twenty rounds.

It didn't take long for our father to rally. "Did I not tell you to go to your room?"

What would strike me afterward was the innocence of it. If I had children and they stayed up late, singing a song about a bird, I believe I would find it charming. *I knew I had those two for a reason*, I think I'd say to myself. I might go so far as to secretly record them and submit the tape in a My Kids Are Cuter Than Yours competition. My dad, by contrast, clearly didn't see it that way, which was strange to me. It's not like we were ruining his TV reception. He couldn't even hear us from that distance, so what did he have to complain about? "All right, sonny, I'm giving you ten seconds. One. Two ... "

I guess what he resented was being dismissed. Had our mother told us to shut up, we'd probably have done it. He, on the other hand, sitting around in his underpants—it just didn't seem that important.

At the count of six I pushed back the covers. "I'm going," I spat, and once again I followed my father downstairs.

Ten minutes later, I was back. Amy cleared a space for me, and we picked up where we had left off. "Laugh,Kookaburra! Laugh, Kookaburra! Gay your life must be."

Actually, maybe it was that last bit that bothered him. An eleven-year-old boy in bed with his sister, not just singing about a bird but doing it as best he could, rocking back and forth and imagining himself onstage, possibly wearing a cape and performing before a multitude.

The third time he came into the room, our father was a wild man. Even worse, he was wielding a prop, the dreaded fraternity paddle. It looked like a beaver's tail made out of wood. In my memory, there were Greek letters burned into one side, and crowded around them were the signatures of other Beta Epsilons, men we'd never met, with old-fashioned nicknames like Lefty and Slivers—names, to me, as synonymous with misfortune as Smith & Wesson. Our father didn't bring out the paddle very often, but when he did, he always used it.

"All right, you, let's get this over with." Amy knew that she had nothing to worry about. He was after me, the instigator, so she propped herself against the pillows, drawing up her legs as I scooted to the other side of the bed, then stood there, dancing from foot to foot. It was the worst possible strategy, as evasion only made him angrier. Still, who in his right mind would surrender to such a punishment?

He got me eventually, the first blows landing just beneath my knee caps. Then down I went, and he moved in on my upper thigh. *Whap, whap, whap.* And while it certainly hurt, I have to say that he didn't go overboard. He never did. I asked him about it once, when I was around fourteen, and he chalked it up to a combination of common sense and remarkable self-control. "I know that if I don't stop myself early I'll kill you," he said.

As always after a paddling, I returned to my room vowing never to talk to my father again. To hell with him, to hell with my mother, who'd done nothing to stop him, to hell with Amy for not taking a few licks herself, and to hell with the others, who were, by now, certainly whispering about it.

I didn't have the analogy of the stove top back then, but what I'd done was turn off the burner marked "family." Then I'd locked my door and sat there simmering, knowing even then that without them, I was nothing. Not a son or a brother but just a boy—and how could that ever be enough? As a full-grown man it seems no different. Cut off your family, and how would you know who you are? Cut them off in order to gain success, and how could that success be measured? What would it possibly mean?

I thought of this as the kookaburra, finally full, swallowed his last strip of duck meat, and took off over the lake. Inside the restaurant, our first courses had arrived, and I watched through the window as Hugh and Pat considered their plates. I should have gone inside right then, but I needed another minute to take it all in and acknowledge, if only to myself, that I really did have it made. A storybook town on the far side of the world, enough in my pocket to shout a fancy lunch, and the sound of that bird in the distant trees, laughing. Laughing.

Just a Quick E-mail

Hey, Robin,

Just a quick e-mail to thank you for the wedding gift, or "wedding gift *certificate*," I guess I should say. Two free pizzas—how thoughtful of you. And how generous: any toppings we want!

Maybe you hadn't heard that I'd registered at Tumbridge & Colchester. Last June, I think it was, just before we announced the engagement. Not that the pizzas didn't come in handy; they did, though in a slightly indirect way. Unlike you, who're so wonderfully unconcerned with what other people think, I'm a bit vain, especially when it comes to my figure. That being the case, I used the certificates to feed our workmen, who are currently building a small addition.

I know you thought our house was big enough already. "Tara meets Dress Barn" was how I heard you so cleverly describe it at the wedding. "I mean, really," you said. "How much room do two people need?"

Or did you say, "Two *thin* people"? What with the band

playing and everyone in the world shouting their congratulations, it was a little hard to hear. Just like it is at our ever-expanding house—the workers all hammering away! What they've done is tear down the wall between the kitchen and the breakfast nook. That'll give us room for a walk-in silverware drawer and this new sixteen-burner stove I've been eyeing. Plus it will allow us to expand the counter space, put in a second dishwasher, and install an electric millstone for grinding blue corn. (Homemade tortillas, anyone?) Then we're going to enclose that useless deck, insulate it, and create a separate dining room for when we go Asian. This will eliminate that ramp you're so fond of, but it's not like we see you all that often and I don't think it will kill you to crawl up a half dozen stairs. As a matter of fact, as long as they're clean, I actually think it might be good for you.

Seeing as we're on this subject, Robin, is it right to insist on all this special treatment? More than that, is it *healthy?* It's been almost a year since the car accident. Don't you think it's time you moved on with your life? Do I need to remind you of all *my* injuries: the dislocated shoulder, the practically broken wrist that still tingles when I do something strenuous like whisk in damp weather? On top of that, it took me days to wash your blood out of my hair. The admitting nurse put me down as a redhead—that's how bad it was—your left front tooth practically embedded in my skull! It's no severed spinal cord, of course, but like Dr. Gaffney says, the ball is in *your* court now. Either you can live in the past as a lonely, bitter paraplegic, or you can live in the present as one. I dusted myself off and got back on the proverbial horse, so why can't you?

In other news, did you get the postcard I sent from our honeymoon? Iraq was beautiful, just as I imagined it would be, but there were *so many* Americans there! I said to Philip,

"Is nowhere safe? I mean, really. In terms of the crowds, we might as well have gone to Paris!" Then, of course, we *did* go to Paris, but it was for work rather than vacation. Philip had a client he needed to meet, an American in town for some big Chablis auction. He once defended her on a drunk-driving charge, and successfully too, this despite her Breathalyzer results and some pretty bad behavior, some of which was caught on video. Now they're suing the people she hit, or at least the one who lived, and it looks like they've got a fairly good chance of winning. This is not to worry you in any way. What with the addition on the house and the million and a half other things on my to-do list, a lawsuit is the last thing on my mind. Not that it wasn't proposed.

While my hardworking husband consulted with his client, I, alone, wandered the quays, stopping every now and then to duck into a boutique. And more than once I thought of you. For Paris, I remembered, is where *you* and Philip honeymooned. That was in the good old days, when the dollar and the euro were practically even. Now it costs a king's ransom just for a cup of coffee and a croque madame, so a pair of shoes from Christian Louboutin—well, you can just imagine! I suppose that for you it would make sense, but for someone who walks the way I do, someone known to practically gallop when there's a sale taking place—the shoes I got are good for one, maybe two seasons at the most. Still, though, what could I do? Iraq had been totally picked over by the time we arrived, and I wanted a little something to remind me of my trip.

After returning stateside Philip went right to work. His number one job: to make me happy. First, we started on the addition ($$$$$$$), then came a successful effort to erase that DWI from my driving record. It wasn't easy, but legal matters rarely are. All I can say is that if it helps to have friends, it helps even more to have friends who are governors!

None of this will get you out of your wheelchair, but it *will* restore my self-confidence and what I like to think of as my good name. It means, as well, that you'll have to stop calling me the "drunken bitch" who "took away" your legs and then "stole" your husband. "Drunk," it seems, is a relative term, and if I were you I'd watch how I used it. The leg bit is an exaggeration, as you clearly still *have* them (big purple veins and all). As for the stealing, Philip came to me of his own volition—one adult to another, no coercion involved. In the end all you're left with is the single word "bitch," which could mean any number of things. I myself would use it to describe someone whose idea of an appropriate wedding present is a gift certificate for two pizzas! Offering it to your ex-husband, I can understand, but to your own sister? That's just tacky.

Gotta run!

—Ronda

A Guy Walks into a Bar Car

In the golden age of American travel, the platforms of train stations were knee-deep in what looked like fog. You see it all the time in black-and-white movies, these low-lying eddies of silver. I always thought it was steam from the engines, but now I wonder if it didn't come from cigarettes. You could smoke everywhere back then: in the dining car, in your sleeping berth. Depending on your preference, it was either absolute heaven or absolute hell.

I know there was a smoking car on the Amtrak I took from Raleigh to Chicago in 1984, but seven years later it was gone. By then if you wanted a cigarette, your only option was to head for the bar. It sounds all right in passing, romantic even—"the baron the Lake Shore Limited"— but in fact it was rather depressing. Too bright, too loud, and full of alcoholics who commandeered the seats immediately after boarding and remained there, marinating like cheap kebabs, until they reached their destinations. At first their voices might strike you as jolly: the warm tones of strangers becoming friends.

Then the drinkers would get sloppy and repetitive, settling, finally, on that cross-eyed mush that passes for alcoholic sincerity.

On the train I took from New York to Chicago in early January 1991, one of the drunks pulled down his pants and shook his bare bottom at the woman behind the bar. I was thirty-four, old enough to know better, yet I laughed along with everyone else. The trip was interminable—almost nineteen hours, not counting any delays—but nothing short of a derailment could have soured my good mood. I was off to see the boyfriend I'd left behind when I moved to New York. We'd known each other for six years, and though we'd broken up more times than either of us could count, there was the hope that this visit might reunite us. Then he'd join me for a fresh start in Manhattan, and all our problems would disappear.

It was best for both of us that it didn't work out that way, though of course I couldn't see it at the time. The trip designed to bring us back together tore us apart for good, and it was a considerably sorrier me that boarded the Limited back to New York. My train left Union Station in the early evening. The late-January sky was the color of pewter, and the ground beneath it—as flat as rolled-out dough—was glazed with slush. I watched as the city receded into the distance, and then I went to the bar car for a cigarette. Of the dozen or so drunks who'd staggered on board in Chicago, one in particular stood out. I've always had an eye for ruined-looking men, and that's what attracted me to this guy—I'll call him Johnny Ryan— the sense that he'd been kicked around. Once he hit thirty, a hardness would likely settle about his mouth and eyes, but as it was—at twenty-nine—he was right on the edge, a screw-top bottle of wine the day before it turns to vinegar.

It must have been he who started the conversation, as I'd never have had the nerve. Under different circumstances I might have stammered hello and run back to my seat, but my breakup convinced me that something major was about to happen. The chance of a life time was coming my way, and in order to accept it I needed to loosen up, to stop being so "rigid." That was what my former boyfriend had called me. He'd thrown in "judgmental" while he was at it, another of those synonyms for "no fun at all." The fact that it stung reaffirmed what I had always suspected: It was all true. No one was duller, more prudish and set in his ways, than I was. Johnny didn't strike me as gay, but it was hard to tell with alcoholics. Like prisoners and shepherds, many of them didn't care who they had sex with, the idea being that what happens in the dark stays in the dark. It's the next morning you have to worry about— the name-calling, the slamming of doors, the charge that you somehow cast a spell. I must have been desperate to think that such a person would lead me to a new life. Not that Johnny was bad company—it's just that the things we had in common were all so depressing. Unemployment, for instance. My last job had been as an elf at Macy's.

"Personal assistant" was how I phrased it, hoping he wouldn't ask for whom.

"Uh—Santa?"

His last job had involved hazardous chemicals. An accident at Thanksgiving had caused boils to rise on his back. A few months before that, a tankard of spilled benzene had burned all the hair off his arms and hands. This only made him more attractive. I imagined those smooth pink mitts of his opening the door to the rest of my life.

"So are you just going to stand here smoking all night?" he asked.

Normally I waited until nine o'clock to start drinking, but "What the heck," I said. "I'll have a beer. Why not?" When a couple of seats opened up, Johnny and I took them. Across the narrow carriage a black man with a bushy mustache pounded on his Formica tabletop. "So a nun goes into town," he said, "and sees a sign reading, 'Quickies—twenty-five dollars.' Not sure what it means, she walks back to the convent and pulls aside the mother superior. 'Excuse me,' she asks, 'but what's a quickie?'

"And the old lady goes, 'Twenty-five dollars. Just like in town.'"

As the room filled with laughter, Johnny lit a fresh cigarette. "Some comedian," he said. I don't know how we got onto the subject of gambling—perhaps I asked if he had a hobby.

"I'll bet on sporting events, on horses and greyhounds—hell, put two fleas on the table and I'll bet over which one can jump the highest. How about you?"

Gambling to me is what a telephone pole might be to a groundhog. He sees that it's there but doesn't for the life of him understand why. Friends have tried to explain the appeal, but still I don't get it. Why take chances with money? Johnny had gone to Gamblers Anonymous, but the whining got on his nerves and he quit after his third meeting. Now he was on his way to Atlantic City, where he hoped to clean up at the craps table.

"All right," called the black man on the other side of the carriage. "I've got another one: What do you have if you have nuts on a wall?" He lit a cigarette and blew out the match. "Walnuts!"

A red-nosed woman in a decorative sweatshirt started talking, but the black fellow told her that he wasn't done yet. "What do you have if you have nuts on your chest?" He waited a beat. "Chestnuts! What do you have when you have nuts on your chin?" He looked from face to face. "A dick in your mouth!"

"Now that's good," Johnny said. "I'll have to remember that."

"I'll have to remind you," I told him, trembling a little at my forwardness. "I mean ... I'm pretty good at holding on to jokes."

As the black man settled down, I asked Johnny about his family. It didn't surprise me that his mother and father were divorced. Each of them was fifty-four years old, and each was currently living with someone much younger. "My dad's girlfriend—fiancée, I guess I should call her—is no older than me," Johnny said. "Before losing my job I had my own place, but now I'm living with them. Just, you know, until I get back on my feet."

I nodded.

"My mom, meanwhile, is a total mess," he said. "Total pot-head, total motormouth, total perfect match for her asshole thirty-year-old boyfriend."

Nothing in this guy's life sounded normal to me. Take food: He could recall his mother rolling joints on the kitchen counter, but he couldn't remember her cooking a single meal, not even on holidays. For dinner they'd eat take-out hamburgers or pizzas, sometimes a sandwich slapped together over the sink. Johnny didn't cook either. Neither did his father or future stepmother. I asked what was in their refrigerator, and he said, "Ketchup, beer, mixers—what else?" He had no problem referring to himself as an alcoholic. "It's just a fact," he said. "I have blue eyes and black hair too. Big deal."

"Here's a clean one," the black man said. "A fried-egg sandwich walks into a bar and orders a drink. The bartender looks him up and down, then goes, 'Sorry, we don't serve food here.'"

"Oh, that's old," one of his fellow drunks said. "Not only that, but it's supposed to be a hamburger, not a fried-egg sandwich."

"It's supposed to be *food*, is what it's supposed to be," the black man told him. "As to what that food is, I'll make it whatever the hell I want to."

"Amen," Johnny said, and the black man gave him a thumbs-up.

His next joke went over much better. "What did the leper say to the prostitute? 'Keep the tip.'"

I pictured what looked like a mushroom cap resting in the palm of an outstretched hand. Then I covered my mouth and laughed so hard that beer trickled out of my nose. I was just mopping it up when the last call was announced, and everyone raced to the counter to stock up. Some of the drinkers would beat it until morning when the bar reopened, while others would find their assigned seats and sleep for a while before returning.

As for Johnny, he had a fifth of Smirnoff in his suitcase. I had two Valiums in mine, and, because of my ugly past history with sedatives, the decision to share them came easily. An hour later, it was agreed that we needed to smoke some pot. Each of us was holding, so the only question was where to smoke it—and how to get there from the bar. Since taking the Valium, drinking six beers, and following them with straight vodka, walking had become a problem for me. I don't know what it took to bring down Johnny, but he wasn't even close yet. That's what comes with years of socking it away—you should be unconscious, but instead you're up, and full of bright ideas. "I think I've got a place we can go to," he said.

I'm not sure why he chose the women's lounge rather than the men's. Perhaps it was closer or maybe there was no men's lounge. One way or the other, even now, all these many years later, it shames me to think of it. The idea of holing up in a bathroom, of hogging the whole thing just so that you can hang out with someone who will never, under any circumstances, return your interest, makes me cringe. Especially given that this—the "dressing room," it was called—was Amtrak's one meager attempt to recapture some glamour. It amounted to a small chamber with a window —a space not much bigger than a closet. There was an area to sit while brushing your hair or applying makeup, and a mirror to look into while you did it. A second, inner door led to a sink and toilet, but we kept that shut and installed ourselves on the carpeted floor.

Johnny had brought our plastic cups from the bar, and after settling in, he poured us each a drink. I felt boneless, as if I'd been filleted; yet still I managed to load the pipe and hold my lighter to the bowl. Looking up through the window, I could see the moon, which struck me, in my half-conscious state, as flat and unnaturally bright, a sort of glowing Pringle.

"Do you think we can turn that overhead light off?" I asked.

"No problem, Chief."

It was he who brought up the subject of sex. One moment I was asking if his mom gave him a discount on his drugs, and the next thing I knew he was telling me about this woman he'd recently slept with. "A fatty," he called her. "A bloodsucker." Johnny also told me that the older he got, the harder it was to get it up. "I'll be totally into it and then it's like, 'What the fuck?' You know?"

"Oh, definitely," I said.

He poured more vodka into his plastic cup and swirled it around, as if it were a fine cognac that needed to breathe. "You get into a lot of fights?" he asked.

"Arguments?"

"No," he said. "I mean with your fists. You ever punch people?"

I relit the pipe and thought of the dustup my former boy-friend and I had had before I left. It was the first time since the fifth grade that I'd hit someone not directly related to me, and it left me feeling like a Grade A moron. This had a lot to do with my punch, which was actually more of a slap. To make it worse, I'd then slipped on the icy sidewalk and fallen into a bank of soft gray snow.

There was no need to answer Johnny's fist fight question. The subject had been raised for his benefit rather than mine, an excuse to bemoan the circumference of his biceps. Back when he was boxing, the one on the right had measured seventeen and a half inches. "Now it's less than fourteen," he told me. "I'm shrinking before my very fucking eyes."

"Well, can't you fatten it back up somehow?" I asked. "You're young. I mean, just how hard can it be to gain weight?"

"The problem isn't gaining weight, it's gaining it in the right place," Johnny said. "Two six-packs a day might swell my stomach, but it's not doing shit for my arms."

"Maybe you could lift the cans for a while before opening them," I offered. "That should count for something, shouldn't it?"

Johnny flattened his voice. "You're a regular comedian, aren't you? Keep it up and maybe you can open for that asshole in the bar." A minute of silence and then he relit the pipe, took a hit, and passed it my way. "Look at us," he said, and he let out a long sigh. "A couple of first-class fucking losers."

I wanted to defend myself, to at least point out that we were in *second* class, but then somebody knocked on the door. "Go away," Johnny said. "The bathroom's closed until tomorrow." A minute later there came another knock, this one harder, and before we could respond a key turned and a security guard entered. It wouldn't have worked to deny anything: the room stunk of pot and cigarette smoke. There was the half-empty bottle of vodka, the plastic cups turned on their sides. Put a couple of lamp shades on our heads, and the picture would have been complete.

I suppose the guard could have made some trouble—confiscated our dope, had us arrested at the next stop—but instead he just told us to take a hike, no easy feat on a train. Johnny and I parted without saying good night, I staggering off to my assigned seat, and he going, I assumed, to his. I saw him again the following morning, back in the bar car. Whatever spell had been cast the night before was broken, and he was just another alcoholic starting his day with a shot and a chaser. As I ordered a coffee, the black man told a joke about a witch with one breast.

"Give it a rest," the woman in the decorative sweatshirt said.

I smoked a few cigarettes and then returned to my seat, nursing what promised to be a two-day headache. While slumped against the window, trying unsuccessfully to sleep, I thought of a trip to Greece I'd taken in August 1982. I was twenty-five that summer and flew by myself from Raleigh to Athens. A few days after arriving, I was joined by my father, my brother, and my sister Lisa. The four of us traveled around the country, and when they went back to North Carolina I took a bus to the port city of Patras. From there I sailed to Brindisi, Italy, wondering all the while why I hadn't returned with the rest of my family. In theory it was wonderful —a European adventure. I was too self-conscious to enjoy it, though, too timid, and it stymied me that I couldn't speak the language.

A bilingual stranger helped me buy a train ticket to Rome, but on the return to Brindisi I had no one but myself to rely on. The man behind the counter offered me three options, and I guess I said yes to the one that meant "No seat for me, thank you. I would like to be packed as tightly as possible alongside people with no access to soap or running water."

It was a common request, at least among the young and foreign. I heard French, Spanish, German, and a good many languages I couldn't quite identify. What was it that sounded like English played backward? Dutch? Swedish? If I found the crowd intimidating, it had more to do with my insecurity than with the way anyone treated me. I suppose the others seemed more deserving than I did, with their faded bandannas and goatskin bags sagging with wine. While I was counting the days until I could go back home, they seemed to have a real talent for living.

When I was a young man my hair was dark brown and a lot thicker than it is now. I had one continuous eyebrow instead of two separate ones, and this made me look as though I sometimes rode a donkey. It sounds odd to say it—conceited, even—but I was cute that August when I was twenty-five. I wouldn't have said so at the time, but reviewing pictures taken by my father in Athens, I think, *That was me? Really?* Looks-wise, I feel that single month constituted my moment, a peak from which the descent has been both swift and merciless.

It's only three hundred and fifty miles from Rome to Brindisi, but, what with the constant stopping and starting, the train took forever. We left, I believe, at around eight thirty p.m., and for the first few hours, everyone stood. Then we sat with our legs crossed, folding them in a little bit tighter when one person, and then another, decided to lie down. As my fellow passengers shifted position, I found myself pushed toward the corner, where I brushed up against a fellow named Bashir.

Lebanese, he said he was, en route to a small Italian university, where he planned to get a master's in engineering. Bashir's English was excellent, and in a matter of minutes we formed what passes between wayfarers in a foreign country as a kind of automatic friendship. More than a friendship, actually—a romance. Coloring everything was this train, its steady rumble as we passed through the dark Italian countryside. Bashir was—how to describe him? It was as if you had coaxed the eyes out of Bambi and resettled them, half asleep, into a human face. Nothing hard or ruined-looking there; in fact it was just the opposite—angelic, you might call him, pretty.

What was it that he and I talked about so intently? Perhaps the thrill was that we *could* talk, that our tongues, each flabby from lack of exercise, could flap and make sounds in their old familiar way. Three hours into our conversation, he invited me to get off the train in his college town and spend some-time, as much as I liked, in the apartment that was waiting for him. It wasn't the offer you'd make to a backpacker but something closer to a proposal. "Be with me" was the way I interpreted it.

At the end of our train car was a little room, no more than a broom closet, really, with a barred window in it. It must have been four a.m. when two disheveled Germans stepped out, and we moved in to take their place. As would later happen with Johnny Ryan, Bashir and I sat on the floor, the state of which clearly disgusted him. Apart from the fact that we were sober, and were pressed so close that our shoulders touched, the biggest difference was that our attraction was mutual. The moment came when we should have kissed—you could practically hear the surging strings—but I was too shy to make the first move, and so, I guess, was he. Still I could feel this thing between us, not just lust but a kind of immediate love, the sort that, like instant oatmeal, can be realized in a matter of minutes and is just as nutritious as the real thing. *We'll kiss . . . now,* I kept thinking. Then, *Okay . . . now.* And on it went, more torturous by the second.

The sun was rising as we reached his destination, the houses and church spires of this strange city —a city I could make my own—silhouetted against the weak morning sky. "And so?" he asked.

I don't remember my excuse, but it all came down to cowardice. For what, really, did I have to return to? A job pushing a wheelbarrow on Raleigh construction sites? A dumpy one-bedroom next to the IHOP?

Bashir got off with his three big suitcases and became a perennial lump in my throat, one that rises whenever I hear the word "Lebanon" or see its jittery outline on the evening news. *Is that where you went back to?* I wonder. *Do I ever cross your mind? Are you even still alive?*

Given the short amount of time we spent together, it's silly how often, and how tenderly, I think of him. All the way to Penn Station, hungover from my night with Johnny Ryan, I wondered what might have happened had I taken Bashir up on his offer. I imagined our apartment overlooking a square: the burbling fountain, the drawings of dams and bridges piled neatly on the desk.

When you're young it's easy to believe that such an opportunity will come again, maybe even a better one. Instead of a Lebanese guy in Italy it might be a Nigerian one in Belgium, or maybe a Pole in Turkey. You tell yourself that if you traveled alone to Europe this summer, you could surely do the same thing next year, and the year after that. Of course you don't, though, and the next thing you know you're an aging, unemployed elf so desperate for love you spend your evening mooning over a straight alcoholic.

The closer we got to New York, the more miserable I became. Then I thought of this guy my friend Lily and I had borrowed a ladder from a few months earlier, someone named Hugh. I'd never really trusted people who went directly from one relationship to the next, so after my train pulled into Penn Station, and after I'd taken the subway home, I'd wait a few hours, or maybe even a full day, before dialing his number and asking if he'd like to hear a joke.

Standing By

It was one of those headaches that befall every airline passenger. A flight is delayed because of thunderstorms or backed-up traffic—or maybe it's canceled altogether. Maybe you board two hours late, or maybe you board on time and spend the next two hours sitting on the runway. When it happens to you it's a national tragedy—*Why aren't the papers reporting this?* you wonder.

Only when it happens to someone else do you realize what a dull story it really is. "They told us we'd leave at three instead of two thirty, so I went to get a frosted-pecan wrap, and when I came back they changed the time to four on account of the plane we'd be riding on hadn't left Pittsburgh yet. Then I was like, 'Why didn't you tell us that an hour ago?' and they were like, 'Ma'am, just stand away from the counter, please.'"

Because I'm in the air so often, I hear this sort of thing a lot. In line for a coffee. In line for a newspaper or a gunpowder test on the handle of my public radio totebag: everywhere I go someone in an eight-dollar T-shirt is whipping out a cell

301

phone and delivering the fine print of his or her delay. One can't help but listen in, but then my focus shifts and I find myself staring. I should be used to the way Americans dress when traveling, yet it still manages to amaze me. It's as if the person next to you had been washing shoe polish off a pig, then suddenly threw down his sponge saying, "Fuck this. I'm going to Los Angeles!"

On Halloween, when I see the ticket agents dressed as hags and mummies, I no longer think, *Nice costume*, but, *Now we have to tag our own luggage?*

I mean that I mistake *them* for *us*.

The scariness, of course, cuts both ways. I was on a plane in the spring of 2003 when the flight attendant asked us to pray for our troops in Iraq. It was a prickly time, but brand-new war or no brand-new war, you don't ever want to hear the word "pray" from a flight attendant.

You don't want to hear the phrase "I'll be right back" either. That's code for "Go fuck yourself," according to a woman who used to fly for Northwest and taught me several terms specific to her profession.

"You know how a plastic bottle of water will get all crinkly during a flight?" she asked. "Well, it happens to people too, to our insides. That's why we get all gassy."

"All right," I said.

"So what me and the other gals would sometimes do is fart while we walked up and down the aisle. No one could hear it on account of the engine noise, but anyway that's what we called 'crop dusting.'"

When I asked another flight attendant, this one male, how he dealt with a plane full of belligerent passengers, he said, "Oh, we have our ways. The next time you're flying and are about to land, listen closely as we make our final pass through the cabin."

*

In the summer of 2009, I was trying to get from North Dakota to Oregon. There were thunderstorms in Colorado, so we were two hours late leaving Fargo. This caused me to miss my connecting flight, and upon my arrival in Denver I was directed to the customer service line. It was a long one—thirty, maybe thirty-five people, all of them cranky and exhausted. In front of me stood a woman in her midseventies, accompanying two beautifully dressed children, a boy and a girl. "The airlines complain that nobody's traveling, and then you arrive to find your flight's been oversold!" the woman griped. "I'm trying to get me and my grandkids to San Francisco, and now they're telling us there's nothing until tomorrow afternoon."

At this, her cell phone rang. The woman raised it to her ear, and a great many silver bracelets clattered down her arm. "Frank? Is that you? What did you find out?"

The person on the other end fed her information, and as she struggled to open her pocketbook, I held out my pad and pen. "A nice young man just gave me something to write with, so go ahead," the woman said. "I'm ready." Then she said, "*What?* Well, *I* could have told you that." She handed me back my pad and pen and, rolling her eyes, whispered, "Thanks anyway." After hanging up she turned to the kids. "Your old grandmother is so sorry for putting you through this. But she's going to make it up to you, she swears."

They were like children from a catalog. The little girl's skirt was a red-and-white check, and matched the ribbon that banded her straw hat. Her brother was wearing a shirt and tie. It was a clip-on, but still it made him and his sister the best-dressed people in line, much better than the family ten or so places ahead of them. That group consisted of a couple in their midfifties and three teenagers, two of whom were obviously brothers. The third teenager, a girl, was holding a very young baby. I suppose it could have been a loaner, but the way she engaged with it—the obvious pride and pleasure she was radiating—led me to believe that the child was hers. Its father, I guessed, was the kid standing next to her. The young man's hair was almost orange and drooped from his head in thin, lank braids. At the end of each one, just above the rubber band, was a colored bead the size of a marble. Stevie Wonder wore his hair like that in the late '70s, but he's black. And blind. Then too, Stevie Wonder didn't have acne on his neck and wear baggy denim shorts that fell midway between his knees and his ankles. Topping it off was the kid's T-shirt. I couldn't see the front of it, but printed in large letters across the back were the words "Freaky Mothafocka."

I didn't know where to start with that one. Let's see, I'm flying on a plane with my parents and my infant son, so should I wear the T-shirt that says, "Orgasm Donor," "Suck All You Want, I'll Make More," or, no, seeing as I'll have the beaded cornrows, I think I should go with "Freaky Mothafocka."

As the kid reached over and took the baby from the teenage girl, the woman in front of me winced. "Typical," she groaned.

"I beg your pardon."

She gestured toward the Freaky Mothafocka. "The only ones *having* babies are the ones who *shouldn't* be having them." Her gaze shifted to the adults. "And look at the stupid grandparents, proud as punch."

It was one of those situations I often find myself in while traveling. Something's said by a stranger I've been randomly thrown into contact with, and I want to say, "Listen. I'm with you on most of this, but before we continue, I need to know who you voted for in the last election."

If the grandmother's criticism was coming from the same place as mine, if she was just being petty and judgmental, we could go on all day, perhaps even form a friendship.

If, on the other hand, it was tied to a conservative

agenda, I was going to have to switch tracks and side with the Freaky Mothafocka, who was, after all, just a kid. He may have looked like a Dr. Seuss character, but that didn't mean he couldn't love his baby —a baby, I told myself, who just might grow up to be a Supreme Court justice or the president of the United States. Or, at least, I don't know, someone with a job.

Of course you can't just *ask* someone whom they voted for. Sometimes you can tell by looking, but the grandmother with the many bracelets could have gone either way. In the end, I decided to walk the center line. "What gets me is that they couldn't even spell 'motherfucker' right," I whispered. "I mean, what kind of example is that setting for our young people?"

After that, she didn't want to talk anymore, not even when the line advanced and Mothafocka and company moved to one of the counter positions. Including the baby, there were six in their party, so I knew it was going to take forever. *Where do they need to go, anyway?* I asked myself. *Wherever it is, would it have killed them to drive?*

Fly enough, and you learn to go brain-dead when you have to. It's sort of like time travel. One minute you're bending to unlace your shoes, and the next thing you know you're paying fourteen dollars for a fruitcup, wondering, *How did I get here?*

No sooner had I alienated the grandmother in Denver than I was trapped by the man behind me, who caught my eye and, without invitation, proceeded to complain. He had been passed over for a standby seat earlier that morning and was not happy about it. "The gal at the gate said she'd call my name when it came time to board, but hell, she didn't call me."

I tried to look sympathetic.

"I should have taken her name," the man continued. "I should have reported her. Hell, I should have punched her is what I should have done!"

"I hear you," I said.

Directly behind him was a bald guy with a silver mustache, one of those elaborate jobs that wander a while before eventually morphing into sideburns. The thing was as curved and bushy as a squirrel's tail, and the man shook crumbs from it as the fellow who'd lost his standby seat turned to engage him.

"Goddamn airline. It's no wonder they're all going down the toilet."

"None of them want to work, that's the problem," the bald man with the mustache said. "All any of them care about is their next goddamn coffee break." He looked at the counter agents with disdain and then turned his eye on the Freaky Mothafocka. "That one must be heading back to the circus."

"Pathetic," the man behind me said. He himself was wearing pleated khaki shorts and a blue T-shirt. A baseball cap hung from his waistband, and his sneakers, which were white, appeared to be brand-new. Like a lot of men you see these days, he looked like a boy, suddenly, shockingly, set into an adult body. "We got a kid looks like him back in the town I come from, and every time I see him I just thank God he isn't mine."

As the two started in on rap music and baggy trousers, I zoned out and thought about my last layover in Denver. I was on the people mover, jogging toward my connection at the end of Concourse C, when the voice over the PA system asked Adolf Hitler to pick up a white courtesy phone. *Did I hear that correctly?* I remember thinking. It's hard to imagine anyone calling their son Adolf Hitler, so the person must have changed it from something less provocative, a category that includes pretty much everything. Weirder still was hearing the name in the same sentence as the word "courtesy." I imagined a man picking up the receiver, his voice made soft by surprise and the possibility of bad news. "Yes, hello, this is Adolf Hitler."

Thinking of it made me laugh, and that brought me back to the present and the fellow behind me in the khaki shorts. "Isn't it amazing how quickly one man can completely screw up a country?" he said.

"You got that right," Mr. Mustache agreed. "It's a god damn mess is what it is."

I assumed they were talking about George Bush but gradually realized it was Barack Obama, who had, at that point, been in office for less than six months.

The man with the mustache mentioned a GM dealership in his hometown. "They were doing fine, but now the federal government's telling them they have to close. Like this is Russia or something, a Communist country!"

The man in the khaki shorts joined in, and I wished I'd paid closer attention to the auto bailout stuff. It had been on the radio and in all the papers, but because I don't drive and I always thought that car dealerships were ugly, I'd let my mind wander or moved on to the next story, which was unfortunate, since I'd have loved to have turned around and given those two what for. Then again, even if I were informed, what's the likelihood of changing anyone's opinion, especially a couple of strangers'? If my own little mind is nailed shut, why wouldn't theirs be?

"We've got to take our country back," the man with the mustache said. "That's the long and short of it, and if votes won't do the trick then maybe we need to use force."

What struck me with him, and with many of the conservatives I'd heard since the election, was his overblown, almost egocentric take on political outrage, his certainty that no one else had quite experienced it before. What, then, had I felt during the Bush-Cheney years? Was that somehow secondary? "Don't tell me I don't know how to hate," I wanted to say. Then I stopped and asked myself, *Do you really want that to be your message? Think you can out-hate me, asshole? I was fucking hating people before you were even born!*

We're forever blaming the airline industry for turning us into monsters: it's the fault of the ticket agents, the baggage handlers, the slowpokes at the newsstands and the fast-food restaurants. But what if this is who we truly are, and the airport's just a forum that allows us to be our real selves, not just hateful but gloriously so?

Would Adolf Hitler please meet his party at Baggage Claim Four? Repeat. Adolf Hitler can meet his party at Baggage Claim Four.

It's a depressing thought, and one that proved hard to shake. It was with me when I boarded my flight to Portland and was still on my mind several hours later, when we were told to put our tray tables away and prepare for landing. Then the flight attendants, garbage bags in hand, glided down the aisle, looking each one of us square in the face and whispering, without discrimination, "Your trash. You're trash. Your family's trash."

Understanding Understanding Owls

Does there come a day in every man's life when he looks around and says to himself, *I've got to weed out some of these owls?* I can't be alone in this, can I? And, of course, you don't want to hurt anyone's feelings. Therefore you keep the crocheted owl given to you by your second youngest sister and accidentally on purpose drop the mug that reads "Owl Love You Always" and was sent by someone who clearly never knew you to begin with. I mean, mugs with words on them! Owl cocktail napkins stay, because everyone needs napkins. Ditto owl candle. Owl trivet: take to the charity shop along with the spool-size Japanese owl that blinks his eyes and softly hoots when you plug him into your computer.

Just when you think you're making progress, you remember the owl tobacco tin and the owl tea cozy. Then there are the plates, the coasters, the Christmas ornaments. This is what happens when you tell people you like something. For my sister Amy, that thing was rabbits. When she was in her late thirties, she got one as a pet, and before it had chewed through its first phone cord, she'd been given rabbit slippers, cushions, bowls, refrigerator magnets, you name it. "Really," she kept insisting, "the live one is enough." But nothing could stem the tide of crap.

Amy's invasion started with a live rabbit, while Hugh's and mine began, in the late 1990s, with decorative art. We were living in New York then, and he had his own painting business. One of his clients had bought a new apartment, and on the high, domed ceiling of her entryway she wanted a skyful of birds. Hugh began with warblers and meadowlarks. He sketched some cardinals and blue tits for color and was just wondering if it wasn't too busy when she asked if he could add some owls. It made no sense naturewise—owls and song birds work different shifts, and even if they didn't they would still never be friends. No matter, though. This was her ceiling, and if she wanted turkey vultures—or, as was later decided, bats—that's what she would get. All Hugh needed was a reference, so he went to the Museum of Natural History and returned with *Understanding Owls*. The book came into our lives almost fifteen years ago, and I've yet to go more than a month without mentioning it. "You know," I'll say. "There's something about nocturnal birds of prey that I *just don't get*. If only there was somewhere I could turn for answers."

"I wish I could help you," Hugh will say, adding, a second or two later, "Hold on a minute ... what about ... *Understanding Owls?*"

We've performed this little routine more times than I can count, but back then, when the book was still fresh-smelling and its pages had not yet yellowed, I decided that because Hugh actually *did* get a kick out of owls, I would try to find him a stuffed one. My search turned up plenty of ravens. I found pheasants and ducks, and foot-tall baby ostriches. I found a freeze-dried turkey's head attached to its own foot, but owls, no luck. That's when I learned that it's illegal to own them in the United States. Even if one dies naturally of a stroke or old age. If it chokes on a mouse or gets kicked by a horse. Should one fly against your house, break its neck, and land like magic on your front stoop, you're still not allowed to stuff it or even to store its body in your freezer. Technically, you're not even allowed to keep one of its feathers—that's how protected they are. I learned this at a now-defunct taxidermy shop in midtown Manhattan. "But if you're *really* interested," the clerk I spoke to said, "I've got a little something you might want to see." He stepped into the back room and returned with what I could only identify as a creature. "What we've done," he boasted, "is stretch a chicken over an owl *form*."

"That's really ... something," I said, groping for a compliment. The truth was that even a child would have seen this for what it was. The beak made from what looked to be a bear claw, the feet with their worn-down, pedestrian talons: I mean, *please!* This was what a chicken might wear to a Halloween party if she had ten minutes to throw a costume together. "Let me think about it," I said.

Years later we moved to Paris, where, within my first week, I found an albino peacock. I found swans and storks and all manner of seabirds but, again, no owls, because stuffing them is forbidden in France. In the U.K., though, it's a slightly different story. You can't go out and shoot one, certainly. They're protected in life just as they are in the U.S., but afterward, in death, things loosen up a bit. Most of the owls I saw in Great Britain had been stuffed during the Victorian era. I'd see them at English flea markets and in Scottish antique shops, but, as is always the case, the moment you decide to buy one they're nowhere to be had. I needed one—or decided I did—in

February 2008. Hugh and I were moving from our apartment to a house in Kensington, and, after going through our owl objects and deciding we could do without nine-tenths of them, I thought I'd get him the real thing for Valentine's Day. I should have started looking a month or two in advance, but with Christmas and packing and helping to ready our new place, it had slipped my mind. Thus I wound up on February 13 calling a London taxidermy shop and asking if they had any owls. The person who answered the phone told me he had two of them, both recent specimens, and free-standing, not behind glass as most of the old ones are. The store was open only by appointment, and after arranging to come by the following afternoon, I went to where Hugh was packing books in the next room and said, "I am giving you the best Valentine's Day gift *ever*."

This is one of those things I do and immediately hate myself for. How is the other person supposed to respond? What's the point? For the first sixteen years we were together, I'd give Hugh chocolates for Valentine's Day, and he'd give me a carton of cigarettes. Both of us got exactly what we wanted, and it couldn't have been easier. Then I quit smoking and decided that in place of cigarettes I needed, say, an eighteenth-century scientific model of the human throat. It was life-size, about four inches long, and, because it was old, handmade, and designed to be taken apart for study, it cost quite a bit of money. "When did Valentine's Day turn into *this?*" Hugh asked when I told him that he had to buy it for me.

What could I say? Like everything else, holiday gifts escalate. The presents get better and better until one year you decide you don't need anything else and start making donations to animal shelters. Even if you hate dogs and cats, they're somehow *always* the ones who benefit. "Eventually we'll celebrate by spaying a few dozen kittens," I said, "but until that day comes, *I want that throat.*"

On Valentine's Day, I carried a few boxes from our apartment to the house we'd bought. It looked like the sort of place where Scrooge might have lived—a narrow brick building, miserly in terms of space, and joined to identical, equally grim houses on either side of it. From there I walked around the corner and got on the Underground. The taxidermy shop was on a quiet street in North London, and as I approached I saw a man and his two sons with their faces pressed against the barred front windows. "A polar bear!" one of the boys shouted. The other tugged on his father's coat. "And a penguin! Look at the baby penguin!"

My heart raced.

The man who owned the shop was so much taller than me that, in order to look him in the eye, I had to throw my head all the way back, like I do at the dentist's office. He had enviably thick hair, and as he opened the door to let me in I noticed an orange kitten positioned on the floor beside a dalmatian puppy. Casting a shadow upon them was a rabbit standing upright on its hind legs, and above him, on a shelf, sat two tawny owls, each mounted to a stump and standing around twenty inches high. Both were females, and in great shape, but what I'd really wanted was a barn owl. Those are the ones with spooky white faces, like satellite dishes with eyes.

"We do get those from time to time, but they're rare," the taxidermist said. Above his head hung a massive seagull with its beak open, and next to him, on a tabletop, lounged a pair of hedgehogs.

I've seen better variety, but there was no denying that the man did beautiful work. Nothing had crooked eyes or bits of exposed plaster at the corners of its mouth. If seen in a photo, you'd think that these animals were alive and had gathered peacefully to boast about their excellent health. The taxidermist and I discussed the owls, and when my eyes cut to a glass-doored cabinet with several weather-beaten skulls inside it, he asked if I was a doctor.

"Me?" For some reason I looked at my hands. "Oh, goodness no."

"Then your interest in those skulls is nonprofessional?"

"Exactly."

The taxidermist's eyes brightened, and he led me to a human skeleton half hidden in the back of the room. "Who do you think this was?" he asked.

Being a layman, all I had to go by was the height—between four and a half and five feet tall. "Is it an adolescent?"

The taxidermist invited me to guess again, but before I could he blurted, "It's a Pygmy!" He then told me that in the nineteenth century the English went to what is now the Congo and hunted these people, tracked them down and shot them for sport.

Funny how quickly this changed the mood. "But he *could* have died of a heart attack, right?" I said. "I mean, how are we to know for certain that he was murdered?"

"Oh, we know, all right," the taxidermist told me. It would have been disturbing to see the skeleton of a slain Pygmy in a museum, but finding him in a shop, for sale, raised certain questions, uncomfortable ones, like *How much is he?*

"If you like the odd bits and pieces, I think I've got something else you might enjoy." The taxidermist retreated to the area behind his desk and pulled a plastic bag off an overhead shelf. It was, I noticed, from Waitrose, a grocery store described to me upon my move to England as "a cut above." From the bag he removed what looked like a platter with an oblong glass dome over it. Inside was a man's forearm,

complete with little hairs and a smudged tattoo. The taxidermist said, completely unnecessarily, "Now there's a story
behind this." For what human limb in a Waitrose bag is *not*
without some sort of story?

He placed the platter on the table, and as the lid was lifted
and set to the side, I was told that, a hundred years ago, the
taxidermist's grandfather witnessed a bar fight between two
sailors. One was armed with a saber, and the other, apparently, was disarmed with one. After it happened, the crowd
went wild. The amputee fell on his back, and as he lay there in
shock, bleeding to death, the taxidermist's grandfather looked
down at the floor, at the blood-soaked fingers that may have
still been twitching, and likely thought, *Well, it's not like it's
doing him any good.*

The story sounds a bit far-fetched, but there was no denying that the arm was real. The cut had been made two inches
south of the elbow, and the exposed end, with its cleanly severed radius and ulna, reminded me of ossobuco. "It was my
grandfather who mummified it," the taxidermist said. "You
can see it's not the best job in the world, but it's really rather
good for a first attempt."

I leaned closer.

"Touch it," he whispered.

As if I were under a spell, I did, shuddering a little at the feel
of the hairs. Equally creepy was the arm's color, which was
not Caucasian flesh tone but not brown either, the way most
desiccated body parts are. This was the same slightly toasted
shade as a spray-on tan.

"I think I'll just take one of those owls," I said. "The one
on the left, if that's okay."

The taxidermist nodded. Then he reached to an even higher
shelf and brought down another plastic grocery bag, this one
from Tesco, which is decidedly less upscale. "Now, a smell is

going to hit you when I open this up, but don't worry," he said. "It's just the smoke they used to preserve the head."

That's a phrase you don't hear too often, so it took a moment for it to sink in. When he opened the bag, I saw that he might more accurately have said "the head of this teenage girl," for she'd been no older than fourteen at the time of her death. This sounds super grisly but is, I propose, just medium grisly. The head was four hundred years old and came from somewhere in South America—Peru, I think he said. The skin was dry and thin, like leather on an old worn-out purse. Parts of it were eaten away, exposing the skull beneath it, but what really struck me was her hair, which was sleek and black, divvied into delicate, slender braids.

I didn't ask the price but said a little more emphatically, "I really think the owl will do it for me today. It's a Valentine's Day present—perfect for our new place. A house, actually— no basement, and three stories tall." I wasn't trying to be boastful. I just wanted him to know that I was loved, and that I lived above ground.

A few minutes later, the owl secured in a good-size cardboard box, I headed back to the Underground. Ordinarily I'd be elated—I'd been determined to find Hugh the perfect present, and, by golly, I had done it—but instead I felt unhinged, not by the things I had seen so much as by the taxidermist. It's common to be misread by people who don't know you. "Like to try Belligerent, the new fragrance for men?" I'll be asked in a department store. And I always think, *Really? Do I seem like the kind of guy who would wear cologne?* Hotel operators so often address me as "Mrs. Sedaris" that I no longer bother to correct them. I've been mistaken for a parent, a pickpocket, and even, God forbid, an SUV owner, and I've always been able to brush it off. What's rare is *not* to be misread. The taxidermist knew me for less time than it took to wipe my feet on his mat, and, with no effort whatsoever, he looked into my soul and recognized me for the person I really am: the type who'd actually love a Pygmy and could easily get over the fact that he'd been murdered for sport, thinking breezily, *Well, it was a long time ago.* Worse still I would flaunt it, hoping in the way a Porsche owner does that this would become a part of my identity. "They say he has a Pygmy," I could imagine my new neighbors whispering as I walked down the street. "Hangs him plain as day in the corner of his living room, next to the musket he was shot with."

I'd love to be talked about in this way, but how did the taxidermist know? Plenty of people must go into his store, ask for a kitten or a seagull or whatever, and walk out five minutes later knowing nothing about the human parts. Why show *me* the head in the grocery bag? As for the arm, how had he known I'd been dying to touch it? I hadn't said anything one way or the other, so what was the giveaway?

At the station I went through the turnstile and stood on the platform until a train arrived. The owl wasn't heavy—in fact it was surprisingly light—but the box was cumbersome, so I was happy to find a seat. At our first stop, a teenage girl in a school uniform got on and took the spot across from me. Deal with a kid her age today and the thought of her head winding up behind some shop counter in a plastic bag might not be all that troubling. I mean, the mouths on some of them! That said, it shouldn't be just *any* kid that age. The one the taxidermist showed me, for instance—what was *her* story?

Fourteen-year-olds existed four hundred years ago, but teenagers, with their angst and rebelliousness, their rage and Ritalin and very own version of *Vogue* magazine, are a fairly recent construct. In the seventeenth-century jungles of Peru, a girl that age would have babies already. Half her life would probably be over, and that's if she was lucky. To have your chopped-off head preserved and then wind up in a Tesco bag some six thousand miles away—that was the indignity. Tesco! At least the arm was in a Waitrose bag.

It bothered me that the bag bothered me more than the head did, but what are you going to do? A person doesn't consciously choose what he focuses on. Those things choose you, and, once they do, nothing, it seems, can shake them. Find someone with a similar eye, and Christmas shopping is a breeze. I can always spot something for my sisters Gretchen and Amy. The three of us can walk into a crowded party and all zoom in on the person who's missing a finger, or who has one regular-size ear and one significantly smaller one, while my sister Lisa will pick up something else entirely.

Hugh and I don't notice the same things either. That's how he can be with me. Everything the taxidermist saw is invisible to him: my superficiality, my juvenile fascination with the abnormal, my willingness to accept and sometimes even celebrate evil—point this out, and he'll say, "David? *My* David? Oh no. He's not like that at all."

A person who's that out of it deserves both an owl *and* chocolate, so I got off the train at Piccadilly Circus and picked him up a box. Then I caught a bus and hurried toward home, thinking about love, and death, and about that throat, so elegant in its detail, which was, no doubt, awaiting me.

Now We Are Five

In late May 2013, a few weeks shy of her fiftieth birthday, my youngest sister, Tiffany, committed suicide. She was living in a room in a beat-up house on the hard end of Somerville, Massachusetts, and had been dead, the coroner guessed, for at least five days before her door was battered down. I was given the news over a white courtesy phone while at the Dallas airport. Then, because my plane to Baton Rouge was boarding and I wasn't sure what else to do, I got on it. The following morning, I boarded another plane, this one to Atlanta, and the day after that I flew to Nashville, thinking all the while about my ever-shrinking family. A person expects his parents to die. But a sibling? I felt I'd lost the identity I'd enjoyed since 1968, when my brother was born. "Six kids!" people would say. "How do your poor folks manage?"

There were a lot of big families in the neighborhood I grew up in. Every other house was a fiefdom, so I never gave it much thought until I became an adult and my friends started having children. One or two seemed reasonable, but anything beyond that struck me as outrageous. A couple Hugh and I knew in Normandy would occasionally come to dinner with their wrecking crew of three, and when they'd leave several hours later every last part of me would feel violated.

Take those kids, double them, and subtract the cable TV: that's what my parents had to deal with. Now, though, there weren't six, only five. "And you can't really say, 'There *used* to be six,'" I told my sister Lisa. "It just makes people uncomfortable."

I recalled a father and son I'd met in California a few years back. "So are there other children?" I asked.

"There are," the man said. "Three who are living and a daughter, Chloe, who died before she was born, eighteen years ago."

That's not fair, I remember thinking. Because, I mean, what's a person supposed to do with *that?*

Compared to most forty-nine-year-olds, or even most forty-nine-*month*-olds, Tiffany didn't have much. She did leave a will, though. In it, she decreed that we, her family, could not have her body or attend her memorial service.

"So put *that* in your pipe and smoke it," our mother would have said. A few days after getting the news, my sister Amy drove to Somerville with a friend and collected two boxes of things from Tiffany's room: family photos, many of which had been ripped into pieces; comment cards from a neighborhood grocery store; notebooks; receipts. The bed, a mattress on the floor, had been taken away and a large industrial fan had been set up. Amy snapped some pictures while she was there and, individually and in groups, those of us left studied them for clues: a paper plate on a dresser that had several drawers missing, a phone number written on a wall, a collection of mop handles, each one a different color, arranged like cattails in a barrel painted green.

Six months before our sister killed herself, I had made plans for us all to gather at a beach house on Emerald Isle, off the coast of North Carolina. My family used to vacation there every summer, but after my mother died we stopped going, not because we lost interest but because it was she who always made the arrangements and, more important, paid for it. The place I found with the help of my sister-in-law, Kathy, had six bedrooms and a small swimming pool. Our week-long rental period began on Saturday, June 8, and we arrived to find a delivery woman standing in the driveway with seven pounds of seafood, a sympathy gift sent by friends. "They's slaw in there too," she said, handing over the bags.

In the past, when my family rented a cottage, my sisters and I would crowd the door like puppies around a food dish. Our father would unlock it, and we'd tear through the house claiming rooms. I always picked the biggest one facing the ocean, and just as I'd start to unpack, my parents would enter and tell me that this was *theirs*. "I mean, just who the hell do you think you are?" my father would ask. He and my mother would move in, and I would get booted to what was called "the maid's room." It was always on the ground level, a kind of dank shed next to where the car was parked. There was never an interior stairway leading to the upper floor. Instead, I had to take the outside steps and, more often than not, knock on the locked front door like a beggar hoping to be invited in.

"What do *you* want?" my sisters would ask. "I want to come inside."

"That's funny," Lisa, the eldest, would say to the others, who were gathered like disciples around her. "Did you hear something, a whining sound? What is it that makes a noise like that? A hermit crab? A little sea slug?" Normally there was a social divide between the three oldest and three youngest children in my family. Lisa, Gretchen, and I treated the others like servants and did very well for ourselves. At the beach, though, all bets were off, and it was just upstairs against downstairs, meaning everyone against me.

This time, because I was paying, I got to choose the best room. Amy moved in next door, and my brother, Paul; his wife; and their ten-year-old daughter, Maddy, took the spot next to her. That was it for oceanfront. The others arrived later and had to take the leftovers. Lisa's room faced the street, as did my father's. Gretchen's faced the street and was intended for someone who was paralyzed. Hanging from the ceiling were electric pulleys designed to lift a harnessed body into and out of bed.

Unlike the cottages of our youth, this one did not have a maid's room. It was too new and fancy for that, as were the homes that surrounded it. Traditionally, the island houses were on stilts, but more and more often now the ground floors are filled in. They all have beachy names and are painted beachy colors, but most of those built after Hurricane Fran hit the coast in 1996 are three stories tall and look almost suburban. This place was vast and airy. The kitchen table sat twelve, and there was not one but *two* dishwashers. The pictures were ocean-related: seascapes and lighthouses, all with the airborne Vs that are shorthand for seagull. A sampler on the living room wall read OLD SHELLERS NEVER DIE, THEY SIMPLY CONCH OUT. On the round clock beside it, the numbers lay in an indecipherable heap, as if they'd come unglued. Just above them were printed the words WHO CARES?

This was what we found ourselves saying whenever anyone asked the time.

"Who cares?"

*

The day before we arrived at the beach, Tiffany's obituary ran in the *Raleigh News & Observer*. It was submitted by Gretchen, who stated that our sister had passed away peacefully at her home. This made it sound as if she were very old and had a house. But what else could you do? People were leaving responses on the paper's website, and one fellow wrote that Tiffany used to come into the video store where he worked in Somerville. When his glasses broke, she offered him a pair she had found while foraging for art supplies in somebody's trash can. He said she also gave him a *Playboy* magazine from the 1960s that included a photo spread titled "The Ass Menagerie."

This was fascinating, as we didn't really know our sister very well. All of us had pulled away from the family at some point in our lives—we'd had to in order to forge our own identities, to go from being *a* Sedaris to our own specific Sedaris. Tiffany, though, stayed away. She might promise to come home for Christmas, but at the last minute there'd always be some excuse: she missed her plane, she had to work. The same would happen with our summer vacations. "The rest of us managed to make it," I'd say, aware of how old and guilt-trippy I sounded.

We'd all be disappointed by her absence, though for different reasons. Even if you weren't getting along with Tiffany at the time, you couldn't deny the show she put on—the dramatic entrances, the nonstop professional-grade insults, the chaos she'd inevitably leave in her wake. One day she'd throw a dish at you, and the next she'd create a mosaic made of the shards. When allegiances with one brother or sister flamed out, she'd take up with someone else. At no time did she get along with everybody, but there was always someone she was in contact with. Toward the end it was Lisa, but before that we'd all had our turn.

The last time she joined us on Emerald Isle was in 1986. "And, even then, she left after three days," Gretchen reminded us.

As kids, we spent our beach time swimming. Then we became teenagers and devoted ourselves to tanning. There's a certain kind of talk that takes place when you're lying, dazed, in the sun, and I've always been partial to it. On the first afternoon of our most recent trip, we laid out one of the bedspreads we'd had as children and arranged ourselves side by side on it, trading stories about Tiffany.

"What about the Halloween she spent on that Army base?"

"And the time she showed up at Dad's birthday party with a black eye?"

"I remember this girl she met years ago at a party," I began when my turn came. "She'd been talking about facial scars and how terrible it would be to have one, so Tiffany said, 'I have a little scar on my face and I don't think it's so awful.'

"'Well,' the girl said, 'you would if you were pretty.'"

Amy laughed and rolled over onto her stomach. "Oh, that's a good line!"

I rearranged the towel I was using as a pillow. "Isn't it, though?" Coming from someone else the story might have been upsetting, but not being pretty was never one of Tiffany's problems, especially when she was in her twenties and thirties, and men tumbled helpless before her.

"Funny," I said, "but I don't remember a scar on her face."

I stayed in the sun too long that day and got a burn on my forehead. That was basically it for me and the beach blanket. I made brief appearances for the rest of the week, stopping to dry off after a swim, but mainly I spent my days on a bike, cycling up and down the coast and thinking about what had happened. While the rest of us seem to get along effortlessly, with Tiffany it always felt like work. She and I usually made up after arguing, but our last fight took it out of me, and at the time of her death we hadn't spoken in eight years. During that period, I regularly found myself near Somerville, and though I'd always toy with the idea of contacting her, I never did, despite my father's encouragement. Meanwhile I'd get reports from him and Lisa: Tiffany had lost her apartment, had gone on disability, had moved into a room found for her by a social service agency. Perhaps she was more forthcoming with her friends, but her family got things only in bits and pieces. She didn't talk *with* us so much as *at* us, great blocks of speech that were by turns funny, astute, and so contradictory it was hard to connect the sentence you were hearing with the one that preceded it. Before we stopped speaking I could always tell when she was on the phone. I'd walk into the house and hear Hugh say, "Uh-huh ... uh-huh ... uh-huh ... "

In addition to the two boxes that Amy had filled in Somerville, she also brought down our sister's 1978 ninth-grade yearbook. Among the messages inscribed by her class-mates was the following, written by someone who had drawn a marijuana leaf beside her name:

Tiffany. You are a one-of-a-kind girl so stay that way you unique ass. I'm only sorry we couldn't have partied more together. This school sux to hell. Stay
- *cool*
- *stoned*
- *drunk*
- *fucked-up*

Check your ass later.

Then there's:

Tiffany,
   I'm looking forward to getting high with you
this summer.

Tiffany,
   Call me sometime this summer and we'll go out and
get blitzed.

A few weeks after these messages were written, Tiffany ran away and was subsequently sent to a disciplinary institution in Maine called Élan. According to what she told us later, it was a horrible place. She returned home in 1980, having spent two years there, and from that point on none of us can recall a conversation in which she did not mention it. She blamed the family for sending her off, but we, her siblings, had nothing to do with it. Paul, for instance, was ten when she left. I was twenty-one. For a year, I sent her monthly letters. Then she wrote and told me to stop. As for my parents, there were only so many times they could apologize. "We had other kids," they said in their defense. "You think we could let the world stop on account of any one of you?"

We were at the beach for three days before Lisa and our father, who is now ninety, joined us. Being on the island meant missing the spinning classes he takes in Raleigh, so I found a fitness center not far from the rental cottage, and every afternoon he and I would spend some time there. On the way over we'd talk to each other, but as soon as we mounted our stationary bikes we'd each retreat in to our own thoughts. It was a small place, not very lively. A mute television oversaw the room, tuned to the Weather Channel and reminding us that there's always a catastrophe somewhere or other, always someone flooded from his home or running for his life from a funnel-shaped cloud. Toward the end of the week, I came upon my father in Amy's room, sifting through the photos that Tiffany had destroyed. In his hand was a fragment of my mother's head with a patch of blue sky behind her. *Under what circumstances had this been ripped up?* I wondered. It seemed such a melodramatic gesture, like throwing a glass against a wall. Something someone in a movie would do.

"Just awful," my father whispered. "A person's life reduced to one lousy box." I put my hand on his shoulder. "Actually there are two of them."

He corrected himself. "Two lousy boxes."

One afternoon on Emerald Isle, we all rode to the Food Lion for groceries. I was in the produce department, looking at red onions, when my brother sneaked up from behind and let loose with a loud "Achoo," this while whipping a bouquet of wet parsley through the air. I felt the spray on the back of my neck and froze, thinking a very sick stranger had just sneezed on me. It's a neat trick, but he also doused the Indian woman who was standing to my left. She was wearing a blood-colored sari, so she got it on her bare arm as well as her neck and the lower part of her back.

"Sorry, man," Paul said when she turned around, horrified. "I was just playing a joke on my brother."

The woman had many thin bracelets on, and they jangled as she brushed her hand against the back of her head.

"You called her 'man,'" I said to him after she walked off. "For real?" he asked.

Amy mimicked him perfectly. "For real?"

Over the phone, my brother, like me, is often mistaken for a woman. As we continued shopping, he told us that his van had recently broken down and that when he called for a tow truck the dispatcher said, "We'll be right out, sweetie." He lowered a watermelon into the cart and turned to his daughter. "Maddy's got a daddy who talks like a lady, but she don't care, do she?" Giggling, she punched him in the stomach, and I was struck by how comfortable the two of them are with each other. Our father was a figure of authority, while Paul is more of a playmate.

When we went to the beach as children, on or about the fourth day, our father would say, "Wouldn't it be nice to buy a cottage down here?" We'd get our hopes up, and then he would bring practical concerns into it. They weren't petty—buying a house that will eventually get blown away by a hurricane probably isn't the best way to spend your money—but still we wanted one desperately. I told myself when I was young that one day *I* would buy a beach house and that it would be everyone's, as long as they followed my draconian rules and never stopped thanking me for it. Thus it was that on Wednesday morning, midway through our vacation, Hugh and I contacted a real estate agent named Phyllis, who took us around to look at available properties. On Friday afternoon, we made an offer on an oceanfront cottage not far from the one we were renting, and before sunset our bid was accepted. I made the announcement at the dinner table and got the reaction I had expected.

"Now, wait a minute," my father said. "You need to think clearly here."

"I already have," I told him.

"OK, then, how old is the roof? How many times has it been replaced in the last ten years?"

"When can we move in?" Gretchen asked.

Lisa wanted to know if she could bring her dogs, and Amy asked what the house was named.

"Right now it's called Fantastic Place," I told her, "but we're going to change it." I used to think the ideal name for a beach house was the Ship Shape. Now, though, I had a better idea. "We're going to call it the Sea Section."

My father put down his hamburger. "Oh no, you're not."

"But it's perfect," I argued. "The name's supposed to be beachy, and if it's a pun, all the better."

I brought up a cottage we'd seen earlier in the day called Dune Our Thing, and my father winced. "How about naming it Tiffany?" he said.

Our silence translated to: *Let's pretend we didn't hear that.*

He picked his hamburger back up. "I think it's a great idea. The perfect way to pay our respects."

"If that's the case we could name it after Mom," I told him. "Or half after Tiffany and half after Mom. But it's a house, not a tombstone, and it wouldn't fit in with the names of the other houses."

"Aw, baloney," my father said. "Fitting in—that's not who we are. That's not what we're about."

Paul interrupted to nominate the Conch Sucker.

Amy's suggestion had the word "Seaman" in it, and Gretchen's was even dirtier.

"What's wrong with the name it already has?" Lisa asked. "No, no, no," my father said, forgetting, I think, that this wasn't his decision. A few days later, after the buyer's remorse had kicked in, I'd wonder if I hadn't bought the house as a way of saying, *See, it's just that easy. No hemming and hawing. No asking to look at the septic tank. Rather, you make your family happy and iron out the details later.* The cottage we bought is two stories tall and was built in 1978. It's on proper stilts and has two rear decks, one above the other, overlooking the ocean. It was rented to vacationers until late September, but Phyllis allowed us to drop by and show it to the family the following morning, after we checked out of the house we'd been staying in. A place always looks different—worse, most often—after you've made the commitment to buy it, so while the others raced up and down the stairs, claiming their future bedrooms, I held my nose to a vent and caught a whiff of mildew. The sale included the furniture, so I also made an inventory of the Barcaloungers and massive TVs I would eventually be getting rid of, along with the shell-patterned bedspreads and cushions with anchors on them. "For our beach house, I want to have a train theme," I announced. "Trains on the curtains, trains on the towels—we're going to go all out."

"Oh brother," my father moaned.

We sketched a plan to return for Thanksgiving, and after saying goodbye to one another, my family splintered into groups and headed off to our respective homes. There'd been a breeze at the beach house, but once we left the island the air grew still. As the heat intensified, so did the general feeling of depression. Throughout the sixties and seventies, the road back to Raleigh took us past Smithfield and a billboard on the outskirts of town that read WELCOME TO KLAN COUNTRY. This time we took a different route, one my brother recommended. Hugh drove, and my father sat beside him. I slumped down in the backseat next to Amy, and every time I raised my head, I'd see the same soybean field or low-slung cinder-block building we'd seemingly passed twenty minutes earlier.

We'd been on the road for a little more than an hour when we stopped at a farmers' market. Inside an open-air pavilion, a woman offered complimentary plates of hummus served with a corn and black-bean salad, so we each accepted one and took seats on a bench. Twenty years earlier, the most a place like this might have offered was fried okra. Now there was organic coffee and artisanal goat cheese. Above our heads hung a sign that read WHISPERING DOVE RANCH, and just as I thought that we might be anywhere, I noticed that the music piped through the speakers was Christian—the new kind, which says that Jesus is awesome.

Hugh brought my father a plastic cup of water. "You OK, Lou?"

"Fine," my father answered.

"Why do you think she did it?" I asked as we stepped back into the sunlight. For that's all any of us were thinking, *had been* thinking, since we got the news. Mustn't Tiffany have hoped that whatever pills she'd taken wouldn't be strong enough and that her failed attempt would lead her back into our fold? How could anyone purposefully leave us—*us*, of all people? This is how I thought of it, for though I've often lost faith in myself, I've never lost faith in my family, in my certainty that we are fundamentally better than everyone else. It's an archaic belief, one I haven't seriously reconsidered since my late teens, but still I hold it. Ours is the only club I'd ever wanted to be a member of, so I couldn't imagine quitting. Backing off for a year or two was understandable, but to want out so badly that you'd take your own life?

"I don't know that it had anything to do with us," my father said. But how could it have not? Doesn't the blood of every suicide splash back on our faces?

At the far end of the parking lot was a stand selling reptiles. In giant tanks were two pythons, each as big around as a fire hose. The heat seemed to suit them, and I watched as they raised their heads, testing the screened ceilings. Beside the snakes was a low pen corralling an alligator with its mouth banded shut. It wasn't full-grown but perhaps an adolescent, around three feet long and grumpy-looking. A girl had stuck her arm through the wire and was stroking the thing's back while it glared, seething. "I'd like to buy everything here just so I could kill it," I said.

My father mopped his forehead with a Kleenex. "I'm with you, brother."

When we were young and would set off for the beach, I'd look out the window at all the landmarks we drove by—the Purina silo on the south side of Raleigh, the Klan billboard—knowing that when we passed them a week later, I'd be miserable. Our vacation over, now there'd be nothing to live for until Christmas. My life is much fuller than it was back then, yet this return felt no different. "What time is it?" I asked Amy.

And instead of saying "Who cares?" she snapped, "You tell me. You're the one with a watch on."

At the airport a few hours later, I picked sand from my pockets and thought of our final moments at the beach house I'd bought. I was on the front porch with Phyllis, who had just locked the door, and we turned to see the others in the driveway below us. "So is that one of your sisters?" she asked, pointing to Gretchen.

"It is," I said. "And so are the two women standing on either side of her."

"Then you've got your brother," she observed. "That makes five—wow. Now, *that's* a big family."

I looked at the sunbaked cars we would soon be climbing into—furnaces, every one of them—and said, "Yes. It certainly is."

A House Divided

Because I'd accumulated so many miles, they bumped me to first class on the flight from Atlanta to Raleigh. I had assumed that our plane would be on the small side, but instead, owing to Thanksgiving and the great number of travelers, it was full-size. I was seated in the second row, in front of a woman who looked to be in her early sixties and was letting her hair fade from dyed red to gray. After she'd settled in she started a conversation with the fellow beside her. That's how I learned that she lived in Costa Rica. "It's on account of my husband," she said. "He's military, well, *retired* military, though you never really leave the Marine Corps, do you?"

She started explaining what had taken her from North Carolina to Central America, but then the flight attendant came to take a drink order from the guy next to me, and I missed it. Just as I was tuning back in, a man across the aisle tried to open his overhead bin. It was stuck for some reason and he pounded on it, saying to anyone who would listen, "This is like Obamacare: broken."

Several of the passengers around me laughed, and I noted their faces, vowing that in the event of a crisis, I would not help lead them to an emergency exit. *You people are on your own,* I thought, knowing that if anything bad *did* happen, it would likely be one of them who'd save me. It would be just my luck. I had passed judgment, so fate would force me to eat my words.

After we took off from Atlanta I pulled out my notebook, half making a list of things we'd need for Thanksgiving and half listening to the woman behind me, who continued to talk throughout the entire flight. I guessed she was drinking, though I could have been wrong. Perhaps she was always this loud and adamant. "I never said I'd spend the rest of my *life* there, that's not what I meant *at all.*"

It was dark by the time we landed in Raleigh, and as we taxied to the gate, one of the flight attendants made an announcement. The "remain seated until the FASTEN SEAT BELT sign has been turned off" part was to be expected, but then she added that we had some very special passengers on board.

Oh no, I thought. *Please don't embarrass me.* I was just wondering who the other important person might be when she said, "With us today is the outstanding soccer team from ... " She named a high school in the Triangle Area and concluded with, "Let's give them all a great big hand!"

The woman behind me whooped and cheered, and when no one joined her, she raised her voice, shouting, "You people are ... *assholes!* I mean, what the hell, you can't even applaud for your own *teenagers?*"

I'd meant to but figured the team was back in coach. They wouldn't have heard me one way or the other, so what difference did it make?

"Pathetic," the woman spat. "Too wrapped up in your ...

smartphones and iPads to congratulate a group of high school athletes."

You couldn't say she hadn't nailed us. Still I had to bite my hand to keep from laughing. It's so funny to be called an asshole by someone who doesn't know you, but then again knows you so perfectly.

"See that woman?" I said to Hugh when he met me at the baggage claim a few minutes later.

I told him what had happened on the plane, and he folded his arms across his chest, the way he always does before lecturing me. "She was right, you know. You should have applauded."

"We've been apart for two months," I reminded him. "Would it kill you to take my side in this?"

He apologized, but after I'd wrestled my bag off the carousel and we'd started toward the parking lot, he added quietly, but not so quietly that I couldn't hear him, "You really should have clapped." From the airport we drove to my brother Paul's. There we met up with my sister Gretchen, who had a cast on her right forearm and held it aloft, like someone perpetually being sworn in. "It helps ease the pain," she explained.

I hadn't seen Gretchen since the previous spring and was startled by her appearance. For as long as I could remember she'd worn her hair long, and though it still fell to below her shoulder blades in the back, the top was now cropped and stood from the crown of her head like the fur of a graying German shepherd. Odder still, she had a sun visor on. "Since when have you had this mullet?" I asked.

Only when she lifted it off did I realize she was wearing a cap, the sort sold in joke shops. "The hair is attached to the top of it. See? I got it at the beach last month."

I hadn't been to our house on Emerald Isle—the Sea

Section—since we'd bought it five months earlier, though Hugh had. He'd flown over in late September to start making improvements. Gretchen joined him for a few days shortly before Halloween and fell into a rut while walking on the beach. That's how she broke her arm. "Can you believe it?" she asked. "No one has worse luck than me."

When there's no traffic, it's a two-and-a-half-hour drive from Raleigh to Emerald Isle. We left at around eight p.m., and on the way, I asked Gretchen about her job. She works as a horticulturalist for the city of Raleigh and had recently discovered a campsite in one of its larger parks. That's common enough, but this one was occupied by someone we once knew. His name was familiar, but I couldn't picture his face until Gretchen put him in context. "He used to come over to the house and hang out with Mom."

"Oh, right," I said.

Kids like to believe that their parents will get lonely after they leave the house, but I think my mother actually did. She delighted in her children and always enjoyed talking to our friends and the people we were going out with. "Why don't you invite Jeff to dinner?" I remember her asking Gretchen one night in the late seventies.

"Because we broke up a month ago and I've been in my room crying ever since?"

"Well, he still needs to *eat*," my mother said.

The fellow who wound up living in a city park—Kevin, I'll call him—started dropping by in the early eighties. His parents and mine owned some rental property together, and over the years both he and I performed odd jobs there. I remembered him as directionless and guessed from what my sister told me that he pretty much stayed that way. Still, it seemed incredible to me that something like this could happen, for we were middle-class and I'd been raised to believe that our social status inoculated us against severe misfortune. A person might be *broke* from time to time—who wasn't?—but you could never be poor the way that *actual* poor people were: poor with lice and missing teeth. Your genes would reject it. Slip too far beneath the surface, and wouldn't your family resuscitate you with a loan or rehab or whatever it was you needed to get back on your feet? Then there'd be friends, hopefully ones who went to college and might at the very least view you as a project, the thing they'd renovate after the kitchen was finished.

At what point had I realized that class couldn't save you, that addiction or mental illness didn't care whether you'd taken piano lessons or spent a summer in Europe? Which drunk or junkie or unmedicated schizophrenic was I crossing the street to avoid when I put it all together? I didn't know what the story was with Kevin. The two of us had had every advantage, yet now he was living in a thicket three miles from the house he grew up in.

My siblings and I used to worry that once our father was gone a similar fate might befall our sister Tiffany, who had committed suicide six months earlier. Like all of us, she received an inheritance a few years after our mother died. It wasn't a fortune, but it was certainly more than I had ever seen. The money arrived just after I really needed it, at a moment when, for the first time in my adult life, I was finally on my feet. I paid off my student loan with a portion of it. My father wanted me to invest the rest, but I didn't want the *idea* of money, I wanted the real thing, so I parked it in my checking account and would go to an ATM sometimes twice a day just to look at my balance on the screen. A year earlier the most I'd had was a hundred dollars. Now this.

It was interesting to see what we all did with our inheritance.

Pragmatic Lisa put her check in the bank. Gretchen moved south and saw to some bills while Amy and Paul essentially spent their money on candy. Tiffany was the only one who quit her job, thinking, I guess, that she was set. Within two years she was broke, but rather than rejoining the workforce, she decided that money was evil, as were most of the people who had it. She canceled her checking account and started bartering, exchanging a day's work for a carton of cigarettes or a bag of groceries. At night she'd go through people's trash cans, looking for things she could sell. It's like she saw poverty as an accomplishment. "I'll be out at one in the morning, knee-deep in a Dumpster and elbowing aside some immigrant Haitian lady for the good stuff," she boasted once when I visited her in Somerville.

"Maybe the Haitian woman *has* to be there," I said. "She has nothing at her disposal, while you have an education. You had braces on your teeth. You speak good English." My argument was an old and stodgy one: the best thing you can do for the poor is avoid joining their ranks, thus competing with them for limited goods and services.

On that same visit Tiffany explained that poor people refuse to answer surveys. "When census takers come to our doors, we ignore them." She spoke the way a tribal leader might to a visiting anthropologist. "We Pawnees grind our corn with a rock!"

Every time I visited, her apartment was more of a wreck, not just messy but filthy. "How can you live like this?" I asked the last time I was there.

"We poor people don't have the energy to clean up after ourselves," she told me.

After she was evicted, she lived in a series of single rooms, with people just as badly off as herself. According to Tiffany, the only thing wrong with her was her back—that's why at the age of forty-three she went on disability, she said. Since when, though, do they prescribe lithium and Klonopin for back pain? If she'd been more forthright, we could have put her behavior in context, could have said, when she tested our patience, "That's her illness talking." As it was, it didn't add up. "Why can't a grown woman hold a job?" we wondered. "Why does she have so many restraining orders against people?"

Tiffany would have inherited money from our father someday, though she likely would have burned right through it. "You want a car?" she'd have said, perhaps to someone she met in a parking lot. "I'll buy you a fucking Bronco or whatever. Is that what you want?"

Word would have gotten out that some lady was buying people Broncos, and in no time she'd have been penniless again and feeling just fine about it.

An hour before arriving at the beach, Hugh stopped at a fast-food place called Hardee's so I could get a coffee. The town we were in was small and grim, and the restaurant was deserted except for us. Inside the front door stood a Christmas tree, over-decorated in a majestic combination of red and gold. "How long has this been up?" I asked the black woman behind the counter.

She scratched at the tattoos on her left forearm, initials that looked like they'd been done at home with a sewing needle. "Since last Tuesday maybe?" She turned to the fellow cleaning the grill. "Do that sound right?"

"Just about," he said.

"Will you have a tree at home?" I asked. "Have you put it up yet?"

This is the sort of thing that drives Hugh crazy—*What does it matter if her Christmas tree is up?*—but there was no one in line behind me, and I was genuinely curious.

"I think it's too early," the woman said. "My kids is all excited for one, but we ain't even had Thanksgiving yet."

Gretchen ran her good hand over the false hair on top of her head. "Will you cook a turkey on Thursday or go for something else?"

"Are you two happy now?" Hugh asked when we finally returned to the car. "Need to go back in and learn what everyone's doing for New Year's, or do you think we can leave?"

Gretchen propped up her broken arm on the narrow window ledge. "If he thinks *we're* bad, he should spend more time with Lisa."

"That's true," I agreed. "Lisa's the master. I left her at a Starbucks for ninety seconds last year, and when I returned the woman behind the counter was saying to her, 'My gynecologist told me that exact same thing.'"

I normally don't believe in drinking coffee in the car. Most often, I spill more than I swallow, but without it I'd have fallen asleep and then had to revive myself once we reached the house. It was after eleven when we arrived, and I was pleasantly surprised by all the changes. The place we bought is two stories tall and divided down the middle into equal-size units. You can pass back and forth between one half and the other by way of a hotel-style connecting door in the living room, but it's inconvenient if you're upstairs. The two kitchens are another problem, as we really only need one. Our initial idea was to knock down some walls and transform it into a single six-bedroom home. Then I recalled our last trip to the beach and the number of times I found my brother lying on the sofa with his shoes on, and decided that two separate halves was probably a good idea. The left side, which was softly lit and decorated with carefully chosen midcentury furniture, was mine and Hugh's, while the junky right side was for everyone else. Of course other people could stay in our half, but only when we were there to monitor and scold them.

Because everyone was coming for Thanksgiving, the house was going to be full. The family was arriving in dribs and drabs, so for the first night it was just the three of us. On the second day, late in the afternoon, Lisa pulled up. I helped her unload her car, and then we took a walk on the beach. It was cold enough to see our breath, and a strong wind was blowing. "Did I tell you I got Tiffany's toxicology report?" she asked a while after we'd left the house. "They also sent me her death certificate, and apparently—"

At that moment a Labrador retriever bounded up, tail wagging, a middle-aged woman in a baseball cap trotting behind it. "Brandy, *no*," she scolded, adding as she unfurled her leash, "I'm sorry."

"For what?" Lisa gathered the dog's head in her hands. "You're beautiful, aren't you?" she trilled in the melodic voice she uses for things with tails. "Yes, you are, and you know it." She turned to the owner. "How old is she?"

"Two years this February," the woman said.

"I have one that age," Lisa told her. "And she's a real handful."

I have no patience for this kind of talk and turned to face the ocean, waiting for the conversation to end. Hopefully then I could learn what our sister had used to kill herself with. We figured she had taken pills—Klonopin, most likely—and though it technically didn't matter if she'd mixed it with other things, we still wanted to know.

Behind me, Lisa was telling the strange woman that the Newfoundland water dog she had before the one she has now died after swallowing all her husband Bob's high blood pressure medication.

"My God," the woman said. "That must have been awful!"

"Oh, it was," Lisa told her. "We just felt so guilty."

The woman with the Labrador wished us a happy Thanksgiving, and as she headed down the beach, Lisa continued her story. "So they sent me the death certificate, and the cause isn't listed as a drug overdose but as asphyxiation."

"I don't get it," I said.

She sniffed her hands for dog and then stuffed them into her coat pockets. "After taking the Klonopin, Tiffany put a plastic bag over her head." Lisa paused a moment to let that sink in. "I wrote to the state trooper who found her body and sent him a picture of her in her twenties, the pretty one we ran with her obituary. I just wanted him to know she was more than what he walked in on."

I've always liked to think that before killing myself I'd take the time to really mess with people. By this I mean that I'd leave them things, and write letters, nice ones, apologizing for my actions and reassuring them that there was nothing they could have said or done to change my mind. In the fantasy I'd leave money to those who'd have never expected it. *Who's he?* they'd wonder after opening the envelope. It might be a Polish lifeguard at the pool I used to go to in London, or a cashier I was quietly fond of. Only lately do I realize how ridiculous this is. When you're in the state that my sister was in, and that most people are in when they take their own lives, you're not thinking of anything beyond your own pain. Thus the plastic bag—the maximizer, as it were—the thing a person reaches for after their first attempt at an overdose fails and they wake up sick a day later thinking, *I can't even kill myself right.*

It's hard to find a bag without writing on it—the name of a store, most often. LOWE'S, it might read. SAFEWAY. TRUE VALUE. Does a person go through a number of them before making a selection, or, as I suspect, will any bag do, regardless of the ironic statement it might make? This is what was going through my mind when Lisa stopped walking and turned to me, asking, "Will you do me a favor?"

"Anything," I said, just so grateful to have her alive and beside me.

She held out her foot. "Will you tie my shoe?"

"Well ... sure," I said. "But can you tell me why?"

She sighed. "My pants are tight and I don't feel like bending over."

I knelt down into the damp sand and did as she'd asked. It was almost dark, and as I stood back up, I looked at the long line of houses stretching to the pier. One of them belonged to us, but I couldn't have begun to guess which one it was. Judging by distance was no help either, as I had no idea how long we'd been walking. Lisa hadn't spent any more time at the Sea Section than I had, so she wasn't much help. "Does our place have one deck or two?" she asked.

"Two?" I said. "Unless it has only one?"

The houses before us were far from identical. They were painted every color you could think of, yet in the weak light, reduced to basic shapes, their resemblance was striking. All were wooden, with prominent picture windows. All had staircases leading to the beach, and all had the air of a second home, one devoted to leisure rather than struggle. They likely didn't contain many file cabinets, but if you were after puzzles or golf clubs or board games, you'd come to the right place. The people in the houses looked similar as well. We could see them in their kitchens and family rooms, watching TV or standing before open refrigerators. They were white, for the most part, and conservative, the sort of people we'd grown up with at the country club, the kind who'd have sat in the front of the plane and laughed when the man across the aisle compared his broken overhead bin to Obamacare. That said, we could have knocked on any of these doors, explained our situation, and received help. "These folks have a house but don't know which one it is!" I could imagine a homeowner shouting over his shoulder into the next room. "Remember when that happened to us?"

It's silly, but after a while I started to panic, thinking, I guess, that we could die out there. In the cold. Looking for one of my houses. I was just condemning Lisa for not bringing her phone when I spotted the broken fishing rod tied to our railing. I'd noticed it earlier that day and had made a mental note to remove it. "Paul put it there so he'd be able to tell which house was ours," Gretchen had told me.

I'd said, "Well, we'll see about *that*." Now here I was, seeing about it.

Hugh was in the kitchen on our side of the house, making soup, when we walked in. "We got lost!" Lisa told him. "Were you worried about us?"

He dried his hands on his apron and tried to pretend he'd known we were out. "Was I ever!" The air smelled pleasantly of chicken stock and onions. On the radio it was announced that the president would be pardoning a turkey and that its name was Popcorn.

"That's nice," Lisa said.

While she went to her room to change, I walked through the connecting door and into the second kitchen. There I found Gretchen standing at the counter before a bowl of sliced apples.

"Did Lisa by any chance tell you about Tiffany?" I asked. "The plastic bag, you mean?" Gretchen nodded. "She told me on the phone last week. I try not to think of it, but it's pretty much all I *can* think about. Our own sister, ending up that way."

I walked to the window and looked at the sky, which had

now gone from bruise-colored to black. "Someone told me," I said, "that in Japan, if you commit suicide by throwing yourself in front of a train, your family gets fined the equivalent of eighty thousand dollars for all the inconvenience you caused." From behind me, I could hear Gretchen slicing more apples. "Of course," I continued, "if your family was the whole reason you were killing yourself, I suppose it would just be an added incentive."

Out on the beach I could see the beam of a flashlight skittering across the sand. Someone was walking past the house, maybe to their own place, or perhaps to one that they were renting for the long holiday weekend. If it was smaller than the Sea Section, or less well positioned, they maybe looked up into our gaily lit windows and resented us, wondering, as we often did ourselves these days, what we had done to deserve all this.

The Perfect Fit

I'm not sure how it is in small families, but in large ones relationships tend to shift over time. You might be best friends with one brother or sister, then two years later it might be someone else. Then it's likely to change again, and again after that. It doesn't mean that you've fallen out with the person you used to be closest to but that you've merged into someone else's lane, or had him or her merge into yours. Trios form, then morph into quartets before splitting into teams of two. The beauty of it is that it's always changing.

Twice in 2014, I went to Tokyo with my sister Amy. I'd been seven times already, so was able to lead her to all the best places, by which I mean stores. When we returned in January 2016, it made sense to bring our sister Gretchen with us. Hugh was there as well, and while he's a definite presence, he didn't figure into the family dynamic. Mates, to my sisters and me, are seen mainly as shadows of the people they're involved with. They move. They're visible in direct sunlight. But because they don't have access to our emotional buttons—because they can't make us twelve again, or five, and screaming—they don't really count as players.

Normally in Tokyo we rent an apartment and stay for a week. This time, though, we got a whole house. The neighborhood it was in—Ebisu—is home to one of our favorite shops, Kapital. The clothes they sell are new but appear to have been previously worn, perhaps by someone who was shot or stabbed and then thrown off a boat. Everything looks as if it has been pulled from the evidence rack at a murder trial. I don't know how they do it. Most distressed clothing seems obviously fake, but not theirs, for some reason. Do they put it in a dryer with broken glass and rusty steak knives? Do they drag it behind a tank over a still-smoldering battlefield? How do they get the cuts and stains so ... right?

If I had to use one word to describe Kapital's clothing, I'd be torn between "wrong" and "tragic." A shirt might look normal enough until you try it on and discover that the armholes have been moved and are no longer level with your shoulders, like a capital "T," but further down your torso, like a lowercase one.

Jackets with patches on them might senselessly bunch at your left hip, or maybe they poof out at the small of your back, where for no good reason there's a pocket. I've yet to see a pair of Kapital trousers with a single leg hole, but that doesn't mean the designers haven't already done it. Their motto seems to be "Why not?"

Most people would answer, "I'll tell you why not!" But I like Kapital's philosophy. I like their clothing as well, though I can't say that it always likes me in return. I'm not narrow enough in the chest for most of the jackets, but what was to stop me, on this most recent trip, from buying a flannel shirt made of five differently patterned flannel shirts ripped apart and then stitched together into a kind of doleful Frankentop?

I got hats as well, three of them, which I like to wear stacked up, all at the same time, partly just to get it over with but mainly because I think they look good as a tower.

I draw the line at clothing with writing on it, but numbers don't bother me, so I also bought a tattered long-sleeved T-shirt with "99" cut from white fabric and stitched onto the front before being half burned off. It's as though a football team's plane had gone down and this was all that was left. Finally, I bought what might be called a tunic, made of denim and patched at the neck with defeated scraps of corduroy. When buttoned, the front flares out, making me look like I have a potbelly. These are clothes that absolutely refuse to flatter you, that go out of their way to insult you, really, and still my sisters and I can't get enough.

There are three Kapital stores in Ebisu, and their interior design is as off-putting as their merchandise. Most clothing hangs from the ceiling, though there are a few beat-up racks, and horizontal surfaces that items are strewn across. At one of the shops, the window display consisted of three carved penises arranged from small to large. The most modest was on par with a Coleman thermos, while the king-size one was as long and thick as a wrestler's forearm. Amy's eyes popped out of her head, and before I could stop her, she hoisted the middle one out of the window, crying, "Oh my goodness, it's teak! I thought from out on the sidewalk that it was mahogany!" As if she were a wood expert and saw nothing beyond the grain.

The salesman blinked as Amy turned the dildo upside down. Then she positioned her right hand at the base of the testicles and pretended she was a waitress. "Would anyone care for some freshly ground pepper?"

There are three other branches of Kapital in Tokyo, and we visited them all, and stayed in each one until our finger-prints were on everything. "My God," Gretchen said, trying on a hat that seemed to have been modeled after a used toilet brush and adding it to her pile, "this place is amazing. I had no idea!"

The main reason we asked Gretchen to join us is that she understands shopping. That is to say, she understands there is nothing *but* shopping—unlike our brother Paul or our sister Lisa, whose disinterest in buying things is downright masculine. She and her husband, Bob, don't exchange Christmas gifts but will, rather, "go in" on something: a new set of shelves for the laundry room, for instance, or a dehumidifier. They usually buy whatever it is in midsummer, so by December it's been forgotten. It's the same with their anniversary and birthdays: nothing. "But you can change that," I often tell her. "Right," she says, the way I do when someone suggests I learn how to drive.

And it's not just big-ticket items. She and I were at O'Hare Airport one afternoon and passed a place that sold nuts. "Why don't you get some for Bob?" I asked. "They would be a nice little something to bring him as a gift."

She looked at the stand, a cart, really, and frowned. "I would, but his dentist told him he has brittle teeth."

"He doesn't have to crack them open in his mouth," I said. "Everything here is preshelled."

"That's OK."

I would never leave town and not bring Hugh back a gift. Nor would he do that to me, though in truth I had to train him. He's normally not that much of a shopper, but Tokyo seems to knock something loose in him. Perhaps it's because it's so far away. The difference is that he's ashamed of it. I think it's something he gets from his mother, who considers shopping to be wasteful, or, worse still in her book, "unserious."

"Why go to a store when you could go to a museum?" she might ask.

"Um, because the museum doesn't sell shit?" My sisters and I refuse to feel bad about shopping. And why should we? Obviously we have some hole we're trying to fill, but doesn't everyone? And isn't filling it with berets the size of toilet-seat covers, if not more practical, then at least *healthier* than filling it with frosting or heroin or unsafe sex with strangers?

"Besides," Amy said at the dinner table on the first night of our vacation, "it's not like everything we buy is for ourselves. I'll be getting birthday presents for friends and all sorts of things for my godson."

"You don't have to convince me," I told her, as we're cut from the same cloth. Shopping has nothing to do with money. If you have it, you go to stores and galleries, and if not, you haunt flea markets or Goodwills. Never, though, do you *not* do it, choosing instead to visit a park or a temple or some cultural institution where they don't sell things. Our sister-in-law, Kathy, swears by eBay, but I like the social aspect of shopping, the getting out. The touching things and talking to people. I work at home, so most days the only contact I have, except for Hugh, is with salespeople and cashiers.

My problem is that if someone really engages me, or goes the slightest bit out of his way, I feel I have to buy whatever it is he's selling. Especially if it involves a ladder or a set of keys. That explains the small painting of a forsaken shack I bought on the fourth day of our vacation, at a place I like called On Sundays. It's on an odd-shaped scrap of plywood, and though it's by a contemporary artist I've always gotten a kick out of—an American named Barry McGee—and was probably a very fair price, I bought it mainly because the store manager unlocked the case that it was in.

"I would have got it if you hadn't," Amy, my enabler, said, as I left with the painting in a recently purchased, very pricey tote bag that had cowboys on it.

Then it was on to another one of our favorite places, the Tokyo outpost of the Dover Street Market. The original store, in London, sells both clothing and the kind of objects you might find in a natural history museum. I got the inner ear of a whale there a few years back and a four-horned antelope skull that was found in India in 1890.

The Ginza branch sticks to clothing and accessories. I'd gone with Amy on our first trip together, in 2014, and left with a pair of wide-legged Paul Harnden trousers that come up to my nipples. The button-down fly is a foot long, and when I root around in my pockets for change, my forearms disappear all the way to the elbows. You can't belt something that reaches that high up on your torso, thus the suspenders, which came with the trousers and are beautiful, but still, suspenders! Clown pants is what they are—artfully hand-stitched, lined all the way to the ankle—but clown pants all the same. They cost as much as a MacBook Air, and I'd have walked away from them were it not for Amy saying, "Are you kidding? You *have* to get those."

This time I bought a pair of blue-and-white-polka-dot culottes. Hugh hates this sort of thing and accuses me of transitioning.

"They're just shorts," I tell him. "Bell-bottom shorts, but shorts all the same. How is that *womanly?*"

A year and a half earlier, at this same Dover Street Market, I bought a pair of heavy black culottes. Dress culottes, you could call them, made by Comme des Garçons and also beautifully lined. They made a pleasant whooshing sound as I ran up the stairs of my house, searching in vain for whatever shoes a grown man might wear with them. Hugh disapproved, but again I thought I looked great, much better than I do in regular trousers. "My calves are my one good feature," I reminded him as he gritted his teeth. "Why can't I highlight them every now and then?" The dress culottes weren't as expensive as the pants that come up to my nipples, but still they were extravagant. I buy a lot of what I think of as "at-home clothes," things I'd wear at my desk or when lying around at night after a bath, but never outdoors. These troubling, Jiminy Cricket-style trousers, for instance, that I bought at another of my favorite Japanese stores, 45rpm. They have horizontal stripes and make my ass look like a half dozen coins collected in a sack made from an old prison uniform.

I'd have felt like a fool paying all that money and limiting my nipple-high pants and black dress culottes to home, so I started wearing them onstage, which still left me feeling like a fool but a different kind of one.

"I hate to tell you," a woman said after a show one night, "but those culottes look terrible on you."

I was shattered. "Really?"

"They're way too long," she told me.

And so I had them shortened. Then shortened again, at which point they no longer made the pleasant whooshing sound and were ruined.

"Are these too long for me?" I asked the saleswoman on our most recent trip.

"Not at all," I'm pretty sure she told me.

A few days later, at the big Comme des Garçons shop in Omotesandō, I bought yet another pair of culottes, a fancier pair that are cerulean blue. "What are you *doing?*" Hugh moaned as I stepped out of the dressing room. "That's *three pairs* of culottes you'll own now."

All I could say in my defense was "Maybe I have a busy life."

I then tried on a button-down shirt that was made to be worn backward. The front was plain and almost suggested a straitjacket. You'd have to have someone close you into it and, of course, knot your tie if you were going for a more formal look. I'd have bought it were it not too tight at the neck.

"Maybe it'll fit after you have your Adam's apple shaved off," Hugh said.

Amy loaded up at Comme des Garçons as well, buying, among other things, a skirt that looks to have been made from the insides of suit pockets.

"What just happened?" she asked as we left the store, considerably more broke, and went up a few doors to Yohji Yamamoto, where I bought what Hugh calls a dress but what is most certainly a smock. A denim one that has side pockets. The front closes with snaps and, for whatever reason, the back does as well.

Most days we returned to our rental house groaning beneath the weight of our purchases, things I'd often wind up regretting the moment I pulled them out of their bags: a pair of drawstring jeans two sizes too large, for instance—drawstring jeans!—or a wool shirt that was relatively sober and would have been great were I able to wear wool. As it is, it causes me to itch and sweat something awful. "Then why did you get it?" Hugh asked. "Because everyone else got something," I told him, adding that it was on sale and I could always send it to my father, who might not wear it but would undoubtedly appreciate the gesture.

Shopping with my sisters in Japan was like being in a pie-eating contest, only with stuff. We often felt sick. Dazed. Bloated. Vulgar. Yet never quite ashamed. "I think I need to lie down," I said one evening. "Maybe with that brand-new eighty-dollar washcloth on my forehead."

Nothing was a total waste, I reasoned, as paying for it gave me a chance to practice my Japanese.

"I am buying something now," I'd say as I approached the register. "I have money! I have coins too!"

As if he or she had been handed a script, the cashier would ask where I was from and what I was doing in Tokyo.

"I am American," I would say. "But now I live in England. I am on vacation with my sisters."

"Oh, your sisters!"

Then I started saying, "I am a doctor."

"What kind?" asked a woman who sold me a bandanna with pictures of fruit and people having sex on it.

"A ... children's doctor," I said.

I wouldn't set out to misrepresent myself, but I didn't know the word for "author" or "trash collector." "Doctor," though, was in one of the ninety "Teach Yourself Japanese" lessons I'd reviewed before leaving England.

I loved the respect being a pediatrician brought me in Japan, even when I wore a smock and had a tower of three hats on my head. You could see it in people's faces. I grew before their very eyes.

"Did you just tell that lady you're a doctor?" Amy would ask. "A little," I'd say.

A week after leaving Tokyo, I was on a flight from Hobart, Tasmania, to Melbourne, and when a passenger got sick and the flight attendant asked if there was a physician on board, my hand was halfway to the call button before I remembered that I am not, in fact, a doctor. That I just play one in Japan.

Though it cut into our shopping time, one thing we all looked forward to in Tokyo was lunch, which was always eaten out, usually at some place we'd just chanced upon. One afternoon toward the end of our vacation, settling into my seat at a tempura restaurant in Shibuya, I looked across the table at Amy, who was wearing a varsity sweater from Kapital that appeared to have bloodstains and bits of brain on it, and at Gretchen, with her toilet-brush hat. I was debuting a shirt that fell three inches below my knees. It was black and made me look like a hand puppet. We don't have the same eyes or noses, my sisters and I. Our hairlines are different, and the shapes of our faces, but on this particular afternoon the family resemblance was striking. Anyone could tell that we were related, even someone from another planet who believed that humans were as indistinguishable from one another as acorns. At this particular moment of our lives, no one belonged together more than us.

Who would have thought, when we were children, that the three of us would wind up here, in Japan of all places, dressed so expensively like mental patients and getting along so well together? It's a thought we all had several times a day: *Look how our lives turned out! What a surprise!*

When the menus came, Gretchen examined hers upside down. She had never used chopsticks before coming to Tokyo, and for the first few days she employed them separately, one in each hand, like daggers. Amy was a little better, but when it came to things like rice she tended to give up and just stare at her bowl helplessly. Always, when the food was delivered, we'd take a moment to admire it, so beautifully presented, all this whatever it was: The little box with a round thing in it. The shredded bit. The flat part. Once, we ate in what I'm pretty sure was someone's garage. The owner served only one thing, and we had it seated around a folding table, just us and a space heater. The food was unfailingly good, but what made lunch such a consistent pleasure was the anticipation, knowing that we had the entire afternoon ahead of us and that it might result in anything: Styrofoam boots, a suit made of tape—whatever we could imagine was out there, waiting to be discovered. All we Sedarises had to do was venture forth and claim it.

Leviathan

As I grow older, I find that the people I know become crazy in one of two ways. The first is animal crazy—more specifically, dog crazy. They're the ones who, when asked if they have children, are likely to answer, "A black Lab and a sheltie-beagle mix named Tuckahoe." Then they add—they always add—"They were rescues!"

The second way people go crazy is with their diet. My brother, Paul, for instance, has all but given up solid food, and at age forty-six eats much the way he did when he was nine months old. His nickname used to be the Rooster. Now we call him the Juicester. Everything goes into his Omega J8006—kale, carrots, celery, some kind of powder scraped off the knuckles of bees—and it all comes out dung-colored and the texture of applesauce. He's also taken to hanging upside down with a neti pot in his nose. "It's for my sinuses," he claims.

Then there's all his disease prevention, the things that supposedly stave it off but that the drug companies don't want you knowing about. I've heard this sort of thing from a number of people over the years. "Cancer can *definitely* be cured with a vegan diet," a friend will insist, "only *they* want to keep it a secret." In this case the "they" that doesn't want you to know is the meat industry, or "Big Meat."

"If a vegan diet truly did cure cancer, don't you think it would have at least made the front page of the *New York Times* Science section?" I ask. "Isn't that a paper's job, to tell you the things 'they' don't want you to know?"

Paul insists that apricot seeds prevent cancer but that the cancer industry—Big Cancer—wants to suppress this information, and has quietly imprisoned those who have tried to enlighten us. He orders in bulk and brought a jarful to our house at the beach one late May afternoon. They're horribly bitter, these things, and leave a definite aftertaste. "Jesus, that's rough," my father said after mistaking one for an almond. "How many do you have in a day?"

Paul said four. Any more could be dangerous, since they have cyanide in them. Then he juiced what I think was a tennis ball mixed with beets and four-leaf clovers.

"Add some strawberries and I'll have a glass as well," my sister Lisa said. She's not convinced about the cancer prevention but is intrigued by all the weight our brother has lost. When he got married in 2001, he was close to 200 pounds—which is a lot if you're only five foot two. Now he was down to 135. It's odd seeing him thin again after all these years. I expected him to look the way he did when he was twenty, before he ballooned up, and while he's the same physical size as he was back then, his face has aged and he now looks like that kid's father. It's as if a generation of him went missing.

Part of Paul's weight loss can be attributed to his new liquid diet, but I think that exercise has more to do with it. He bought a complicated racing bike and rides it while wearing what looks like a Spider-Man costume and the type of cycling shoes that have cleats on them. One day that May, as I walked to the post office, he pedaled past without recognizing me. His face was unguarded, and I felt I was seeing him the way other people do, at least superficially: this boyish little man with an icicle of snot hanging off his nose. "Mornin'," he sang as he sped by.

It's ridiculous how often you have to say hello on Emerald Isle. Passing someone on the street is one thing, but you have to do it in stores as well, not just to the employees who greet you at the door but to your fellow shoppers in aisle three. Most of the houses that face the ocean are rented out during the high season, and from week to week the people in them come from all over the United States. Houses near the sound, on the other hand, are more commonly owner-occupied. They have landscaped yards, and many are fronted by novelty mailboxes. Some are shaped like fish, while others are outfitted in cozies that have various messages—BLESS YOUR HEART or SANDY FEET WELCOME!—printed on them.

The neighborhoods near the sound are so Southern that people will sometimes wave to you from *inside* their houses. Workmen, hammers in hand, shout hello from ladders and half-shingled roofs. I'm willing to bet that the local operating rooms are windowless and have doors that are solid wood. Otherwise the surgeons and nurses would feel obliged to acknowledge everyone who passed down the hall, and patients could possibly die as a result.

While the sound side of the island feels like an old-fashioned neighborhood, the ocean side is more like an upscale retirement community. Look out a street-facing window on any given morning, and you'd think they were filming a Centrum commercial. All these hale, silver-haired seniors walking or jogging or cycling past the house. Later in the day, when the heat cranks up, they purr by in golf carts, wearing visors, their noses streaked with sunblock. If you were a teenager, you likely wouldn't give it much thought, but to my sisters and me—people in our mid to late fifties—it's chilling. *That'll be us in, like, eight years,* we think. *How can that be when only yesterday, on this very same beach, we were children?*

Of course, the alternative is worse. When my mother was the age that I am now, she couldn't walk more than ten steps without stopping to catch her breath. And stairs—forget it. In that regard, our father is her opposite. At ninety-one, the only things wrong with him are his toes. "My doctor wants to cut one off, but I think he's overreacting," he said on the second morning of our vacation. The sun shone brightly through the floor-to-ceiling windows, and he was sitting shirtless at the kitchen table on the side of the house that Hugh and I share, wearing black spandex shorts.

The toes he presented for my inspection looked like fingers playing the piano, all of them long and bent and splayed. "How do you fit those things into shoes?" I asked, wincing. "Wouldn't it be easier to go the Howard Hughes route and just wear tissue boxes on your feet?"

Just then, the plumber arrived to look at our broken dishwasher. Randy is huge in every way, and as we shook hands I thought of how small mine must have felt within his, like a paw almost. "So, what seems to be the problem?" he asked.

It's the same story every time: Hugh calls and schedules an appointment regarding something I know nothing about. Then he leaves for God knows where and I'm left to explain what I don't understand. "I guess it's not washing the dishes right, or something?" I said.

Randy pulled a screwdriver from his tool belt and bent

down toward a panel. "I'd have come sooner, but we're still catching up from the winter we had. Pipes frozen, all kinds of mess."

"Was it that cold?" I asked.

"Never seen anything like it," he said.

My father raised his coffee cup. "And they talk about global warming. Ha!" After twenty minutes or so, Randy suggested we get a new dishwasher, a KitchenAid, if possible. "They're not that expensive, and it'll probably be cheaper than fixing this here one." I showed him to the door, and as he made his way down the stairs, my father asked when I was going to have my prostate checked. "You need to get that taken care of ASAP. While you're at it, you might want to get a complete physical. I mean, the works."

What does that have to do with the dishwasher? I wondered.

When Hugh returned, I passed on Randy's suggestion regarding the KitchenAid, and he nodded. "While he was here, did you ask him about the leak under the sink?"

"I didn't know I was supposed to."

"Goddamn it, I told you last night—"

My father tapped me on the shoulder. "You need to call a doctor and get a checkup."

This was my second trip to our house on Emerald Isle, and the second time my entire family, or what was left of it, was assembling here. Summer was still a month away, and already the temperature was in the nineties. The humidity was high, and once you left the beach the breeze disappeared, inviting in its dearth great squadrons of biting flies. Still, I would force myself out every afternoon. On one of my walks, I came across my brother and his daughter, Madelyn, standing on a footbridge a few blocks inland from our house and dropping bread into the brackish canal. I thought they were feeding fish, but it turned out they were throwing the food to turtles, dozens of them. Most had shells between six and eight inches long and are what my sister Gretchen, who owns a lot of reptiles, calls sliders. Then there were the snapping turtles. The largest measured around three and a half feet from nose to tail. Part of his left front foot was missing, and he had a tumor on his head the size of my niece's fist.

"And you're giving them *bread?*" I said to Paul. It made me think of my first visit to Spokane, Washington. I was walking through the park that fronts the river there and happened upon people feeding animals that resembled groundhogs.

"What are these?" I asked a man who was kneeling with his arm outstretched.

"Marmots," he told me. "And what do they eat?"

He reached into a bag he kept at his feet. "Marshmallows." I've subsequently seen people feed all sorts of things to the turtles in the canal on Emerald Isle: dry dog food, Cheerios, Pop-Tarts, potato chips.

"None of that is good for them," Gretchen says. Her turtles eat mainly worms and slugs. They like fruit as well, and certain vegetables. "But potato chips, no."

"What about *barbecue* potato chips?" I asked.

During the week that we spent at the beach, I'd visit the canal every afternoon, sometimes with raw hot dogs, sometimes with fish heads or chicken gizzards. The sliders would poke their heads out of the water, begging, but it was the snappers I was there for. Seeing one was like seeing a dinosaur, for isn't that what they are? Watching as they tore into their food, I'd shiver with fear and revulsion, the way I used to when watching my brother eat. On YouTube there's a video of one biting off a finger, and of the man whose finger it used to be acting terribly surprised, the way that people who offer sandwiches to bears, or jump security fences to pose beside tigers, ultimately are. There are other videos of snapping turtles eating rats and pigeons and frogs, all of which are still alive, their pathetic attempts at self-defense futile. It's a kind of pornography, and after sitting for twenty minutes, watching one poor animal after another being eviscerated, I erase my Internet user history, not wanting to be identified as the person who would find this sort of thing entertaining—yet clearly *being* that person.

Did it help, I wondered, that my favorite turtle was the one with the oversize tumor on his head and half of his front foot missing? Did that make me a friend of the sick and suffering, or just the kind of guy who wants both ice cream *and* whipped cream on his pie? Aren't snapping turtles terrible enough? Did I really need to supersize one with a cancerous growth?

My main reason for buying the house on Emerald Isle was that it would allow my family to spend more time together, especially now, while my father's still around. Instead, though, I was spending all my time with these turtles. Not that we didn't do anything as a group. One afternoon we scattered my mother's ashes in the surf behind the house. Afterward, standing on the shore with the empty bag in my hands, I noticed a trawler creeping across the horizon. It was after shrimp, or some kind of fish, and hovering over it, like flies around a garbage pail, were dozens of screaming seabirds. It made me think of my mother and how we'd follow her even to the bathroom. "Can't I have *five minutes?*" she'd plead from behind the locked door as we jiggled the handle, relating something terribly important about tights, or a substitute teacher, or a dream one of us had had about a talking glove. My mother died in 1991, yet reaching into the bag, touching her remains, essentially throwing her away, was devastating, even after all this time.

Later, drained, we piled into the car and drove to the small city of Beaufort. There we went to a coffee shop and fell in line behind a young man with a gun. It was tucked into a holster he wore belted around his waist, and after he had gotten his order and taken a seat with two people I took to be his parents, we glared at him with what might as well have been a single eye. Even my father, who laughs appreciatively at such bumper stickers as DON'T BLAME ME, I VOTED FOR THE AMERICAN, draws the line at carrying a pistol into a place where lattes are being served. "What's he trying to prove?" he asked. The guy was my height or maybe a little shorter, wearing pressed jeans. "He's obviously got a complex of some kind," my sister-in-law, Kathy, said.

"It's called being a Republican," Lisa offered.

My father frowned into his decaf. "Aw, come on, now."

I mentioned a couple of T-shirts I'd seen people wearing on the pier not far from my turtle spot. INVEST IN HEAVY METALS, read one, and it pictured three bullets labeled BRASS, COPPER, and LEAD. Another showed a pistol above the message WHEN YOU COME FOR MINE, YOU BETTER BRING YOURS.

"Since when is the government coming for anyone's guns in this country?" I asked. "I mean, honestly, can't any of us enter a Walmart right now and walk out with a Sidewinder missile?"

It was a nice moment, all of us on the same page. Then my father ruined it by asking when I'd last had a physical.

"Just recently," I said. "Recently, like when?"

"1987," I told him, adding, after he moaned, "You *do* know this is the fourth time today you've asked me about this, right? I mean, you're not just being ninety-one, are you?"

"No," he said. "I know what I'm saying."

"Well, can you please *stop* saying it?"

"I will when you get a physical."

"Is this really how you want to be remembered?" I asked. "As a nagger ... with hammertoes?"

"I'm just showing my concern," he said. "Can't you see that I'm doing this for your own good? Jesus, son, I want you to have a long, healthy life! I love you. Is that a crime?"

The Sea Section came completely furnished, and the first thing we did after getting the keys was to load up all the televisions and donate them to a thrift shop. It's nice at night to work puzzles or play board games or just hang out, maybe listening to music. The only one this is difficult for is my father. Back in Raleigh, he has two or three TVs going at the same time, all tuned to the same conservative cable station, filling his falling-down house with outrage. The one reprieve is his daily visit to the gym, where he takes part in a spinning class. Amy and I like to joke that his stationary bike has a front wheel as tall as a man and a rear one no bigger than a pie tin—that it's a penny-farthing, the kind people rode in the 1880s. On its handlebars we imagine a trumpet horn with a big rubber bulb on one end.

Being at the beach is a drag for our father. To his credit, though, he never complains about it, just as he never mentions the dozens of aches and pains a person his age must surely be burdened by. "I'm fine just hanging out," he says. "Being together, that's all I need." He no longer swims or golfs or fishes off the pier. We banned his right-wing radio shows, so all that's left is to shuffle from one side of the house to the other, sometimes barefoot and sometimes wearing leather slippers the color of a new baseball mitt.

"Those are beautiful," I said the first time I noticed them. "Where did they come from?"

He looked down at his feet and cleared his throat. "A catalog. They arrived back in the early eighties, but I only just recently started wearing them."

"If anything should ever ... happen to you, do you think that maybe *I* could have them?" I asked.

"What would ever happen to me?"

In the ocean that afternoon, I watched my brother play with his daughter. The waves were high, and as Madelyn hung laughing off Paul's shoulders, I thought of how we used to do the same with our own father. It was the only time any of us ever touched him. Perhaps for that reason I can still recall the feel of his skin, slick with suntan oil and much softer than I had imagined it. Our mother couldn't keep our hands off her. If we'd had ink on our fingers, at the end of an average day she'd have been black, the way we mauled and poked and petted her. With him, though, we never dared get too close. Even in the ocean, there'd come a moment when, without warning, he'd suddenly reach his limit and shake us off, growling, "God almighty, will you just leave me alone?"

He was so much heavier back then, always determined to lose thirty pounds. Half a century later he'd do well to *gain* thirty pounds. Paul embraced him after our sister Tiffany died and reported that it was like hugging a coatrack. "What I do," he says every night while Hugh puts dinner together, "is take a chicken breast, broil it with a little EVOO, and serve it with some lentils—*fan*tastic!" Though my father talks big, we suspect the bulk of his meals come from whatever they're offering as free samples at his neighborhood Whole Foods, the one we give him gift cards for. How else to explain how he puts it away while we're all together, eating as if in preparation for a fast?

"Outstanding," he says between bites, the muscles of his jaws twitching beneath his spotted skin. "My compliments to the chef!"

One night, I looked over and saw that he was wearing a

Cherokee headdress someone had brought to the house for Thanksgiving. Paul had put it on him and, rather than shake it off the way he would have a few years earlier, he accepted it—owned it, really. Just before dessert was served, Amy and I noticed that he was crying. He looked like the Indian from that old "Keep America Beautiful" ad campaign. One single tear running down his cheek. He never blubbered or called attention to himself, so we never asked what the problem was, or if there even *was* a problem. "Maybe he was happy that we were all together," Lisa said when we told her about it. Gretchen guessed that he was thinking about our mother, or Tiffany, while Paul wondered if it wasn't an allergic reaction to feathers.

It's not that our father waited till this late in the game to win our hearts. It's that he's succeeding.

"But he didn't *used* to be this nice and agreeable," I complained to Hugh.

"Well, he is now," he said. "Why can't you let people change?"

This is akin to another of his often asked questions: "Why do you choose to remember the negative rather than the positive?"

"I don't," I insist, thinking, *I will never forget your giving me such a hard time over this.*

Honestly, though, does choice even come into it? Is it my fault that the good times fade to nothing while the bad ones burn forever bright? Memory aside, the negative just makes for a better story: the plane was delayed, an infection set in, outlaws arrived and reduced the schoolhouse to ashes. Happiness is harder to put into words. It's also harder to source, much more mysterious than anger or sorrow, which come to me promptly, whenever I summon them, and remain long after I've begged them to leave.

For whatever reason, I was very happy with my snapping turtles. In the wild, they can live for up to thirty years, though I fear that my favorite, the one with the hideous growth on his head, might not make it that long. There's something wrong with his breathing, though he still manages to mount the females every chance he gets.

"Oh, look," a passerby said, pointing down into the churning water on the last full day of our vacation. "They're playing!"

I looked at the man with an incredulity that bordered on anger. "Snapping turtles don't *play*," I said. "Not even when they're babies. They're reptiles, for Christ's sake."

"Can you believe it?" I said to my father when I got back to the beach house that evening. He was standing beside the sofa, wearing a shirt I clearly remember throwing into his trash can in the summer of 1990, and enjoying a glass of vodka with a little water in it. All around him, people were helping with dinner. Lisa and Amy were setting the table while Gretchen prepared the salad and Paul loaded his juicer with what looked like dirt. Hugh brought fish up from the grill, and as Kathy and Madelyn rounded up chairs, I put on some music. "Attaboy," my father said. "That's just what we needed. Is this Hank Mobley?"

"It is," I told him.

"I thought so. I used to have this on reel-to-reel tape." While I know I can't control it, what I ultimately hope to recall about my late-in-life father is not his nagging or his toes but, rather, his fingers, and the way he snaps them when listening to jazz. He's done it forever, signifying, much as a cat does by purring, that you may approach. That all is right with the world. "Man, oh man," he'll say in my memory, lifting his glass and taking us all in, "isn't this just *fan*tastic?"

A Modest Proposal

London is five hours ahead of Washington, DC, except when it comes to gay marriage. In that case, it's two years and five hours ahead, which was news to me. "Really?" I said, on meeting two lesbian wives from Wolverhampton. "You can do that here?"

"Well, *of course* they can," Hugh said when I told him about it. "Where have you been?"

Hugh can tell you everything about the current political situation in the U.K. He knows who the chancellor of the exchequer is, and was all caught up in the latest election for the whatever-you-call-it, that king-type person who's like the president but isn't.

"*Prime minister?*" he said. "Jesus. You've been here *how* long?"

It was the same when we lived in Paris. Hugh regularly read the French papers. He listened to political shows on the radio, while I was, like, "Is he the same emperor we had last year?"

When it comes to American politics, our roles are reversed.

"What do you mean 'Who's Claire McCaskill?'" I'll say, amazed that I—that *anyone,* for that matter—could have such an ignorant boyfriend.

I knew that the Supreme Court ruling on gay marriage was expected at ten a.m. on June 26, which is three p.m. in Sussex. I'm usually out then, on my litter patrol, so I made it a point to bring my iPad with me. When the time came, I was standing by the side of the road, collecting trash with my grabber. It's generally the same crap over and over— potato-chip bags, candy wrappers, Red Bull cans—but along this particular stretch, six months earlier, I'd come across a strap-on penis. It seemed pretty old and was Band-Aid colored, about three inches long and not much bigger around than a Vienna sausage, which was interesting to me. You'd think that if someone wanted a sex toy she'd go for the gold, sizewise. But this was just the bare minimum, like getting AAA breast implants. Who had this person been hoping to satisfy, her Cabbage Patch doll? I thought about taking the penis home and mailing it to one of my sisters for Christmas but knew that the moment I put it in my knapsack, I'd get hit by a car and killed. That's just my luck. Medics would come and scrape me off the pavement, then, later, at the hospital, they'd rifle through my pack and record its contents: four garbage bags, some wet wipes, two flashlights, and a strap-on penis.

"There must be some mistake," Hugh would tell them. "You said it was *how* big?"

My iPad could get no signal at three p.m., so I continued walking and picking up trash, thinking that, whichever way the Supreme Court went, I never expected to see this day in my lifetime. When I was young, in the early seventies, being gay felt like the worst thing that could happen to a person, at least in Raleigh, North Carolina. There was a rumor that it could be cured by psychiatrists, so for most of my teens that's where I placed my hope. I figured that eventually I'd tell my mother and let her take the appropriate steps. What would kill me would be seeing the disappointment on her face. With my father I was used to it. That was the expression he naturally assumed when looking at me. Her, though! Once when I was in high school she caught me doing something or other, imitating my Spanish teacher, perhaps with a pair of tights on my head, and said, like someone at the end of her rope, "What are you, *a queer?*"

I'd been called a sissy before, not by her but by plenty of other people. That was different, though, as the word was less potent, something used by children. When my mother called me a queer, my face turned scarlet and I exploded. "*Me?* What are you talking about? Why would you even *say* a thing like that?"

Then I ran down to my room, which was spotless, everything just so, the Gustav Klimt posters on the walls, the cornflower-blue vase I'd bought with the money I earned babysitting. The veil had been lifted, and now I saw this for what it was: the lair of a blatant homosexual.

That would have been as good a time as any to say, "Yes, you're right. Get me some help!" But I was still hoping that it might be a phase, that I'd wake up the next day and be normal. In the best of times, it seemed like such a short leap. I *did* fantasize about having a girlfriend—never the sex part, but the rest of it I had down. I knew what she'd look like and how she'd hold her long hair back from the flame when bending over a lit candle. I imagined us getting married the summer after I graduated from college, and then I imagined her drowning off the coast of North Carolina during one of my family's vacations. Everyone needed to be there so they could see just how devastated I was. I could actually make myself cry by picturing it: How I'd carry her out of the water, how my feet would sink into the sand owing to the extra weight. I'd try mouth-to-mouth resuscitation, and keep trying until someone, my father most often, would pull me back, saying, "It's too late, son. Can't you see she's gone?"

It seemed I wanted to marry just so I could be a widower. So profound would be my grief that I'd never look at another woman again. It was perfect, really. Oh, there were variations. Sometimes she'd die of leukemia, as in the movie *Love Story*. Occasionally a madman's bullet would fell her during a hostage situation, but always I'd be at her side, trying everything in my power to bring her back.

The fantasy remained active until I was twenty. Funny how unimportant being gay became once I told somebody. All I had to do was open up to my best friend, and when she accepted it I saw that I could as well.

"I just don't see why you have to rub everyone's noses in it," certain people would complain when I told them. Not that I wore it on T-shirts or anything. Rather, I'd just say "boyfriend" the way they said "wife" or "girlfriend" or "better half." I insisted that it was no different, and in time, at least in the circles I ran in, it became no different.

While I often dreamed of making a life with another man, I never extended the fantasy to marriage or even to civil partnerships, which became legal in France in 1999, shortly after Hugh and I moved to Paris. We'd been together for eight years by that point, and though I didn't want to break up or look for anyone else, I didn't need the government to validate my relationship. I felt the same way when a handful of American states legalized same-sex marriage, only more so: I didn't need a government *or* a church giving me its blessing. The whole thing felt like a step down to me. From the dawn of time, the one irrefutably good thing about gay men and lesbians was that we didn't force people to sit through our weddings. Even the most ardent of homophobes had to hand us that. We were the ones who toiled behind the scenes while straight people got married: the photographers and bakers and florists, working like Negro porters settling spoiled passengers into the whites-only section of the train.

"Oh, Christopher," a bride might sigh as her dressmaker zipped her up, "what would I have ever done without you?"

What saved this from being tragic was that they were doing something we wouldn't dream of: guilt-tripping friends and relatives into giving up their weekends so they could sit on hard church pews or folding chairs in August, listening as the couple mewled vows at each other, watching as they were force-fed cake, standing on the sidelines, bored and sweating, as the pair danced, misty-eyed, to a Foreigner song.

The battle for gay marriage was, in essence, the fight to be as square as straight people, to say things like "My husband tells me that the new Spicy Chipotle Burger they've got at Bennigan's is awesome!"

That said, I was all for the struggle, mainly because it so irritated the fundamentalists. I wanted gay people to get the right to marry, and then I wanted none of us to act on it. I wanted it to be ours to spit on. Instead, much to my disappointment, we seem to be all over it.

I finally got a signal at the post office in the neighboring village. I'd gone to mail a set of keys to a friend and, afterward, I went out front and pulled out my iPad. The touch of a finger and there it was, the headline story on the *New York Times* site: "Supreme Court Ruling Makes Same-Sex Marriage a Right Nationwide."

I read it and, probably like every American gay person,

I was overcome with emotion. Standing on the sidewalk, dressed in rags with a litter picker pinioned between my legs, I felt my eyes tear up, and as my vision blurred I considered all the people who had fought against this and thought, *Take that, assholes.*

The Supreme Court ruling tells every gay fifteen-year-old living out in the middle of nowhere that he or she is as good as any other dope who wants to get married. To me it was a slightly mixed message, like saying we're all equally entitled to wear Dockers to the Olive Garden. Then I spoke to my accountant, who's as straight as they come, and he couldn't have been more excited. "For tax purposes, you and Hugh really need to act on this," he told me.

"But I don't want to," I said. "I don't believe in marriage."

He launched into a little speech, and here's the thing about legally defined couples: they save boatloads of money, especially when it comes to inheriting property. My accountant told me how much we had to gain, and I was, like, "Is there a waiting period? What documents do I need?"

That night, I proposed for the first of what eventually numbered eighteen times. "Listen," I said to Hugh over dinner, "we really need to do this. Otherwise when one of us dies, the other will be clobbered with taxes."

"I don't care," he told me. "It's just money."

This is a sentence that does not register on Greek ears. It's *just* a mango-size brain tumor. It's *just* the person I hired to smother you in your sleep. But since when is money *just* money?

"I'm not marrying you," he repeated.

I swore to him that I was not being romantic about it: "There'll be no rings, no ceremony, no celebration of any kind. We won't tell anyone but the accountant. Think of it as a financial contract, nothing more."

"No."

"Goddamn it," I said. "You are going to marry me whether you like it or not."

"No, I'm not."

"Oh, yes you are."

After two weeks of this, he slammed his fork on the table, saying, "I'll do anything just to shut you up." This is, I'm pretty sure, the closest I'm likely to get to a yes.

I took another ear of corn. "Fine, then. It's settled."

It wasn't until the following day that the reality set in. I was out on the side of a busy road with my litter picker, collecting the shreds of a paper coffee cup that had been run over by a lawn mower, when I thought of having to tick the box that says "married" instead of "single." I always thought there should have been another option, as for the past twenty-four years I've been happily neither. I would never introduce Hugh as my husband, nor would he refer to me that way, but I can easily imagine other people doing it. They'd be the type who so readily embraced "partner" when it came down the pike, in the mid-nineties. Well-meaning people. The kind who wear bike helmets. It occurred to me while standing there, cars whizzing by, that the day I marry is the day I'll get hit and killed, probably by some driver who's texting or, likelier still, sexting. "He is survived by his husband, Hugh Hamrick," the obituary will read, and before I'm even in my grave I'll be rolling over in it.

That night at dinner, neither of us mentioned the previous evening's conversation. We talked about this and that, our little projects, the lives of our neighbors, and then we retreated to different parts of the house—engaged, I suppose, our whole lives ahead of us.

Why Aren't You Laughing?

From the outside, our house on the North Carolina coast—the Sea Section—is nothing much to look at. It might have been designed by a ten-year-old with a ruler, that's how basic it is: walls, roof, windows, deck. It's easy to imagine the architect putting down his crayon and shouting into the next room, "I'm done. Can I watch TV now?"

Whenever I denigrate the place, Hugh reminds me that it's the view that counts: the ocean we look out at. I see his point, but it's not like you have to limit yourself to one or the other. "What about West Sussex?" I say. From the outside our cottage in England resembles something you'd find in a storybook—a home for potbellied trolls, benevolent ones that smoke pipes. Built of stone in the late sixteenth century, it has a pitched roof and little windows with panes the size of playing cards. We lie in bed and consider sheep grazing in the shadow of a verdant down. I especially love being there in winter, so it bothered me when I had to spend most of January and February working in the United States. Hugh came along,

379

and toward the end we found ourselves on Maui, where I had a reading. I'd have been happy just to fly in and fly out, but Hugh likes to swim in the ocean, so we stayed for a week in a place he found online.

"Let me guess," the box-office manager of the theater I performed at said. "It's spread out over at least four levels and paneled in dark wood, like something you'd see on a 1970s TV show, right?"

He'd hit it squarely on the nose, especially the dark part. The wood on the interior walls had been rigorously stained and was almost the color of fudge, a stark contrast to the world outside, which was relentlessly, almost oppressively, bright. As for the various levels, any excuse seemed to have been taken to add stairs, even if only two or three. If you lived there full-time, you'd no doubt get the hang of them. As it was, I tripped or fell down at least twice a day. The house reminded me of the condominium units my family used to rent on Emerald Isle when I was in my twenties, though none of those had a crucifix hanging in the kitchen. This one was ten inches tall and supported a slender, miserable Christ plated in bronze.

That was the only decoration aside from a number of framed photo collages of the owner and his family taken over the years. They were a good-looking group, one that multiplied as the children grew and had kids of their own. The color in the earlier snapshots had faded, just as it has in pictures of my own family: same haircuts, same flared slacks and shirts with long droopy collars, only now drained of their vibrancy, like lawns in winter. Each generation looked healthy and prosperous, yet I found myself wondering what lurked beneath the surface—for surely there was something. "Which of you is in prison now?" I'd ask, glancing up as I tripped on the stairs to the bedroom.

The house was on the ocean, and the beach that began where the backyard ended was shaded with palms. Most often it was deserted, so except for a few short trips up the coast for supplies, Hugh stayed put during our week on Maui. If he wasn't on the deck overlooking the water, he was in the water looking back at the deck. He saw whales and sea turtles. He snorkeled. My only accomplishment was to sign my name to five thousand blank sheets of paper sent by my publisher. "Tip-ins," they're called. A month or two down the line, they'd be bound into copies of the book I had just about finished. There were still a few more weeks to make changes, but they could be only minor grammatical things. Hugh, who is good at spotting typos and used to do so for his father, a novelist, was reading the manuscript for the first time. Whenever I heard him laugh, I'd ask, "What's so funny?" Should five or ten minutes pass with no reaction, I'd call out, "Why aren't you laughing?"

It takes quite a while to sign your name five thousand times, so I set myself a daily goal and would stop whatever I was doing every two hours and pick up my Magic Marker. Often, while autographing, I'd listen to the radio or watch a TV show I like called *Intervention*. In it, real-life alcoholics and drug addicts are seen going about their business. Most are too far gone to hold down jobs, so mainly we see them starting fights, crying on unmade beds, and shooting up in hard-to-spot places like the valleys between their toes. Amazing, to me, is that anyone would allow him or herself to be filmed in this condition. "Did you catch me on TV?" I'd imagine them saying to their friends. "Wasn't it incredible when I shit on that car?"

That's what a thirty-one-year-old drunk woman did in one of the episodes I watched as I signed blank sheets of paper: pulled down her pants, positioned herself just so,

David Sedaris

and defecated on the rear bumper of a parked Audi A4. As she went at it—a diamond shape blurring her from the waist down—I thought of my mother, in part because she was a lady. By this, I mean that she never wore pants, just skirts and dresses. She never left the house without makeup on and her hair styled. Whenever I see a young woman boarding a plane in her pajamas, or a guy in a T-shirt that reads your hole is my goal, I always wonder what Mom would think.

She's been dead almost thirty years, so she missed a lot of the buildup to what is now thought of as less-than-scandalous behavior. I once watched a show in which a group of young men were sent out to collect pubic hair. It was a contest of sorts, and in the end the loser had to put all the spoils on a pizza and eat it. That was in 2003, so, to me, someone on television shitting on a car—*Sure. OK. That makes sense.* To go there straight from *Murder, She Wrote,* however, would be quite a shock.

Another reason *Intervention* makes me think about my mother is that she was an alcoholic. It's a hard word to use for someone you love, and so my family avoided it. Rather, we'd whisper, among ourselves, that mom "had a problem," that she "could stand to cut back."

Sober, she was cheerful and charismatic, the kind of person who could—and would—talk to anyone. Unlike with our father, who makes jokes no one understands and leaves his listeners baffled and eager to get away, it was fun to hear what our mom might come out with. "I got them laughing" was a popular line in the stories she'd tell at the end of the day. The men who pumped her gas, the bank tellers, the receptionists at the dentist's office. "I got them laughing." Her specialty was the real-life story, perfected and condensed. These take work, and she'd go through a half dozen verbal drafts before getting one where she wanted it. Over the course of the day the line she *wished* she'd delivered in response to some question or comment—the zinger—would become the line she *had* delivered. "So I said to him, 'Buddy, that's why they invented the airplane.'"

We'd be on the sidelines, aghast: "That's not how it happened at all!" But what did it matter with such great results?

You'd think my mother could have seen the difference between the sunny, likable her and the dark one who'd call late at night. I could hear the ice cubes in her glass rushing forth whenever she took a sip. In my youth, when she'd join my father for a drink after work—"Just one, I have to get dinner on the table"—that was a happy sound. Now it was like a trigger being cocked.

"The little bitch," my mother would say, her voice slurred, referring to someone she might have spoken to that afternoon, or maybe five years earlier—a shop clerk, a neighbor. "Talking to *me* that way? Like *that?* Like I'm nothing? She doesn't know it, but I could buy and sell her."

Fly home for a visit, and you'd find her in the kitchen, slamming around, replaying some argument she'd had with our father. "Goddamn bastard, shove it up your ass, why don't you, you and your stinking 'Why hire a plumber when I can do it myself?' You *can't* do it yourself, you hear me, buddy? You *can't.*" Late in her life, my mother embraced the word "fuck" but could never quite figure out its place in a sentence. "So I said to him, 'I don't give a damn fuck what you *do* with it, just get it the hell out of my driveway.'"

By that point in the evening she'd look different, raw, like you'd taken the lady she was earlier and peeled her. The loafers she favored would have been kicked off and she'd be in her stocking feet, hands on the counter to steady herself as she raged. She was hardly ever angry at the person she was talking to—exceptions being my brother, Paul; my father; and my sister Tiffany—rather, she'd be looking for support. "Can you believe this shit? I mean, *can you?*" We didn't dare contradict her.

I have an English friend named Ingrid, and her father was an alcoholic. When he lost his license for driving drunk, he got himself a tricycle and would pedal it back and forth to a pub, everyone in the village watching.

"Not a regular bike?" I asked.

"He would have fallen off!" Ingrid told me, relieved to be at the stage where she could laugh about it. Her father was a horrible person, a mean clown, which makes it easier, in a way. Our mother did nothing so cartoonish, and if she had we'd have felt traitorous making fun of her. Instead, we separated her into two people and discounted what the second, drunk one did. For that wasn't really her, we reasoned, but a kind of virus talking. Her father had it too, and drank until men in white coats carted him off to the state hospital, where he received shock treatments. I look at pictures of him after his release and think, *Wait, that's me.* We didn't resemble each other when I was young, but now we could be twins.

The big moment on *Intervention* is when family and friends of the alcoholic or drug addict confront him or her. It's supervised by a counselor and often takes place in a sad hotel conference room with flesh-colored furniture and no windows. The addicts are usually in full blossom, drunk or high or on the nod. "What the hell ... ?" they say, looking around at their parents, their brothers and sisters, their wives or husbands, all together, seated in a semicircle.

The subjects of the intervention already feel ambushed, so steps are taken to keep them from feeling attacked as well. It's easy to lose one's temper in this situation, so the counselor has instructed the friends and family members to organize their thoughts on paper. The letters they read are never wholly negative and usually kick off with a pleasant memory. "I remember when you were brought home from the hospital" is a big one. This is the equivalent of a short story beginning with the main character's alarm clock going off, and though I know I shouldn't get hung up on this part of the show, I do. *Oh please,* I think, rolling my eyes as the combative meth addict is told, "You had a smile that could light up a room."

The authors of the letters often cry, perhaps because what they've written is so poorly constructed. Then again, reality TV is fueled by tears. Take another of the shows I like, *My 600-lb Life,* about morbidly obese people struggling with their weight. At the start of each program loved ones appear, always weeping, always saying the exact same thing: "I don't want to have to bury my own child/sister/nephew, etc."

Yes, well, I wouldn't either, I think. If digging the grave didn't do me in, I'd surely die trying to roll that massive body into it. There's crying on *Hoarders* as well, though rarely by the pack rat, who sees no downside to saving all his used toilet paper.

After everyone on *Intervention* has had their say, the addicts are offered a spot in a rehab center. Not all of them accept, but most do. The places they're sent to tend to be sunny: Arizona, Southern California, Florida. We see them two months into their stay, most looking like completely different people. "Here are the wind chimes I made in my arts-and-crafts group," the woman who earlier in the program was seen shooting speed into her neck says.

Not everyone stays the prescribed ninety days. Some leave early and relapse. Others get out on schedule and relapse a week or six months later. The heartiest of them are revisited several years down the line, still sober, many with jobs now and children. "All that time I wasted," they say. "What on earth was I thinking?"

I asked Ingrid once if she ever talked to her father about his drinking, and I think she was ashamed to answer no. Not that I or anyone in my family ever confronted my mother, no matter how bad it got. Even my dad, who's superdirect and tells complete strangers that they're loud or wrong or too fat for that bolero jacket, said nothing. Then again, it built so gradually. For as long as I was living at home, it never seemed a problem. It was only after five of her six children had left that she upped her quota. The single Scotch before dinner became two, and then three. Her wine intake doubled. Tripled. She was never a quality drinker—quantity was what mattered. She bought jugs, not bottles. After dinner, she'd switch to coffee and then back to Scotch or wine, supplementing the alcohol with pills. "Mom's dolls," we called them.

When she told us that she would no longer drive at night, that she couldn't see the road, we all went along with it, knowing the real reason was that by sunset she was in no shape to get behind the wheel. "Gosh," we said, "we hope that doesn't happen to our eyes when we're your age."

In that respect, you have to hand it to the family members on *Intervention*. Corny letters notwithstanding, they have guts. The person they're confronting might storm out of the room and never talk to them again, but at least they're rolling the dice. Though we never called our mother on her behavior, she knew that we noticed it.

"I haven't had a drink in four days," she'd announce out of nowhere, usually over the phone. You could hear the struggle and the hope in her voice. I'd call her the next night and could tell right away that she'd lost her willpower. *Why aren't you stronger?* I wanted to ask. *I mean, really. Can't you just try harder?*

Of course, I was drunk too, so what could I say? I suppose I felt that my youth made it less sad. The vast plain of adulthood stretched before me, while she was well into her fifties, drinking alone in a house filled with crap. Even sober, she'd rail against that: all the junk my father dragged home and left in the yard or the basement—old newspapers and magazines, toaster ovens picked out of the trash, hoses, sheets of plywood—all of it "perfectly good," all of it just what he needed.

In my mind, our house used to be so merry. There was music playing in every room. The phone was always ringing. People in my family laughed more than people in other families. I was as sure of that as I was of anything. Up and down the street, our neighbors left their dinner tables as soon as they could and beat it for the nearest TV. That's what my father did, while the rest of us stayed put with our mother, vying for her attention as the candles burned down. "Group therapy," she called it, though it was more like a master class. One of us would tell a story about our day and she'd interject every now and then to give notes. "You don't need all that detail about the bedroom," she'd say, or, "Maybe it's best to skip the part about the teacher and just cut to the chase."

"Pour me a cup of coffee," she'd say come ten o'clock, our empty plates still in front of us. "Get me another pack of Winstons from the pantry, will you?" One of the perks of having six kids was that you didn't have to locate anything on your own. "Find my car keys," she'd command, or, "Someone get me a pair of shoes."

There was never a rebellion, because it was *her* asking. Pleasing our mother was fun and easy and made us feel good.

"I'll light her cigarette ... "

"No, *I* will."

Maybe ours wasn't the house I'd have chosen had I been in charge of things. It wasn't as clean as I'd have liked. From the outside, it wasn't remarkable. We had no view, but still it was the place I held in mind, and proudly, when I thought, *Home.* It had been a living organism, but by the time I hit my late twenties it was rotting, a dead tooth in a row of seemingly healthy ones. When I was eleven, my father planted a line of olive bushes in front of the house. They were waist-high and formed a kind of fence. By the mid-eighties they were so overgrown that pedestrians had to quit the sidewalk and take to the street instead. People with trash to drop waited until they reached our yard to drop it, figuring the high grass would cover whatever beer can or plastic bag of dog shit they needed to discard. It was like the *Addams Family* house, which would have been fine had it still been merry, but it wasn't anymore. Our mother became the living ghost that haunted it, gaunt now and rattling ice cubes instead of chains.

I'd come home from Chicago, where I was living, and she would offer to throw a dinner party for my friends. "Invite the Seiglers," she'd say. "And, hey, Dean. Or Lyn. I haven't seen her for a while."

She was lonely for company, so I'd pick up the phone. By the time my guests arrived, she'd be wasted. My friends all noticed it—how could they not? Sitting at the table as she repeated a story for the third time—"I got them laughing"—watching as she stumbled, as the ash of her cigarette fell onto the floor, I'd cringe and then feel guilty for being embarrassed by her. Had I not once worn a top hat to meet her at the airport, a top hat *and* suspenders? With red platform shoes? I was seventeen that year, but still. And how many times had *I* been drunk or high at the table? Wasn't it maybe *my turn* to be the embarrassed one? *Must remain loyal,* I'd think.

The morning after a dinner party, her makeup applied but

still in her robe, my mother would be sheepish. "Well, it was nice to see Dean again." That would have been the perfect time to sit her down, to say, "Do you remember how out of control you were last night? What can we do to help you?" I'm forever thinking of all our missed opportunities—six kids and a husband, and not one of us spoke up. I imagine her at a rehab center in Arizona or California, a state she'd never been to. "Who knew I'd be so good at pottery?" I can hear her saying, and, "I'm really looking forward to rebuilding my life."

Sobriety would not have stopped the cancer that was quietly growing inside her, but it would have allowed her to hold her head up—to recall what it felt like to live without shame—if only for a few years.

"Do you think it was my fault that she drank?" my father asked not long ago. It's the assumption of an amateur, someone who stops after his second vodka tonic and quits taking his pain medication before the prescription runs out. It's almost laughable, this insistence on a reason. I think my mother was lonely without her children—her fan club. But I think she drank because she was an alcoholic.

"How can you watch that garbage?" Hugh would say whenever he walked into the house on Maui and caught me in front of *Intervention*.

"Well, I'm not *only* watching it," I'd tell him. "I'm also signing my name."

This was never enough for him. "You're in Hawaii, sitting indoors in the middle of the day. Get out of here, why don't you? Get some sun."

And so I'd put on my shoes and take a walk, never on the beach but along the road, or through residential neighborhoods. I saw a good deal of trash—cans, bottles, fast-food wrappers—the same crap I see in England. I saw flattened cane toads with tire treads on them. I saw small birds with brilliant red heads. One afternoon, I pushed an SUV that had stalled in traffic. The driver was perhaps in his mid-twenties and was talking on the phone when I offered a hand. He nodded, so I took up my position at the rear and remembered after the first few yards what a complete pain in the ass it is to help someone in need. I thought he'd just steer to the curb, but instead he went another hundred or so feet down the road, where he turned the corner. "Does he expect me to ... push him ... all the way ... home?" I asked myself, panting.

Eventually he pulled over and put on the brake. The guy never thanked me, or even put down his phone. *Asshole,* I thought.

Back at the house, I took another stack of papers and started signing my name to them. "That's not your signature," Hugh said, frowning over my shoulder.

"It's what's *become* of my signature," I told him, looking at the scrawl in front of me. You could sort of make out a "D" and an "S," but the rest was like a silhouette of a mountain range, or a hospital patient's medical chart just before he's given the bad news. In my defense, it never occurred to me that I'd be signing my name five thousand times. In the course of my entire life, maybe, but not in one shot. This was not the adulthood that I had predicted for myself: an author of books, spending a week in Hawaii with his handsome, long-time boy-friend before deciding which house to return to. I had *wished* for it, sure, but I'd also wished for a complete head transplant.

Hugh had made himself a Manhattan and was sitting on the patio with my manuscript. A minute passed, then two. Then five. "Why aren't you laughing?" I called.

I was living in New York, still broke and unpublished, when my mother died. Aside from the occasional Sidney Sheldon novel, she wasn't a reader, so she didn't understand the world I was fluttering around the edges of. If she thought it was hopeless, or that I was wasting my time writing, she never said as much. My father,on the other hand, was more than happy to predict a dismal future. Perhaps it was to spite him that she supported us in our far-fetched endeavors—art school for me and Gretchen, Amy at Second City. Just when we needed money, at the moment before we had to ask for it, checks would arrive. "A little something to see you through," the accompanying notes would read. "Love, your old mother."

Was she sober in those moments? I wondered, signing my name to another sheet of paper. *Was it with a clear mind that she believed in us, or was it just the booze talking?*

The times I miss her most are when I see something she might have liked: a piece of jewelry or a painting. The view of a white sand beach off a balcony. Palm trees. How I'd have loved to spoil her with beautiful things. On one of her last birthdays I gave her a wasp's nest that I'd found in the woods. It was all I could afford—a nursery that bugs made and left behind. "I'll get you something better later," I promised.

"Of course you will," she said, reaching for her glass. "And whatever it is I'm sure I'm going to love it."

The Spirit World

Our house on Emerald Isle is divided down the middle and has an *E* beside one front door and a *W* beside the other. The east side is ruled by Hugh, and the bedroom we share is on the top floor. It opens onto a deck that overlooks the ocean and is next to Amy's room, which is the same size as ours but is shaped differently. Unlike Lisa and Paul, who are on the west side of the house and could probably sleep on burlap without noticing it, Amy likes nice sheets.

She'd packed a new set in her suitcase, and on the night before Thanksgiving, as I helped her make her bed, she mentioned a friend who'd come to her apartment for dinner the previous evening in New York. "He drinks Coke, right, so I went to the store on the corner to buy some," she said. "And you know how those new bottles have names on the labels— Blake or Kelly or whatever?"

I nodded.

"Well, there were only two left on the shelf, one with Mom printed on it, and the other with Tiffany."

393

I reached for a pillowcase. "Do you think if I were dead there would have been three bottles on the shelf instead of two and the third would have had *my* name on it?"

Amy thought for a moment. "Yes."

"So the only Cokes at that store in New York City are for people in our family who have died?"

She smoothed out the bedspread. "Yes."

I couldn't tell if she honestly believed this. It's hard to say with Amy. On the one hand she's very pragmatic, and on the other she's open to just about anything. Astrology, for instance. I wouldn't call her a nut exactly, but she has paid good money to have her chart done, and if you're talking about someone, she'll often ask when this person's birthday is and then say something like "Ah, a Gemini. OK. That makes sense now."

She's big on acupuncture as well, which I also tend to think is dubious, at least for things like allergies. That said, I admire people who are curious and open their minds to new possibilities, especially after a certain age. You have to draw the line somewhere, though, and with me it's my anus. When I was in my early thirties, it became a thing to have colonics. A number of my friends started going to a man in Chicago and discussing the rubble he'd discovered in their lower intestines. "A pumpkin seed, and I haven't eaten pumpkin in eight years!"

Their insides were like pharaohs' tombs, dark catacombs littered with ancient relics. Now people are giving themselves coffee enemas, believing it wards off and even cures cancer.

"I think I'll take the cancer, thank you," my sister Lisa said to me on Thanksgiving morning.

"Amen to that," I agreed.

Lisa's not open to the things that Paul and Amy are, but she has her equivalents. If you told her, for instance, that she was holding her car keys the wrong way and that there were meetings for people like her, she'd likely attend them for at least three months. One of the groups she was going to lately was for mindful eating. "It's not about dieting—we don't believe in that," she said. "You're supposed to carry on as usual: three meals a day, plus snacks and desserts or whatever. The difference is that now you *think* about it." She then confessed that the doughnut she'd just finished had been her sixth of the day. "Who *brought* these?" she asked.

I looked at the box and whimpered a little. "Kathy, I think."

"Goddamn her," Lisa whispered.

A few weeks before we came to the beach, Amy paid a great deal of money to visit a well-known psychic. The woman has a long waiting list, but somebody pulled a few strings, and, not long after getting the idea, Amy had her session, which took place over the phone and lasted for an hour. She sent me a brief email after it was over and went into greater detail as we rode with Gretchen from the Raleigh airport to Emerald Isle the day before Thanksgiving. "So start again from the top," I said. "Was it scary?"

"It was maybe like calling someone in prison and having one person after another get on the line," she said from the backseat. "First I talked to Mom for a while, who's doing well, by the way, and takes credit for setting up you and Hugh. Then Tiffany appeared."

I ripped open a bag of almonds. "Yeah, right."

"Ordinarily I'd be like that too," Amy said, "but the psychic's voice changed after Mom went away. She sounded tough all of a sudden and started by saying, 'I really don't feel like talking to you right now. This is a *favor*, OK?'"

Tiffany thanked Amy for cleaning up the mess she'd left after she'd committed suicide.

"That's strange," I said. "I mean, how would the psychic have known anything about that?"

Amy sat up and moved closer, so that her head was between my seat and Gretchen's. "I know! She said that Tiffany had tried to kill herself before—also true—and that she always knew that she was going to do this, the only question was when. It was crazy how much she got right. 'Your sister was mentally ill,' she said. 'Possibly bipolar, and stopped taking her medication because she didn't want to dull herself.' She said Tiffany felt like everyone was taking from her, using her."

"That was certainly true," I said.

"Most of what Tiffany had to say was directed at you," Amy told me. "She wants you to know that the two of you are OK now, that she's not mad anymore."

"*She's* not mad!" I said. "*Her? I'm* the one who had reason to be mad."

"She said she'd misunderstood you and that lately she's been working on herself."

"You have to work on yourself *after* you're dead?" I asked. It seemed a bit much, like having to continue a diet or your participation in AA. I thought that death let you off the hook when it came to certain things, that it somehow purified you.

"Tiffany's been hanging out a lot with Mom's dad, Grandpa Leonard," Amy told me.

This made me furious for some reason. "But she didn't even *know* him."

"I guess they met there," Amy said. "And where is that?"

Amy shrugged. "I don't know. It's not like you can ask a thousand questions and get them answered. They tell you what they want to tell you and you just listen."

I tried to let that sink in.

"She and Mom are finally getting along," Amy continued.

"She mainly wanted to let you know that she has no hard feelings. The psychic said Tiffany's been trying to tell you this herself and asked if you've had a lot of problems with your phone lately."

"No."

"Power outages?" Again I said no.

"What about butterflies?"

"Are you serious?" I asked. "Our house last winter was loaded with them. I've never seen anything like it. In the summer, fine, but this was crazy. Hugh and I talked about it every day."

Amy crossed her arms. "It was Tiffany. She was trying to contact you."

The appointment with the psychic had unnerved the whole family. "Tiffany was calmer than normal, but still it was like an actual conversation with her," Amy said. "You remember how those were, right? We'd be shaking while they were going on. Then we'd think about them for weeks afterward."

"I remember," Gretchen and I said at the same time.

After Tiffany signed off, Amy spoke to an actor she'd known who died of a heroin overdose a few years back, and to her first serious boyfriend, John Tsokantis, who had a brain aneurysm when he was twenty-five.

Because she'd had a session so recently, I was welcome to cut to the front of the line and have one of my own the following week. "Do you want me to give you the psychic's number?"

I said nothing.

"Is that a no?" Amy asked.

Often, when signing books, I'll pretend to have powers. "Well, look at the Scorpio," I'll say when someone approaches my table. I'm just guessing—I wouldn't know a Scorpio from a double Sagittarius. The key, I learned, is to speak with authority. It's never "Are you a Libra?" but, rather, "It's about time I had a Libra up in here."

Every now and then I'll be right, and the person will be shocked. "How did you know my sign?" they'll ask.

"The same way I know you have a sister."

If I'm right about the sister as well, the person I'm talking to will become like a cat released into a new setting, very low to the ground and suspicious. "Who were you talking to? Did one of my friends put you up to this?"

I met a young woman a few years back, and after being right about both her sign *and* her sister, I said, as if I were trying to recall something I had dreamed, "You were in a ... hospital earlier this week, not for yourself but for someone else. You were ... visiting someone very close to you."

The woman fell apart before my eyes. "My mother has cancer. They operated but ... How do you ... I don't ... What are you doing?"

"I can't help it," I told her. "I know things. I see them."

I don't, of course. Those were just guesses, pulled out of my ass in order to get a rise out of someone.

Hugh said the psychic Amy went to did the same thing, but I'm not sure. "How would she know what Tiffany sounded like?"

"Looked her up on YouTube," he said. "Read one of your stories. These people tell you what you want to hear. It's their way of getting you to come back."

There's something about picking the psychic apart that I don't like. It's cynical and uninteresting. That said, I knew I didn't want to book a session. My mother and I were very close, and though I miss her terribly, I'm not sure I need to talk to her again. Since her death I'd thought of it as an impossibility. Now it felt like a decision, like Mom wants to speak to me and I'm saying no. But what if she's angry at me for some reason? What would I do with that?

As for Tiffany, a few months after she died, a Dutch film crew came to Sussex and followed me around for three days. Our conversation was all over the place—we talked about England, writing, life with Hugh. The last hour was shot on a hilltop overlooking my house. The interviewer, a man named Wim, sat beside me. Off camera he'd mentioned that my sister had recently taken her life. Now he brought it up again. "What if you could ask her one question?"

It seemed like such a television moment, the intimacy unearned—grotesque, almost. And so I paused and blinked hard. Then I said, "I'd ask ... 'Can I have back that money I loaned you?'"

What troubled me most about Amy's talk with the psychic was the notion that the dead are unsettled. That they linger. I said to Lisa at the beach that Thanksgiving, "If they can see us from wherever they are, what's to stop them from watching us on the toilet?" Lisa took a moment to consider this. "I'm guessing that certain places are just ... off-limits."

"And who would make them off-limits?" I asked.

"I don't know," she said. "God, maybe. I mean ... beats me."

We were returning from a walk and came upon our father in the middle of the street a quarter mile from the house. He was dressed in jeans and had a flat-topped cap on his head. His flannel shirt was untucked, and the tail of it drooped from beneath the hem of his Windbreaker. "What are you doing here?" I asked.

"Looking for someone," he said.

Lisa asked who, and he said he didn't know. "I was just hoping somebody might come along and invite me to his house to watch the game. The Panthers are playing this afternoon, and you don't have a goddamn TV."

"You thought someone was just going to say, 'Hey, why don't you come to my place and watch some football?'" Lisa asked.

"I was going to build up to it," my father said. "You know, drop hints and so forth."

The day after Thanksgiving was bright and unseasonably warm. Hugh made ham sandwiches for lunch and we ate on the deck. "We need to have a code word so when the next one of us dies, we'll know if the psychic is for real," Amy said. She turned to Dad, the most likely candidate for ceasing to live. "What'll yours be?"

He gave it no thought. "Ecstasy."

"Like the drug?" I asked.

He picked up his sandwich. "What drug?"

"It should be something you say a lot," I told him. "Something that would let us know it's really you. Maybe ... 'You've gained weight' or 'Obama's from Kenya.'"

"Those are both three words," Lisa noted.

"What about 'Broderson'?" I said, referring to a North Carolina painter whose work my father collected in the 1970s.

"Oh, that's perfect," Amy said.

I went into the kitchen to get another napkin, and by the time I returned, the topic had changed and Dad was discussing someone who goes to his gym. The guy is in his forties and apparently stands too close in the locker room. "He undresses me with his eyes, and it makes me uncomfortable," my father said.

"How does someone undress you with his eyes when you're already undressed?" I asked. "By that point what's he looking at, your soul?"

On our final evening at the beach over the Thanksgiving weekend, Amy and my niece, Madelyn, usually host a spa night. They dress in uniforms and let it be known beforehand that clients are expected to tip, and generously. Facials are given, and Kathy offers foot massages. The treatments feel great, but the best part is listening to Amy, who plays the role of the supervisor. This year, while massaging clay onto my father's face, she asked him if he was alone this evening or with his gay lover. "I know that a lot of men such as yourself also like their testicles waxed," Amy said. "If that is of any interest to you, sir, I can get my trainee, Madelyn, right on it. Maddy, you up for this?"

It's so subversive, not just insisting that our father is gay but that his twelve-year-old granddaughter might want to rip the hair off his balls.

Before the clay is rubbed into our faces, we're outfitted in shower caps, and afterward, while it dries, we lie back with cucumber slices on our eyes. Paul programs his iPad to play spa music, or what passes for music in such places, the sound of a waterfall or rustling leaves. A whale saying something nice to another whale. A harp. This year I lifted the cucumbers off my eyes and saw Lisa and Dad stretched out like corpses, fast asleep. Paul was out as well, and Gretchen, whose legs were shin-deep in the warm whirling bath, was getting there.

It seems there was a perfectly good explanation for all the butterflies in our Sussex house the previous winter. From what I'd read since Amy brought it up, they flew in through our windows in early autumn, then passed into a kind of hibernation. Hugh and I were away until right before Christmas, and when we returned and cranked up the heat, the butterflies, mainly tortoiseshells—dozens and dozens of them—awoke, wrongly believing that spring had arrived. They were on all the second-floor windows, batting against the panes, desperate to get out.

As symbols go, they're a bit too sweet, right for Lisa but all wrong for Tiffany, who'd have been better represented by something more dynamic—crows, maybe. Two big ones flew down the chimney of my office that winter and tore the place apart, systematically overturning and then shitting on everything I cared about.

What, I wondered, placing the cucumbers back over my eyes, *would my symbol be?*

The last time I saw my sister Tiffany was at the stage door at Symphony Hall in Boston. I'd just finished a show and was getting ready to sign books when I heard her say, "David. David, it's me."

We hadn't spoken in four years at that point, and I was shocked by her appearance. Tiffany always looked like my mother when she was young. Now she looked like my mother when she was old, though at the time she couldn't have been more than forty-five. "It's me, Tiffany." She held up a paper bag with the Starbucks logo on it. Her shoes looked like she'd found them in a trash can. "I have something for you."

There was a security guard holding the stage door open, and I said to him, "Will you close that, please?" I had filled the house that night. I was in charge—Mr. Sedaris. "The door," I repeated. "I'd like for you to close it now."

And so the man did. He shut the door in my sister's face, and I never saw her or spoke to her again. Not when she was evicted from her apartment. Not when she was raped. Not when she was hospitalized after her first suicide attempt. She was, I told myself, someone else's problem. I couldn't deal with her anymore.

"Well," the rest of my family said, "it was Tiffany. Don't be too hard on yourself. We all know how she can be."

Perhaps, like the psychic, they were just telling me what I

needed to hear, something to ease my conscience and make me feel that underneath it all I'm no different from anyone else. They've always done that for me, my family. It's what keeps me coming back.

Unbuttoned

I was in Paris, waiting to undergo what promised to be a pretty disgusting medical procedure, when I got word that my father was dying. The hospital I was in had opened in 2000, but it seemed newer. From our vantage point in the second-floor radiology department, Hugh and I could see the cafés situated side by side in the modern, sun-filled concourse below. "It's like an airline terminal," he observed.

"Yes," I said. "Terminal Illness."

Under different circumstances, I might have described the place as cheerful. It was the wrong word to use, though, when I'd just had a CT scan and, in a few hours' time, a doctor was scheduled to snake a multipurpose device up the hole in my penis. It was a sort of wire that took pictures, squirted water, and had little teeth. These would take bites out of my bladder, which would then be sent to a lab and biopsied. So "cheerful"? Not so much, at least for me.

I'd hoped to stick out in the radiology wing, to be too youthful or hale to fit in, but, looking around the waiting

405

area, I saw that everyone was roughly my age, and either was bald or had gray hair. If anybody belonged here, it was me.

The good news was that the urologist I met with later that afternoon was loaded with personality. This made him the opposite of one I'd seen earlier that month, in London, when I'd gone in with an unmistakable urinary-tract infection. The pain was a giveaway, as was the blood that came out when I peed. U.T.I.s are common in women, but in men are usually a sign of something more serious. The London urologist was sullen and Scottish, the first to snake a multipurpose wire up my penis, but, sadly, not the last. The only time he came to life was when the camera started sending images to the monitor he was looking at. "Ah," he trilled. "There's your sphincter!"

I've always figured there was a reason my insides were on the inside: so I wouldn't have to look at them. Therefore I said something noncommittal, like "Great!," and went back to wishing that I were dead, because it really hurts to have a wire shoved up that narrow and uninviting slit.

The urologist we'd come to see in Paris looked over the results of the scan I'd just undergone and announced that they revealed nothing out of the ordinary. He also studied the results of the tests I'd had in London, including one for my prostate. My eyes had been screwed shut while it took place, but I'm fairly certain it involved forcing a Golden Globe Award up my ass. I didn't cry or hit anyone, though. Thus it annoyed me to see what the English radiologist who'd performed the test had written in the comment section of his report: "Patient tolerated the trans-rectal probe poorly."

How dare he! I thought.

In the end, a quick prostate check and the CT scan were the worst I had to suffer that day in Paris. After taking everything into consideration, the French doctor, who was young and handsome, like someone who'd play a doctor on TV, decided it wasn't the right time to take little bites out of my bladder. "Better to give it another month," he said, adding that I shouldn't worry too much. "Were you younger, your urinary-tract infection might not have been an issue, but at your age it's always best to be on the safe side."

That evening, Hugh and I took the train back to London, and bought next-day plane tickets for the U.S. My father was by then in the intensive-care unit, where doctors were draining great quantities of ale-colored fluid from his lungs. His heart was failing, and he wasn't expected to live much longer. "This could be it," my sister Lisa wrote me in an e-mail.

The following morning, as we waited to board our flight, I learned that he'd been taken from intensive care and put in a regular hospital room.

By the time we arrived in Raleigh, my father was back at Springmoor, the assisted-living center he'd been in for the past year. I walked into his room at five in the afternoon and was unnerved by how thin and frail he was. Asleep, he looked long dead, like something unearthed from a pharaoh's tomb. The head of his bed had been raised, so he was almost in a sitting position, his open mouth a dark, seemingly bottomless hole and his hands stretched out before him. The television was on, as always, but the sound was turned off.

"Are you looking for your sister?" an aide asked. She directed us down the hall, where a dozen people in wheelchairs sat watching *The Andy Griffith Show*. Just beyond them, in a grim, fluorescent-lit room, Lisa and my sister-in-law, Kathy, were talking to a hospice nurse they had recently engaged. "What's Mr. Sedaris's age?" the young woman asked, as Hugh and I took seats.

"He'll be ninety-six in a few weeks," Kathy said.

"Height?"

Lisa looked through her papers. "Five feet six."

Really? I thought. My father was never super-tall, but I'd assumed he was at least five-nine. Had he honestly shrunk that much?

"Weight?"

More shuffling of papers.

"One-twenty," Lisa answered.

"Well now he's just showing off," I said.

The hospice nurse needed to record my father's blood pressure, so we went back to his room, where Kathy gently shook him awake. "Dad, were you napping?"

When he came to, my father focused on Hugh. The tubes that had been put down his throat in the hospital had left him hoarse. Speaking was a challenge, thus his "Hey!" was hard to make out.

"We just arrived from England," Hugh said.

My father responded enthusiastically, and I wondered why I couldn't go over and kiss him, or at least say hello. Unless you count his hitting me, we were never terribly physical with each other, and I wasn't sure I could begin at this late date.

"I figured you'd rally as soon as I spent a fortune on last-minute tickets," I said, knowing that if the situation were reversed he'd have stayed put, at least until a discount could be worked out. All he's ever cared about is money, so it had hurt me to learn, a few years earlier, that he'd cut me out of his will. Had he talked it over with me, had he said, for example, that I seemed comfortable enough, it might have been different. But I heard about it secondhand. He'd wanted me to find out after he died. It would be like a scene in a movie, the wealthy man's children crowded into the lawyer's office: "And, to my son David, I leave nothing."

When I confronted him about the will, he said he'd consider

leaving me a modest sum, but only if I promised that Hugh would touch none of the money.

Of course I said no.

"Actually, don't worry," I said, of the plane tickets. "I'll just pay for them with part of my inheritance ... oops."

"Awww, come on now," he moaned. His voice was weak and soft, no louder than rustling leaves.

"I'm going to turn him over and examine his backside for bedsores," the hospice nurse said. "So if any of y'all need to turn away ... "

I was in the far corner of the room, beneath a painting my father had made in the late sixties of a monk with a mustache. Beside me was the guitar I was given in the fifth grade. "What's this doing here?" I asked.

"Dad had it restrung a few months ago and said he was going to learn how to play," Lisa told me. She pointed to a keyboard wedged behind a plaster statue of a joyful girl with her arms spread wide. "The piano, too."

"*Now?*" I asked. "He's had all this time but decided to wait until he was connected to tubes?"

After the hospice nurse had finished, my father's dinner was brought in, all of it puréed, like baby food. Even his water was mixed with a thickener that gave it the consistency of nectar.

"He has a bone that protrudes from the back of his neck and causes food to go down the wrong way," Lisa explained. "So he can't have anything solid or liquid."

As Kathy spooned the mush into my father's mouth, Hugh picked the can of thickener up off the dinner tray, read the ingredients, and announced that it was just cornstarch.

"So how was your flight?" Lisa asked us.

Time crawled. Amber-colored urine slowly collected in the bag attached to my father's catheter. The room was sweltering.

"Was that dinner O.K., Dad?" Lisa asked.

He raised a thumb. "Excellent."

How had she and Paul and Kathy managed to do this day after day? Conversation was pretty much out of the question, so they mainly offered observations in louder than normal voices: "She was nice," or "It looks like it might start raining again."

I was relieved when my father got drowsy, and we could all leave and go to dinner. "Do you want me to turn your TV to Fox News?" Lisa asked, as we put our coats on.

"Fox News," my father mumbled.

Lisa picked up the remote, but when she jabbed it in the direction of the television nothing happened. "I can't figure out which channel that is, so why don't you watch *CSI: Miami* instead?"

Amy arrived from New York at ten the following morning, wearing a black-and-white polka-dot coat she'd bought on our last trip to Tokyo. Instead of taking her straight to Springmoor, Hugh and I drove her to my father's place, where we met up with Lisa and Gretchen. Our dad started hoarding in the late eighties: a broken ceiling fan here, an expired can of peaches there, until eventually the stuff overtook him and spread into the yard. I hadn't been inside the house since before he was moved to Springmoor, and, though Lisa had worked hard at clearing it of junk, the over-all effect was still jaw-dropping. His car, for instance, looked like the one in *Silence of the Lambs* that the decapitated head was found in. You'd think it had been made by spiders out of dust and old pollen. It was right outside the front door, and acted as an introduction to the horrors that awaited us.

"Whose turd is this on the floor next to the fireplace?" I called out, a few minutes after descending the filthy carpeted stairs into the basement.

Amy looked over my shoulder at it, as did Hugh and, finally, Lisa, who said, "It could be my dog's from a few months ago."

I leaned a bit closer. "Or it could be—"

Before I could finish, Hugh scooped it up with his bare hands and tossed it outside. "You people, my God." Then he went upstairs to help Gretchen make lunch.

Continuing through the house, I kept asking the same question: "Why would anyone choose to live this way?" It wasn't just the falling-down ceilings or the ragged spiderwebs draped like bunting over the doorways. It wasn't the tools and appliances he'd found on various curbs—the vacuum cleaners with frayed cords or the shorted-out hair dryers he'd promised himself he would fix—but the sense of hopelessness they conveyed when heaped into rooms that used to seem so normal, no different in size or design from those of our neighbors, but were now ruined. "Whoever buys this house will just have to throw a match on it and start over," Gretchen said.

What struck me most were my father's clothes. Hugh gets after me for having too many, but I've got nothing compared with my dad, who must own twenty-five suits and twice as many sports coats. Dozens of them were from Brooks Brothers, when there was just the one store in New York and the name meant something. Others were from long-gone college shops in Ithaca and Syracuse, the sort that sold smart jackets and white bucks. There were sweaters in every shade: the cardigans on hangers, their sleeves folded in a self-embrace to prevent them from stretching; the V-necks and turtlenecks folded in stacks, a few unprotected, but mostly moth-proofed in plastic bags. There were polo shirts and dress shirts and casual shirts from every decade of postwar America. Some hung like rags—buttons missing, great tears in the backs, as if he'd worn them while running too slowly from bears. Others were still in their wrapping, likely bought two or three years ago. I could remember him wearing most of the older stuff—to the club, to work, to the parties he'd attend, always so handsome and stylish.

Though my mother's clothes had been disposed of—all those shoulder pads moldering in some landfill—my father's filled seven large closets, one of them a walk-in, and hung off the shower-curtain rods in all three bathrooms. They were crammed into dressers and piled on shelves. Hats and coats and scarves and gloves. Neckties and bow ties, too many to count, all owned by the man who since his retirement seemed to wear nothing but the same jeans and same T-shirt with holes in it he'd worn the day before, and the day before that; the man who'd always found an excuse to skimp on others, but allowed himself only the best. There were clothes from his self-described fat period, from the time he slimmed down, and from the years since my mother died, when he's been out-and-out skinny: none of them thrown away or donated to Goodwill, and all of them now reeking of mildew.

I nicked a vibrant red button-down shirt from the fifties, noticing later that it had a sizable hole in the back. Then I claimed the camel-colored, moth-eaten beret I'd bought him on a school trip to Madrid in 1975.

"It suits you," Hugh observed.

"It matches your skin and makes you look bald," Amy said.

We were all in the dining room, going through boxes with more boxes in them, when I glanced over at the window and saw a doe step out of the woods and approach some of the trash on the lawn near the carport, head lowered, as if she'd followed the scent of fifty-year-old house paint hardened in rusted-through cans. "Look," we whispered, afraid our voices from inside the house might frighten her off. "Isn't she beautiful!" We couldn't remember there being deer in the woods when we were young. Perhaps our dogs had scared them off.

"Oh," Lisa said, her voice as soft as our father's. "I hope she doesn't step on a rusty nail."

Gretchen served Greek food for lunch, and afterward we drove to Springmoor. It was a Saturday afternoon in late February, cold and raining. Our father was in his reclining chair covered with a blanket when we arrived, not asleep but not exactly awake, either. It was this new state he occasionally drifted into: neither here nor there. After killing the overhead lights, we seated ourselves around his room and continued the conversation we'd been having in the car.

"I asked Marshall to write Dad's obituary, but he doesn't feel up to it," Gretchen said, referring to her boyfriend of nearly thirty years.

The rest of us glanced over at our father.

"He can't hear us," Gretchen said. She looked at me. "So will *you* write it?"

I've been writing about my father for ages, but when it comes to the details of his life, the year he graduated from college, etc., I'm worthless. Even his job remains a mystery to me. He was an engineer, and I like to joke that up until my late teens I thought that he drove a train. "I don't really know all that much about him," I said, scooting my chair closer to his recliner. He looked twenty years older than he had on my last visit to Raleigh, six months earlier. One change was his nose. The skin covering it was stretched tight, revealing facets I'd never before noticed. His eyes were shaped differently, like the diamonds you'd find on playing cards, and his mouth looked empty, though it was in fact filled with his own teeth. He did this thing now, opening wide and stretching out his lips, as if pantomiming a scream. I kept thinking it was in preparation for speech, but then he'd say nothing.

I was trying to push the obituary off on Lisa when we heard him call for water.

Hugh got a cup, filled it from the tap in the bathroom, and stirred in some cornstarch to thicken it. My father's oxygen tube had fallen out of his nose, so we summoned a nurse, who showed us how to reattach it. When she left, he half raised his hand, which was purpled with spots and resembled a claw.

"What's on your ... mind?" he asked Amy, who had always been his favorite, and was seated a few yards away. His voice couldn't carry for more than a foot or two, so Hugh repeated the question.

"What's on your mind?"

"You," Amy answered. "I'm just thinking of you and wanting you to feel better."

My father looked up at the ceiling, and then at us. "Am I ... real to you kids?" I had to lean in close to hear him, especially the last half of his sentences. After three seconds he'd run out of steam, and the rest was just breath. Plus the oxygen machine was loud.

"Are you what?"

"Real." He gestured to his worn-out body, and the bag on the floor half filled with his urine. "I'm in this new ... life now."

"It'll just take some getting used to," Hugh said. My father made a sour face. "I'm a zombie."

I don't know why I insisted on contradicting him. "Not really," I said. "Zombies can walk and eat solid food. You're actually more like a vegetable."

"I know you," my father said to me. He looked over at Amy, and at the spot that Gretchen had occupied until she left. "I know all you kids so well."

I wanted to say that he knew us superficially at best. It's how he'd have responded had I said as much to him: "You don't *know* me." Surely my sisters felt the way I did, but some-thing—most likely fatigue—kept them from mentioning it.

As my father struggled to speak, I noticed his fingernails, which were long and dirty.

"If I just ... dropped out of the sky like this ... you'd think I was a freak."

"No," I said. "*You'd* think you were a freak, or at least a loser."

Amy nodded in agreement, and I plowed ahead. "It's what you've been calling your neighbors here, the ones parked in the hall who can't walk or feed themselves. It's what you've always called weak people."

"You're a hundred per cent right," he said.

I didn't expect him to agree with me. "You're vain," I continued. "Always were. I was at the house this morning and couldn't believe all the clothes you own. Now you're this person, trapped in a chair, but you're still yourself to us. You're like ... like you were a year ago, but drunk."

"That's a very astute ... observation," my father said. "Still, I'd like to ... apologize."

"For being in this condition?" I asked.

He looked over at Amy, as if she had asked the question, and nodded.

Then he turned to me. "David," he said, as if he'd just realized who I was. "You've accomplished so many fantas-tic things in your life. You're, well ... I want to tell you ... you ... you won."

A moment later he asked for more water, and drifted mid-sip into that neither-here-nor-there state. Paul arrived, and I went for a short walk, thinking, of course, about my father, and about the writer Russell Baker, who had died a few weeks earlier. He and I had had the same agent, a man named Don Congdon, who was in his midseventies when I met him, in

1994, and who used a lot of outdated slang. "The blower," for instance, was what he called the phone, as in "Well, let me get off the blower. I've been gassing all morning."

"Russ Baker's mother was a tough old bird," Don told me one rainy afternoon, in his office on Fifth Avenue. "A real gorgon to hear him tell it, always insisting that her son was a hack and would never amount to anything. So on her deathbed he goes to her saying, 'Ma, look, I made it. I'm a successful writer for the *New York Times*. My last book won the Pulitzer.'"

"She looked up at him, her expression blank, and said, 'Who are you?'"

I've been told since then that the story may not be true, but still it struck a nerve with me. Seek approval from the one person you desperately want it from, and you're guaranteed not to get it.

As for my dad, I couldn't tell if he meant "You won" as in "You won the game of life," or "You won over *me,* your father, who told you—assured you when you were small and then kept reassuring you—that you were worthless." Whichever way he intended those two faint words, I will take them, and, in doing so, throw down this lance I've been hoisting for the past sixty years. For I am old myself now, and it is so very, very heavy.

I returned to the room as Kathy was making dinner reservations at a restaurant she'd heard good things about. The menu was updated Southern: fried oysters served with pork belly and collard greens—that kind of thing. The place was full when we arrived, and the diners were dressed up. I was wearing the red shirt I'd taken from my father's closet, and had grown increasingly self-conscious about how strongly it stank of mildew.

"We all smell like Dad's house," Amy noted.

While eating, we returned to the topic of his obituary, and what would follow. A Greek Orthodox funeral is a relatively sober affair, sort of like a Mass. I'd asked if I could speak at my mom's, just so there'd be a personal touch. If I were to revisit what I read that morning in 1991, I'd no doubt cringe. That said, it was easy to celebrate my mother. Effortless. With my father, I'd have to take a different tone. "I remember the way he used to ram other cars at the grocery store when the drivers—who were always women—took the parking spots he wanted," I could say. "Oh, and the time he found seventeen-year-old Lisa using his shower, and dragged her out naked."

How could I reconcile that perpetual human storm cloud with the one I had spent the afternoon with, the one who never mentioned, and has never mentioned, the possibility of dying, who has taken everything life has thrown at him and found a way to deal with it. Me, on the other hand, after half a dozen medical tests involving the two holes below my waist, before even learning whether or not I *had* cancer, I'd decided I was tired of battling it. "Just let me die in peace," I said to Hugh, after the French urologist stuck his finger up my ass.

Meanwhile, here was my father, tended to by aides, afforded no privacy whatsoever, and determined to get used to it. Where did that come from? I wondered, looking at my fried chicken as it was set before me. And how is it that none of his children, least of all me, inherited it?

Of all us kids, Paul was the only one to fight the do-not-resuscitate order. He wanted all measures taken to keep our father alive. "You have to understand," he said over dinner. "Dad is my best friend." He didn't say it in a mawkish or dramatic way, but matter-of-factly, the way you might identify your car in a parking lot: "It's that one there." The relation-ship between my brother and my father has always been a mystery to my sisters and me. Is it the thickness of their skin? The fact that they're both straight men? On the surface, it seems that all they do is yell at each other: "Shut up." "Go to hell." "Why don't you just suck my dick." It is the vocabulary of conflict, but with none of the hurt feelings or dark intent. While the rest of us may mourn our father's passing, only Paul will truly grieve.

"Hey," he said, taking an uneaten waffle off his daughter's plate. "Did I tell you I just repainted my basement?" He found a picture on his phone and showed me what looked like a Scandinavian preschool, each wall a bold primary color.

"Let me see," Amy said. I handed her the phone and she, in turn, passed it to Lisa. It then went by the spots where Gretchen and Tiffany would be if Tiffany hadn't killed herself and Gretchen hadn't fallen asleep at her boyfriend's house earlier that evening, and on to Kathy, then to my niece, Maddy, and back to Paul.

We were the last party to leave the restaurant, and were standing out front in a light rain, when Amy pointed at the small brick house across the street. "Look," she cried, "a naked lady!"

"Oh, my God," we said, following her finger and lowering our voices the same way we'd done ten hours earlier with the doe on my father's lawn.

"Where?" Lisa whispered.

"Right there, through the window on the ground floor," Hugh told her. He and Amy would later remark that the woman, who was middle-aged and buxom and wore her hair in a style I associate with the nineteen-forties, made them think of a Raymond Chandler novel.

"What's she doing?" I asked, watching as she moved into the kitchen.

"Getting a drink of water?" Lisa guessed.

Paul turned to his daughter. "Look away, Maddy!"

When the light went out, we worried that we had scared the naked woman, but a second later it came back on, and she was joined by a dark-haired man with a towel around his waist. The two of them appeared to speak for a moment. Then he took her by the hand and led her into another room and out of sight.

It was all we talked about as we made our way down the street to our various cars. "Can you believe it? Naked!!" As if we'd seen a flying saucer, or a congregation of pixies. To hear us in a gang like that, the wonder in our voices, the delight and energy, you'd almost think we were children.